IMAGES
of America

MEXICO

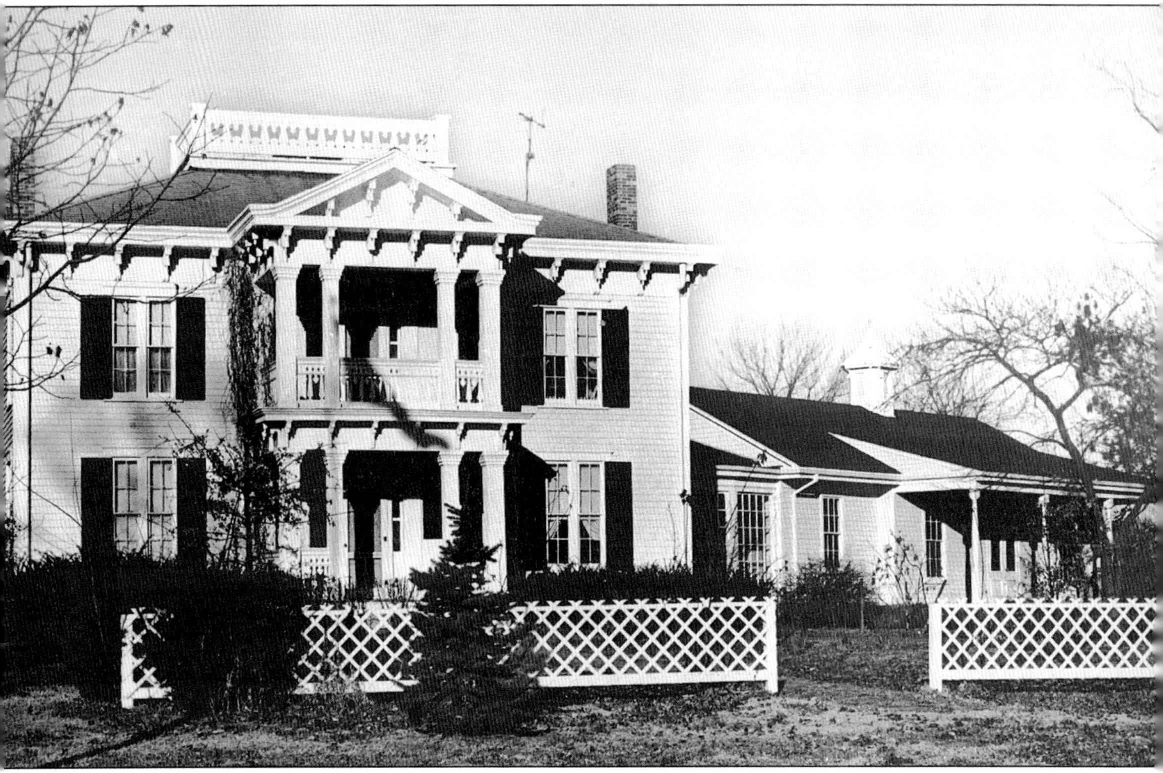

The Audrain County Historical Society Museum Complex is housed in the 11-acre Robert S. Green Memorial Park. Graceland, the museum headquarters, is a Greek Revival home built in 1857 by John P. Clark and is one of the oldest homes in the county. In 1970, the American Saddlebred Horse Museum was built as an addition to Graceland. The Country School, Country Church, a gazebo, and gardens are also part of the complex. In 2008, the museum opened a new wing featuring Audrain County's firebrick industry.

ON THE COVER: Hardin College students celebrate a May Day fete with queen and court in 1921. Students and citizens alike enjoyed the college events.

IMAGES
of America

MEXICO

Vicki Berger Erwin

ARCADIA
PUBLISHING

ISBN 978-0-7385-8448-5

Published by Arcadia Publishing
Charleston SC, Chicago IL, Portsmouth NH, San Francisco CA

Printed in the United States of America

Library of Congress Control Number: 2009943864

For all general information contact Arcadia Publishing at:
Telephone 843-853-2070
Fax 843-853-0044
E-mail sales@arcadiapublishing.com
For customer service and orders:
Toll-Free 1-888-313-2665

Visit us on the Internet at www.arcadiapublishing.com

To all my friends and family in Mexico, Missouri

CONTENTS

ACKNOWLEDGMENTS

My family moved to Mexico when I was four years old, and I attended the Mexico Public Schools, the Audrain County Fair, checked books out of the Mexico (later Audrain County) Library, read the *Ledger*, and shopped the square. Doing the research for this book was a like a trip back home.

My heartiest thanks go to the Audrain County Historical Society (AHS). There would be no book without them! A big thank you goes to Dana Keller, executive director of the society, for opening the doors and the files of the AHS as well as for being a resource and a helping hand. I especially want to thank Janice Robison, assistant director, for her never-flagging assistance and hospitality. She helped me find information and photographs and—most importantly—fed me.

Any factual errors are entirely my responsibility. I have tried to give an overview of the history of the city and, due to space and photographs available, had to make some hard decisions about what to include and what not to include. The information is archival and concentrates on the early history of Mexico versus more recent occurrences.

Thanks to Lewis Melahn for helping make contact with the right people to get this project off the ground, to Ted at Our House Bed and Breakfast for welcoming accommodations and the best breakfasts ever, to Connie Harrison Fennewald for being a cheerleader for the book, and to the staff at Main Street Books in St. Charles, Missouri, for covering work hours for me. Of course, I thank my husband, Jim, and family for just always being there.

All photographs are courtesy of Audrain Historical Society unless otherwise noted.

INTRODUCTION

On April 23, 1836, Robert Mansfield and James Smith officially filed a plat for a new town to be called Mexico. At the same time, they asked that it be selected as the county seat for a soon-to-be-formed county in Missouri. Mansfield and Smith offered to donate a certain number of lots, including a town square, in order to make this happen.

The town's name was originally recorded as New Mexico, but was quickly corrected. Two stories circulate about why the name Mexico was chosen. In one, settlers found a sign reading, "To Mexico" and pointing southwest. In the second and more accepted version, the name was tied to the excitement over Texas seeking independence from the country of Mexico. The founders hoped that the name choice would transfer some of that enthusiasm to their town and bring settlers looking for adventure and prosperity.

Audrain County was organized a few months later, on December 17, 1836, and Mexico was chosen as the county seat. Audrain was named after James H. Audrain, a recently deceased state legislator from St. Charles County. Audrain had served in the War of 1812 before settling in St. Charles, where he built a mill and a distillery and opened an inn. He was elected to the state legislature in 1830 and died in 1831.

Agriculture and basic exchanges of goods were the early enterprises of pioneer families. In the first census taken after the founding of the city, its population was 1,949. The coming of the railroad in 1858 was seen as the essential step in making Mexico a center of commerce. Prior to the railway, goods had to be hauled by wagon and stock driven to market. Stores in town carried few products because of the difficulty in procuring them. The county jumped on board immediately and pledged $50,000 toward extending a rail line if it traveled through Audrain. The indebtedness was quickly retired, and the railroad came directly through town thanks to the donation of the right-of-way by Dr. Nathaniel Allison, whose generosity proved a boon for Mexico.

The railroad also determined the course the Civil War took for Mexicoans. To protect supply lines, Union forces occupied the city for the duration of the war, bringing martial law and a curfew. As a result of split loyalties, an underlying sense of distrust and suspicion—neighbor against neighbor—spread throughout the area. No battles were fought on Audrain soil, but one minor skirmish occurred on July 15, 1861. The Audrain Rangers, a local band of secession sympathizers, ambushed a militia train headed to Mexico to protect the railroad, wounding and killing several soldiers before disappearing into the countryside. This incident set the antagonistic tone for the occupation. Gen. U. S. Grant commanded the Union troops in Mexico for a short period during that summer.

After the war, an era of expansion and success took over. The arrival of Colby Quisenberry and his purebred saddle horses started Mexico on a path that would end up with the city being recognized as the Saddle Horse Capital of the World. Until the 1930s and the growth in automobile popularity, Mexico would give the world many famous champion horses, like Rex McDonald, and many famous trainers and breeders, including the Lee brothers, Bill Cunningham, Tom Bass, Art Simmons, and others.

In 1910, Allen P. Green moved to town, bringing ideas and innovation for the struggling firebrick industry. The county sat upon a deposit of fireclay that when formed into bricks resisted heat and change, an essential ingredient in growing industrial concerns across the nation. Green saw the possibilities and built A. P. Green Fire Brick Company into the largest firebrick manufacturer in the nation while helping make Mexico the "Firebrick Capital of the World."

All good things must come to an end, and the facility closed in 2002, leaving a hole in the employment market. Recently the plant reopened in limited operation under the direction of former employees. Yet agriculture continues to thrive, and new companies are constantly moving in and creating opportunity. Today Mexico considers itself the "Mainstreet of the Midwest."

One

The Courthouse Square

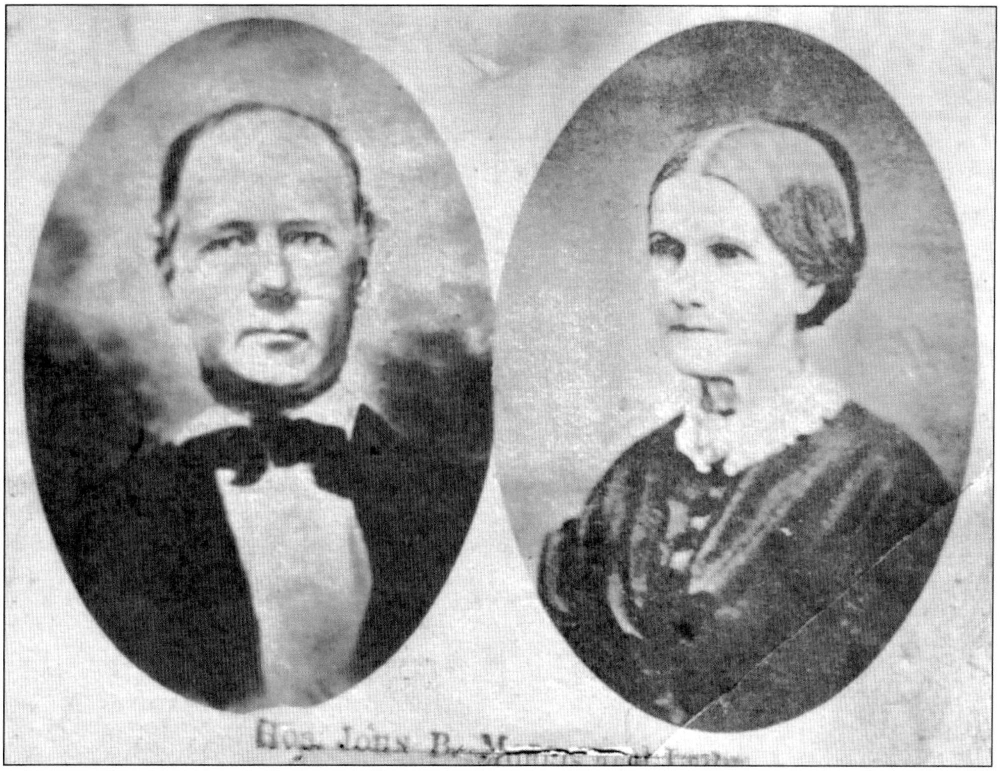

John Bingle Morris, seen here with his wife, Julia, is recognized as a founding father of Mexico. In the block north of Love Street and east of Jefferson Street, he built one of Mexico's first permanent structures, the Green Tree Tavern. It served as his family's home, a general store, a tavern, and the post office. Morris was also the first postmaster and served as both county clerk and county judge.

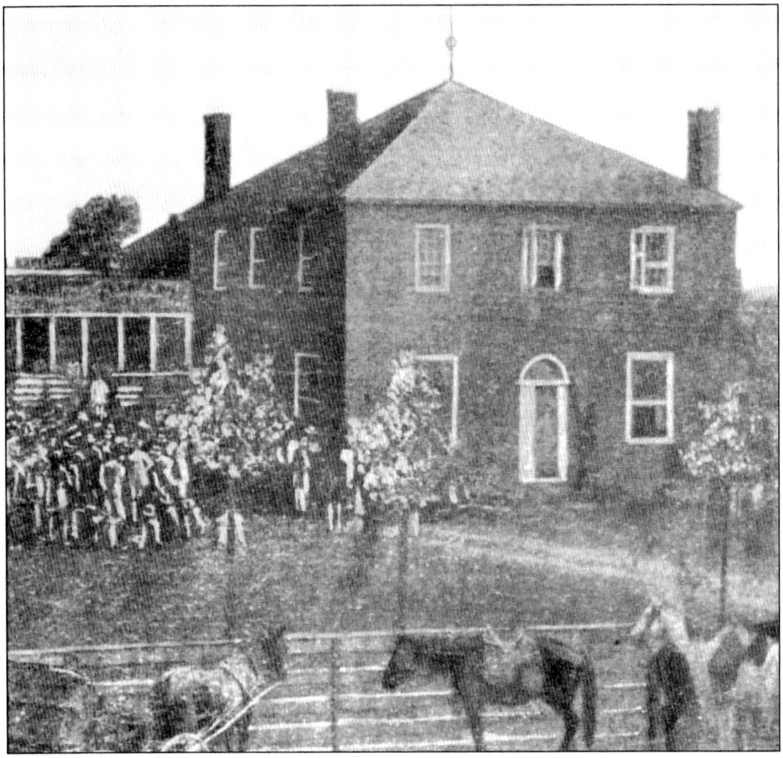

In 1839, the second courthouse, a square brick building, replaced an earlier log structure and was opened for use. It had a courtroom on the first floor and three rooms on the second floor and cost the county $1,600. Used harshly by Federal troops during the Civil War, the building was replaced after the war.

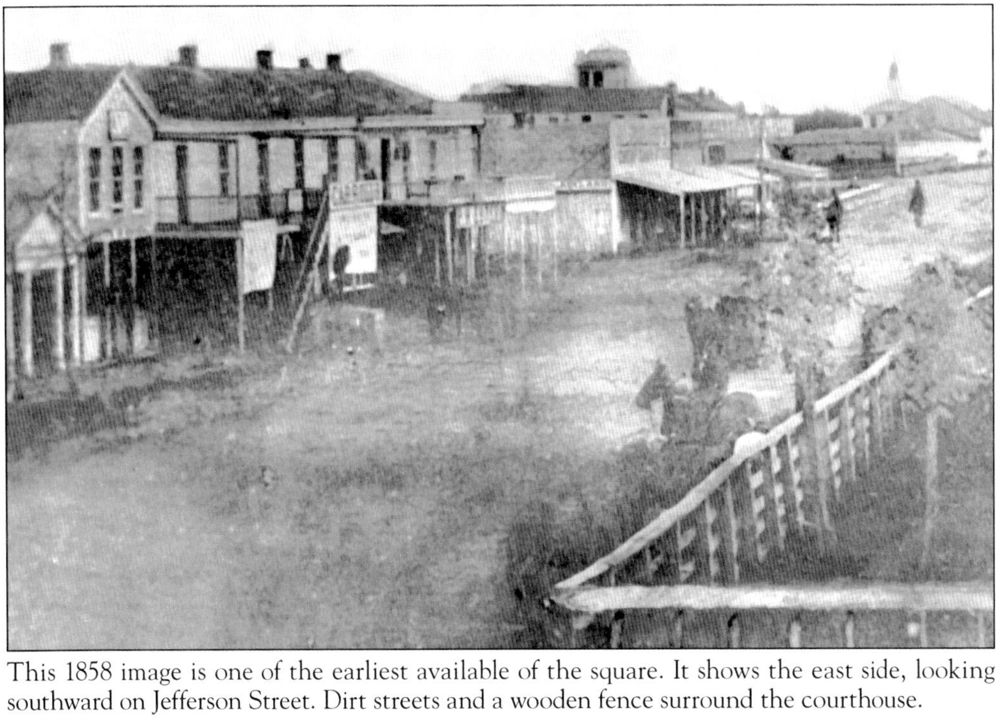

This 1858 image is one of the earliest available of the square. It shows the east side, looking southward on Jefferson Street. Dirt streets and a wooden fence surround the courthouse.

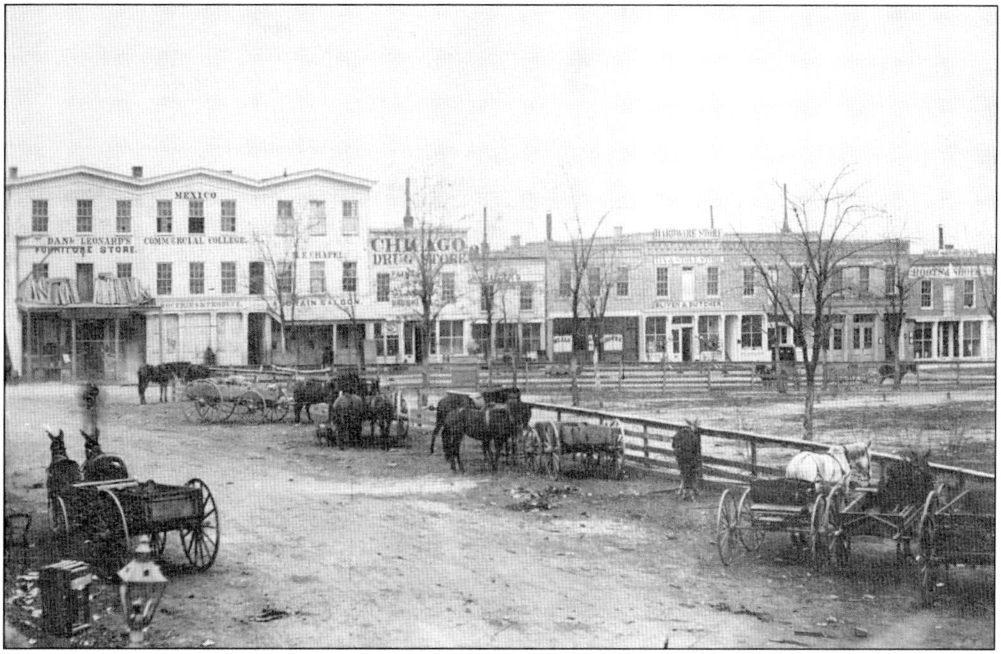

This photograph shows the west side of the square around 1868 about the time construction of a third courthouse began. Buildings and businesses here include a furniture store, commercial college, drugstore, grocery store, and hardware store.

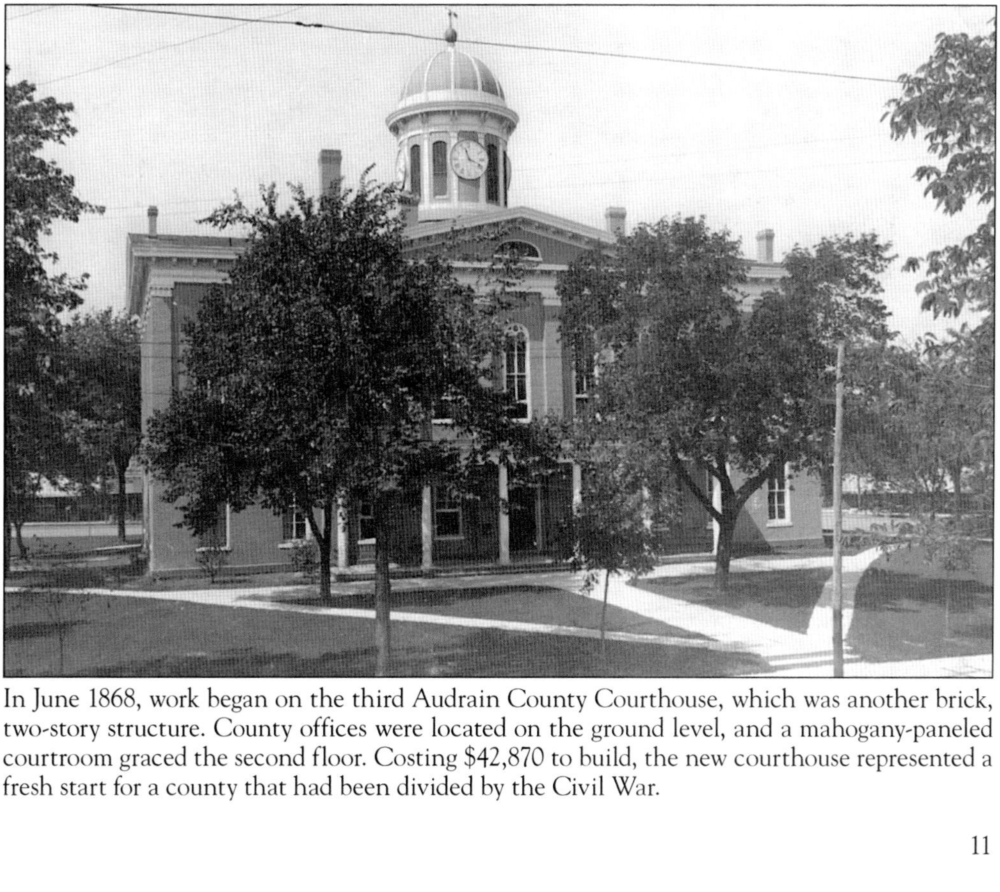

In June 1868, work began on the third Audrain County Courthouse, which was another brick, two-story structure. County offices were located on the ground level, and a mahogany-paneled courtroom graced the second floor. Costing $42,870 to build, the new courthouse represented a fresh start for a county that had been divided by the Civil War.

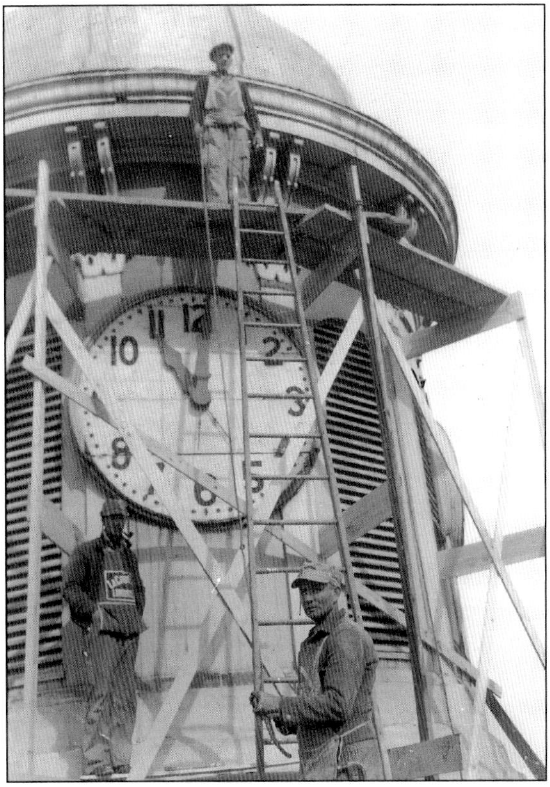

The courthouse dome was highly visible, and the four-faced clock with its ringing iron bell became a city and county institution, keeping residents on time. Because the county refused to move the cupola clock forward, the city remained on standard time for the summer. Federal work-project funding provided the clock with a face-lift in the 1930s, replacing Roman numerals with Arabic, as seen in this *c.* 1939 image.

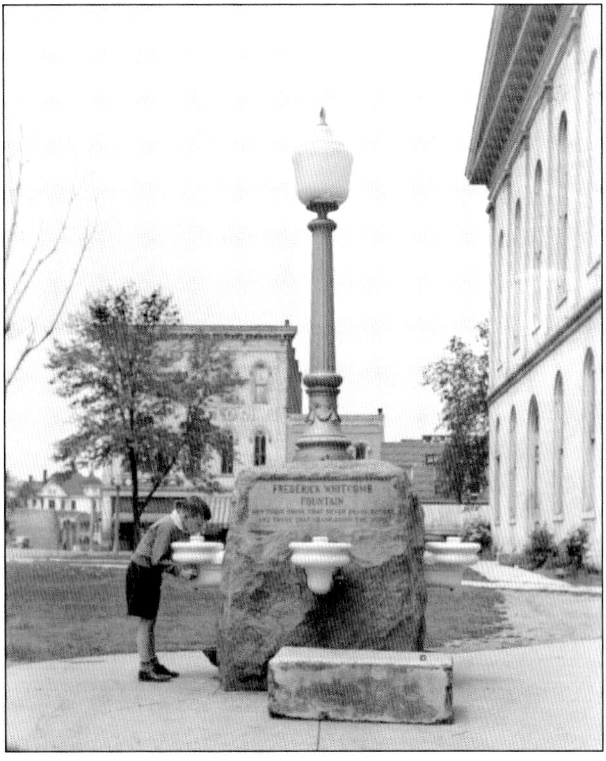

Pictured here around 1937, the Frederick Whitcomb Fountain remains on the grounds of the Courthouse Square—although the third courthouse has been replaced. The carving reads, "Now those drink, That never drank before, And those that drank, Drink the more."

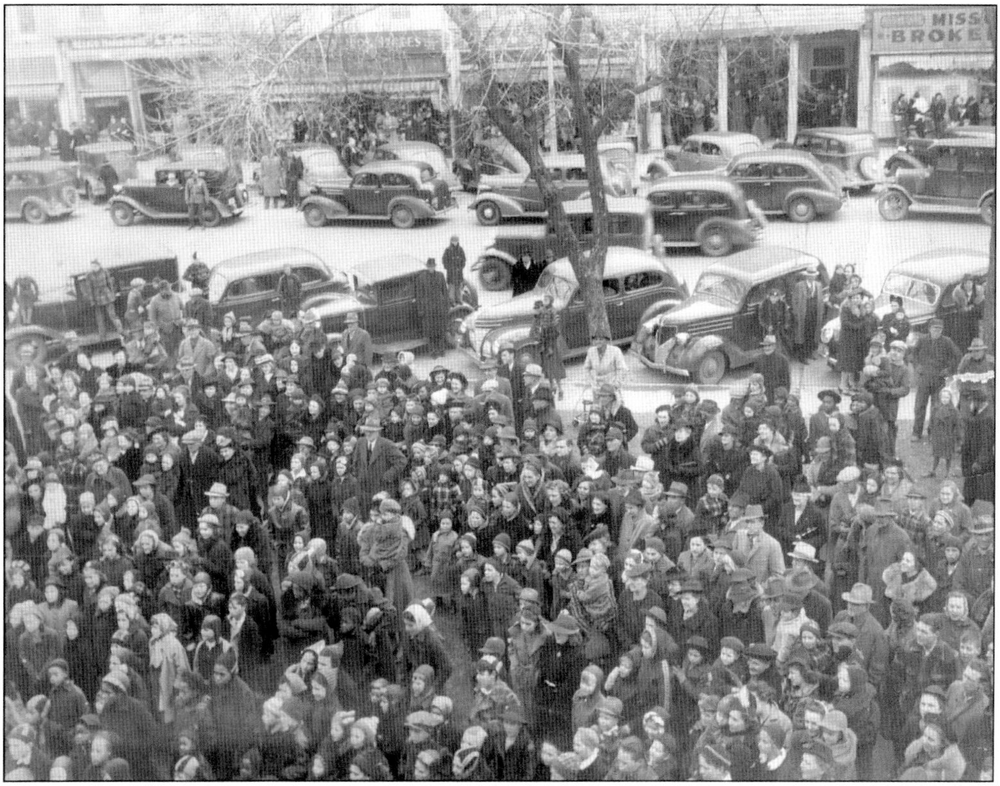

In the 1939 image above, a crowd awaits the official opening of the Christmas season and a special visitor, who, according to many young attendees, resided in the courthouse during December. As vibrantly illustrated in the *c.* 1890s photograph below, the square was the center of economic and social life in Mexico at the turn of the century and beyond.

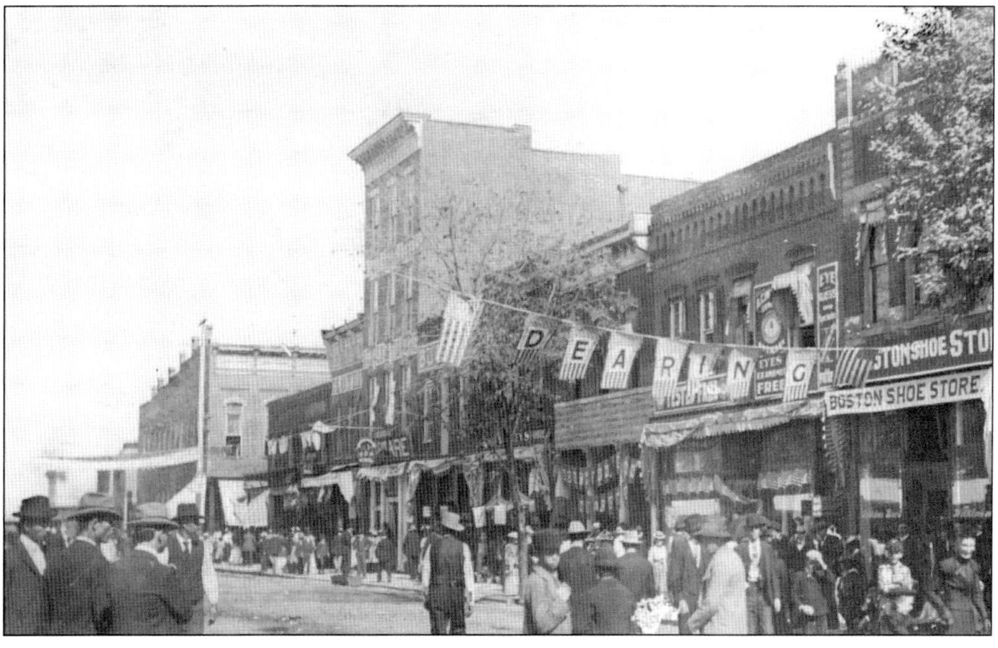

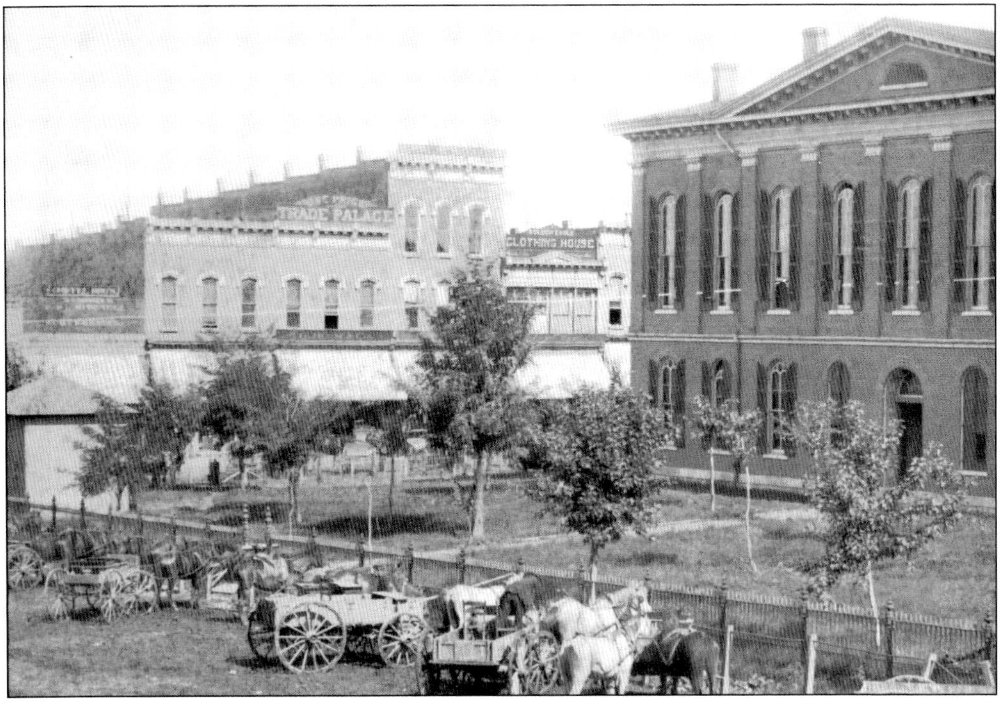

During the 1880s, with the courthouse still surrounded by dirt roads, people walked on plank sidewalks and hitched horses and wagons to racks along the wrought-iron fence surrounding the building. During that era, 80 stores and businesses thrived on the blocks around the square.

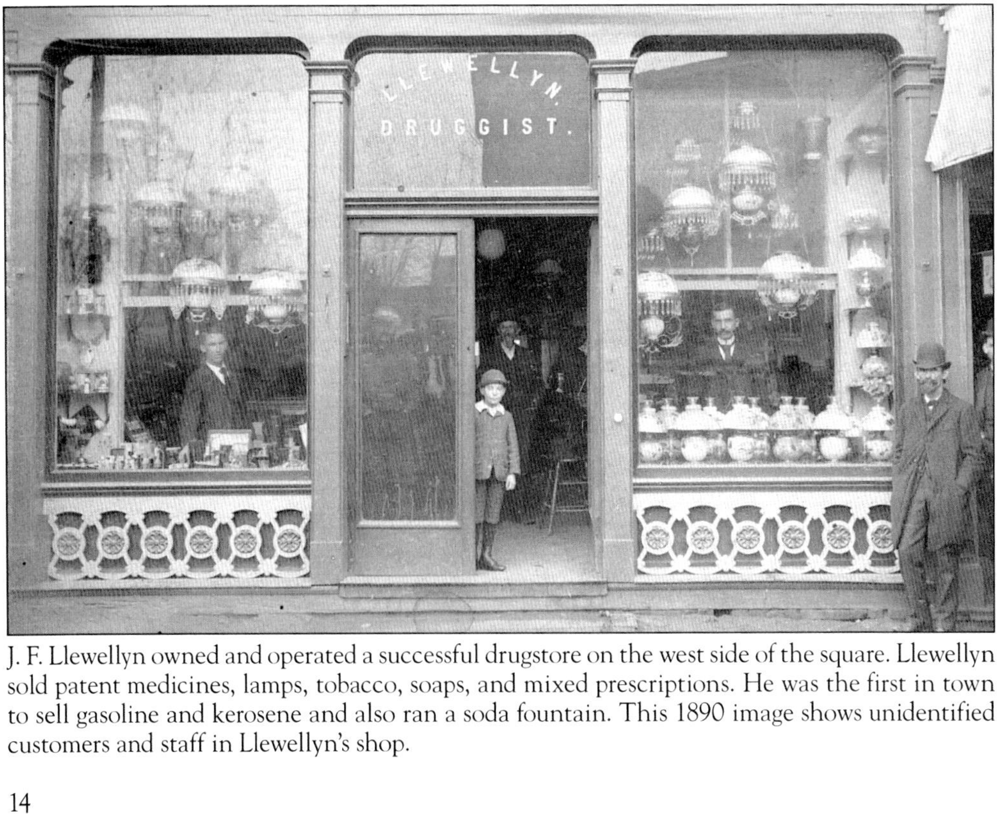

J. F. Llewellyn owned and operated a successful drugstore on the west side of the square. Llewellyn sold patent medicines, lamps, tobacco, soaps, and mixed prescriptions. He was the first in town to sell gasoline and kerosene and also ran a soda fountain. This 1890 image shows unidentified customers and staff in Llewellyn's shop.

Llewellyn was also interested in science. He kept detailed records of local weather and set up an electric plant in the basement of his establishment. Local businesses went together to pay for four streetlights on the square, but the effort failed for lack of payment. In 1887, the city finally contracted with Llewellyn for electricity.

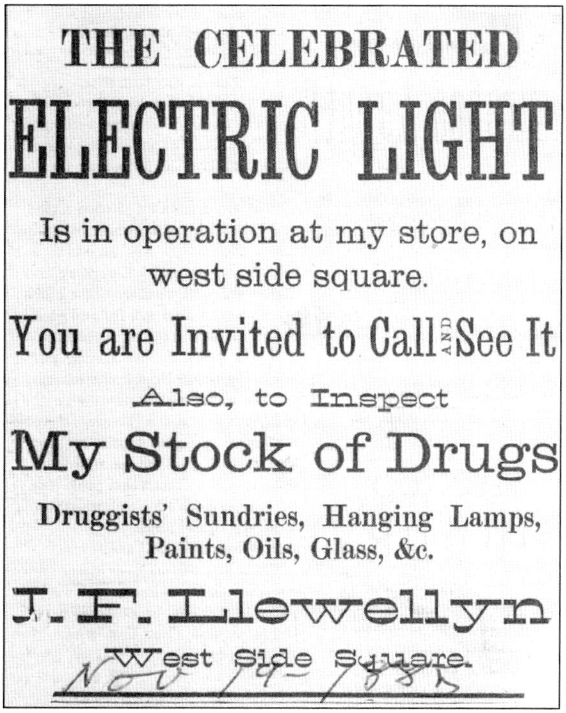

In a special election after her husband's death, Clara (Mrs. J. S.) Snidow was the first woman to be elected to a county office in Missouri. She is shown here in 1899 with Pelide Locke in the county clerk's office.

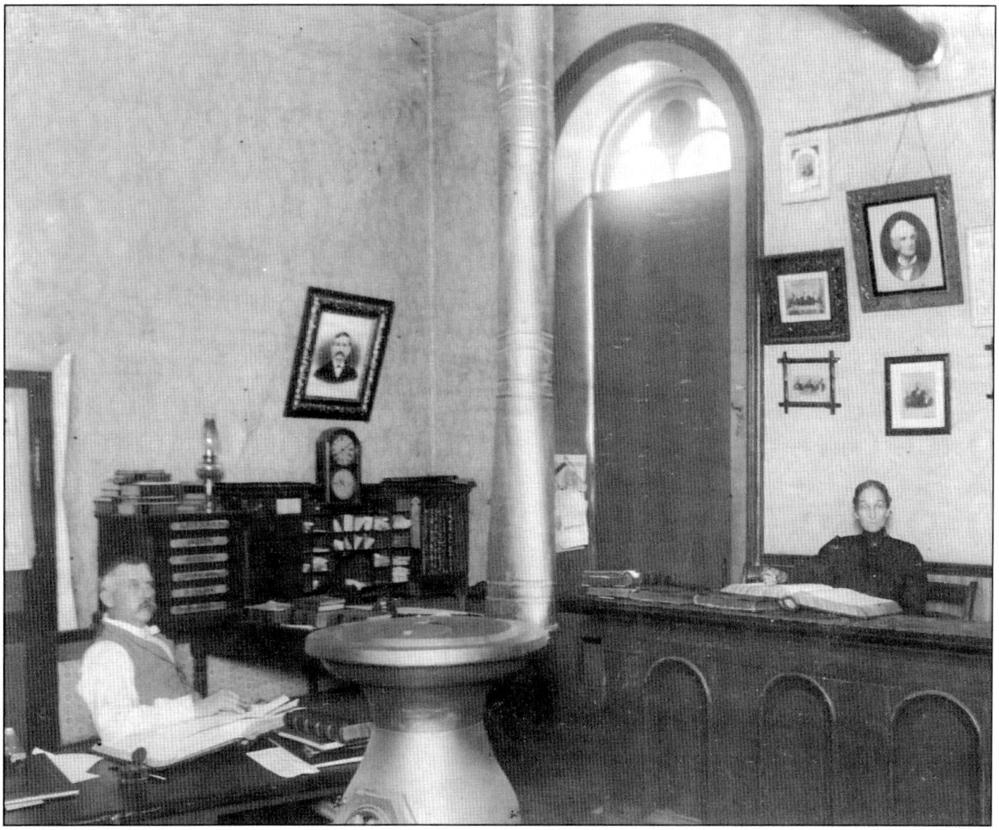

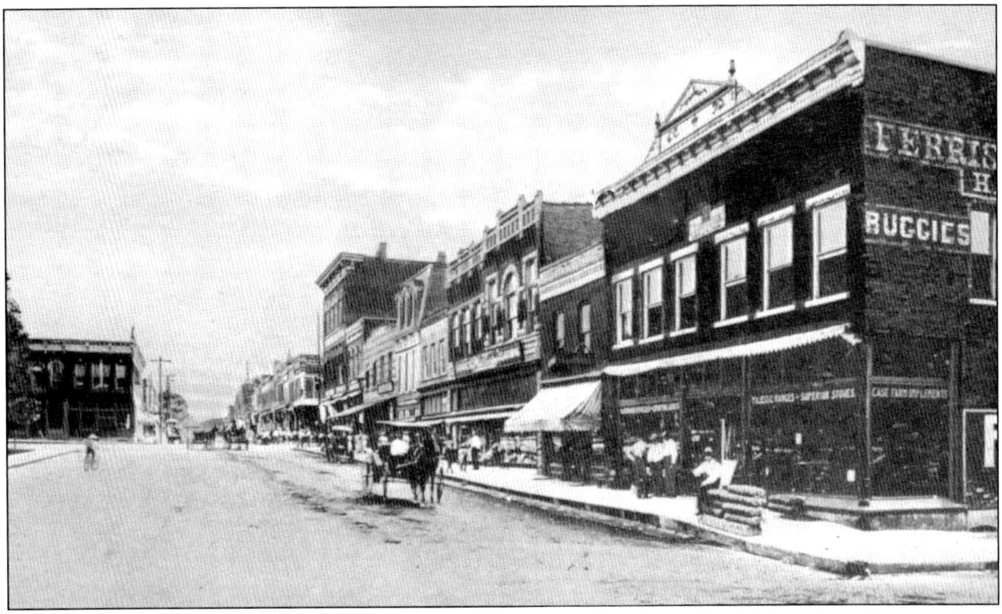

Around 1900, many people in Mexico shopped based on family and neighbor ties, distance from their homes, and church and club memberships more than on price. Pictured here is the west side of the square at that time.

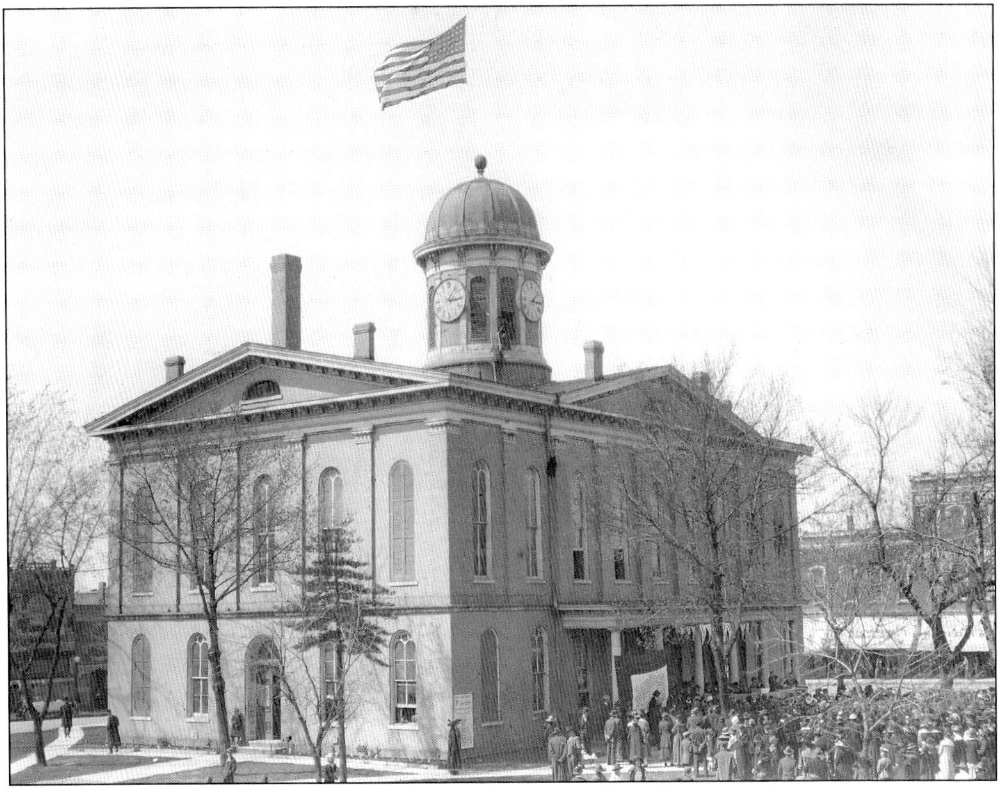

Decorations graced the Courthouse Square at times other than Christmas. Here, crowds celebrate the Fourth of July in 1908.

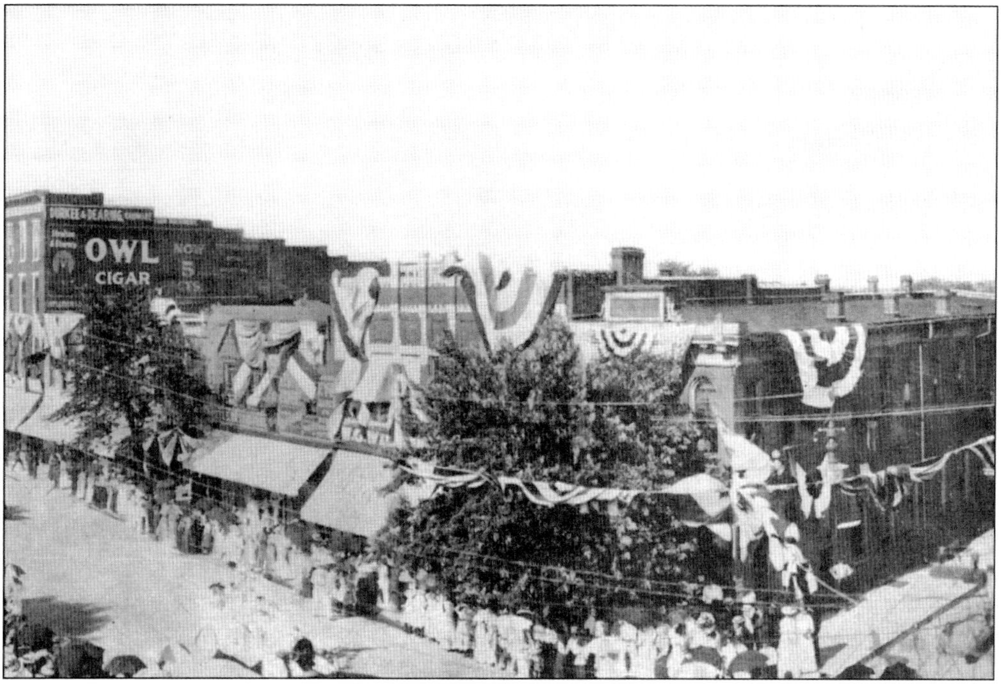

Spectators line the east side of the square for the 1908 Fourth of July parade.

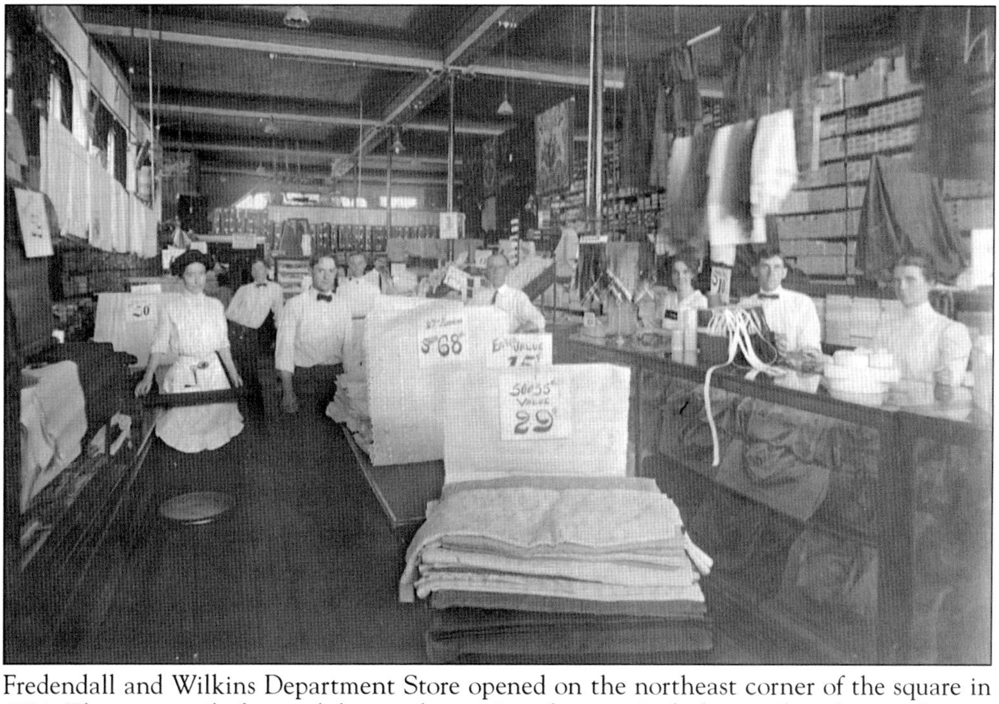

Fredendall and Wilkins Department Store opened on the northeast corner of the square in 1901. The mercantile featured dry goods, men's and women's clothing, a hat shop, and, most memorably, a cash trolley that ran on cables through the store to the mezzanine. The business closed in February 1978.

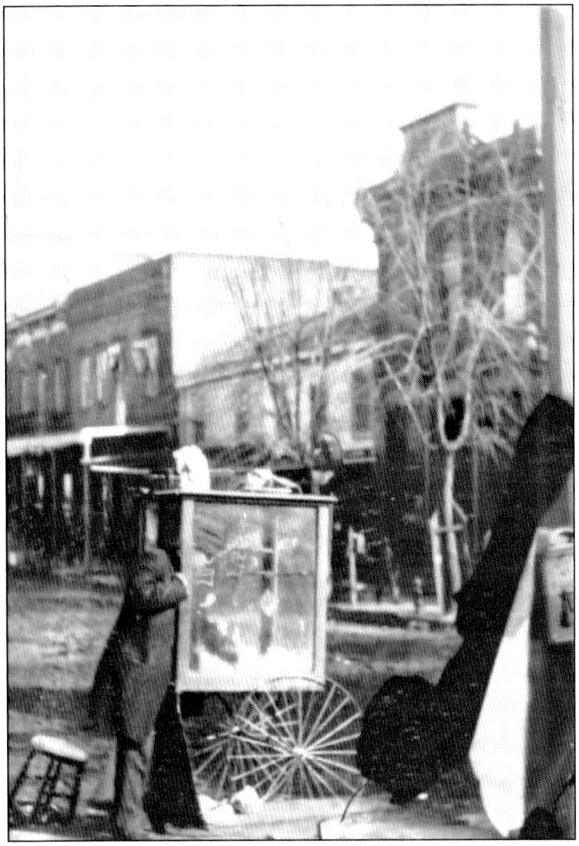

Some vendors did not bother with permanent buildings. Mr. Dryden sold popcorn from a cart on the square.

Parades have been perennially popular around the square. This photograph shows a Flower Parade around 1900.

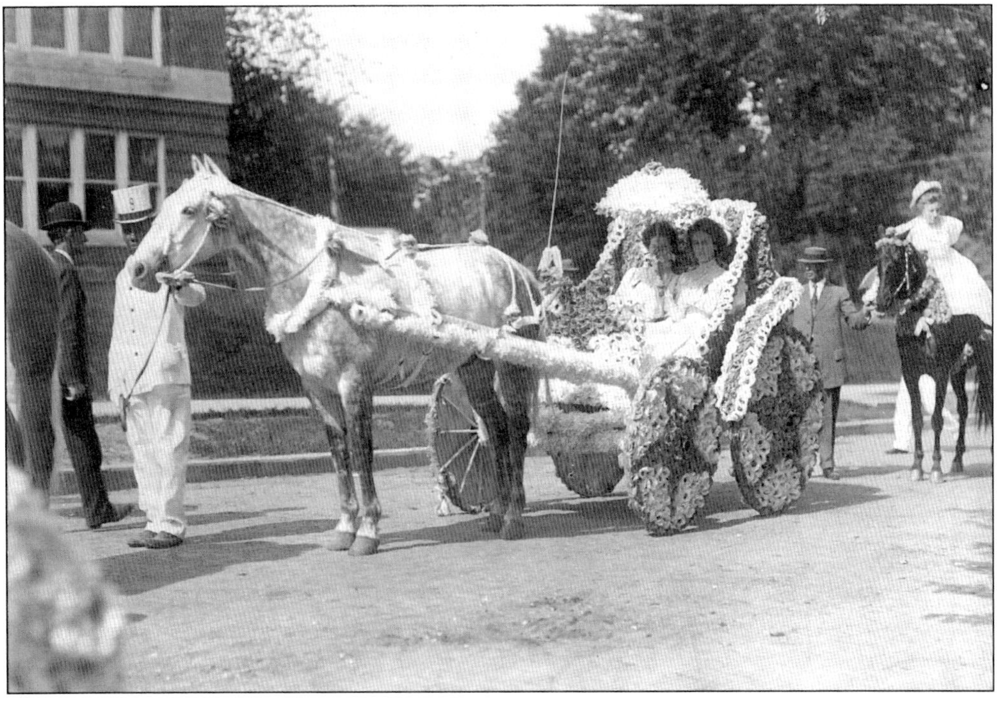

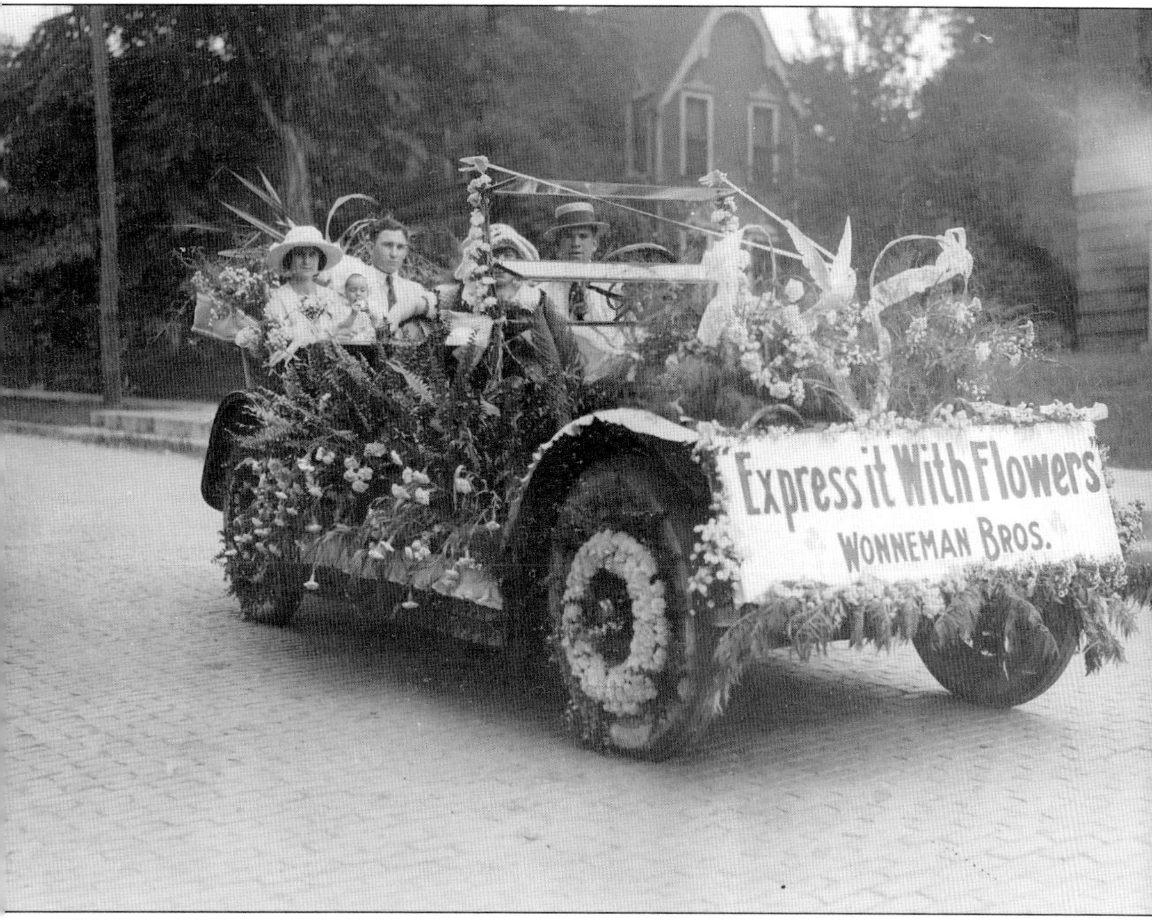

Wonneman Brothers tells the community to "Express it With Flowers" in its entry in the July 4, 1920, American Legion Parade. Wonneman Brothers is still in business as a florist today.

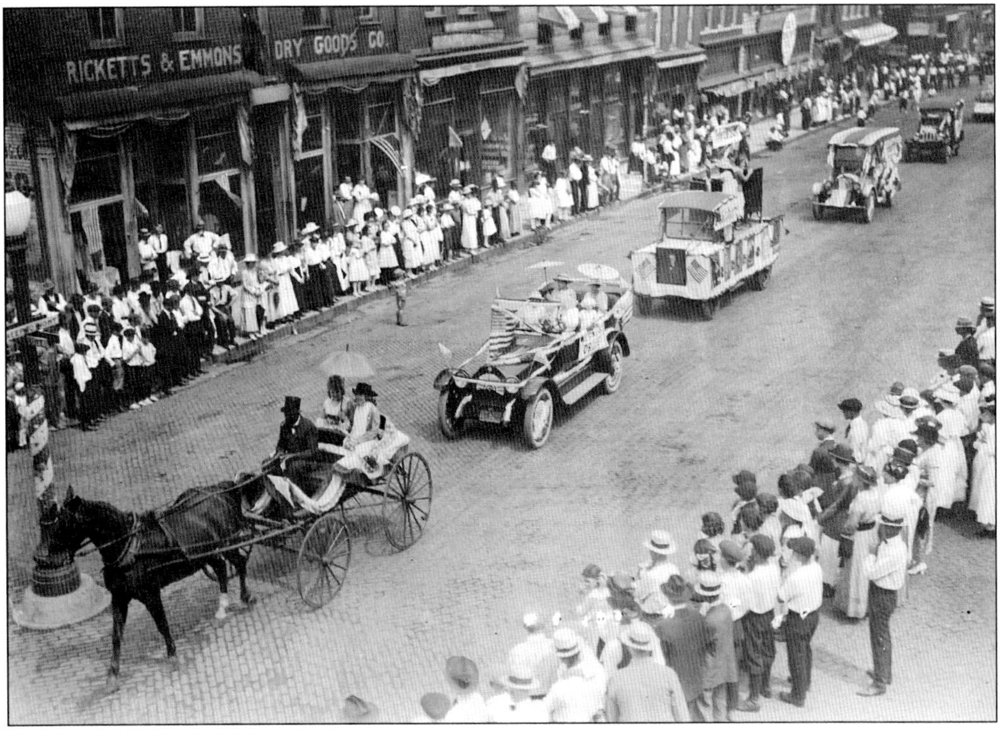

Here is a glimpse of the American Legion Parade in 1920.

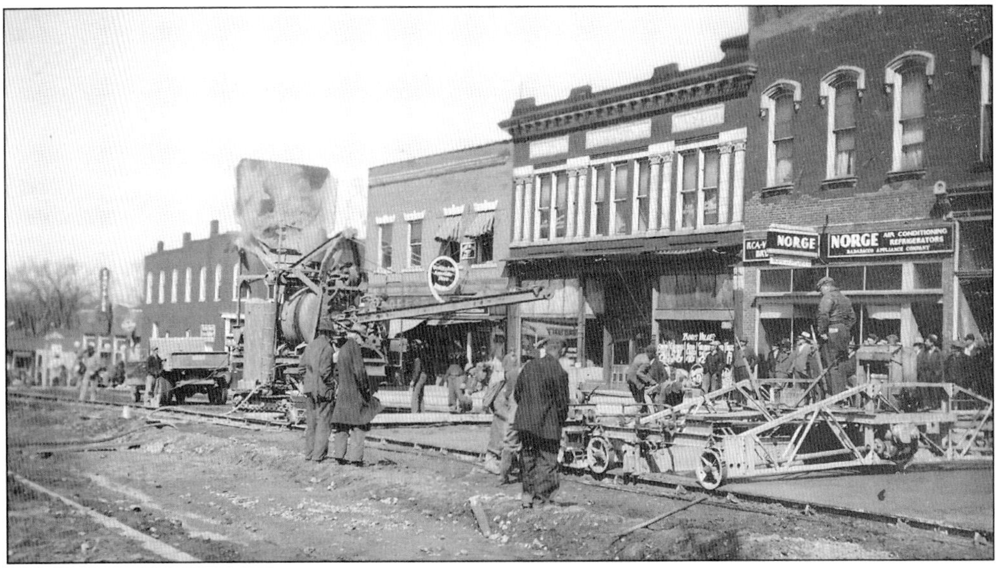

In 1938, the repaving of the square was funded as a federal works project. Laborers were paid 30¢ an hour for 15 hours per week. Shown here is repaving in progress on the north side of the square.

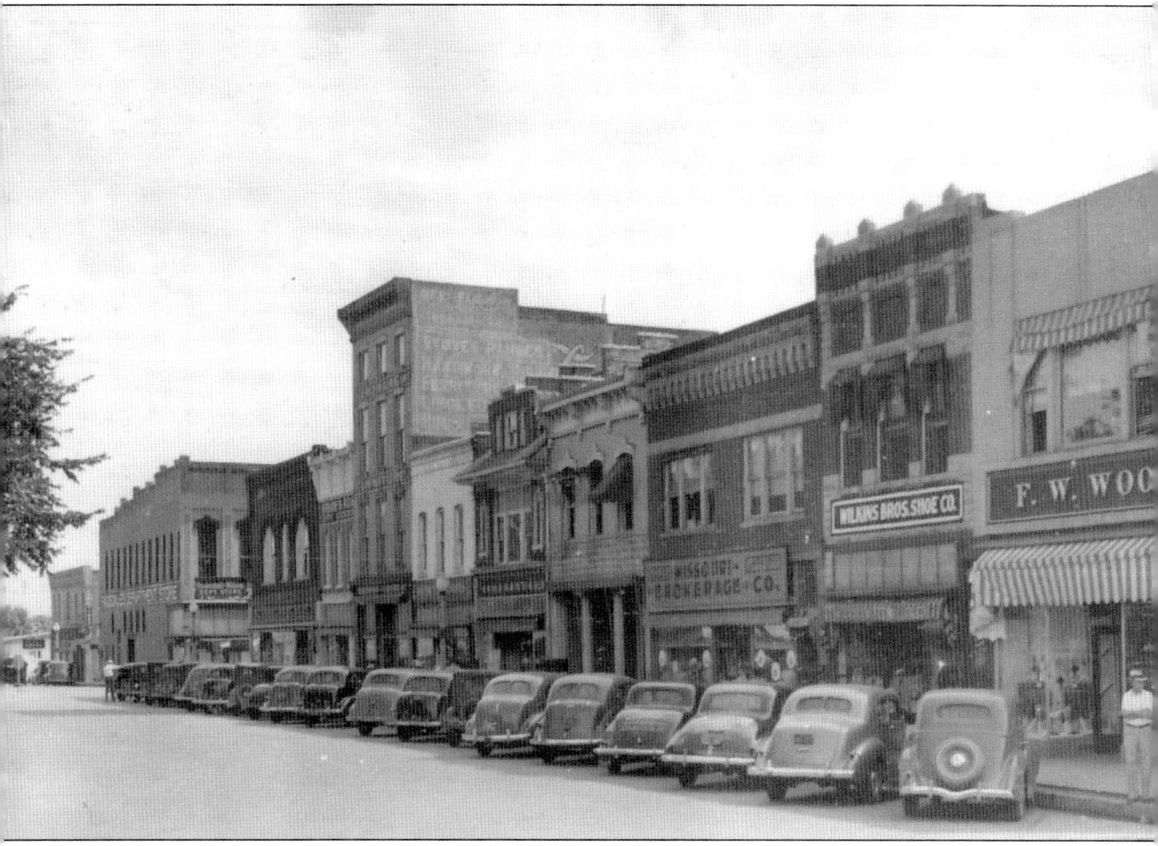

The next five photographs as a group show the four sides of the square in 1938, as well as an aerial view. The east side was anchored on the south by F. W. Woolworth, a five-and-dime, and on the north by Fredendall and Wilkins Department Store.

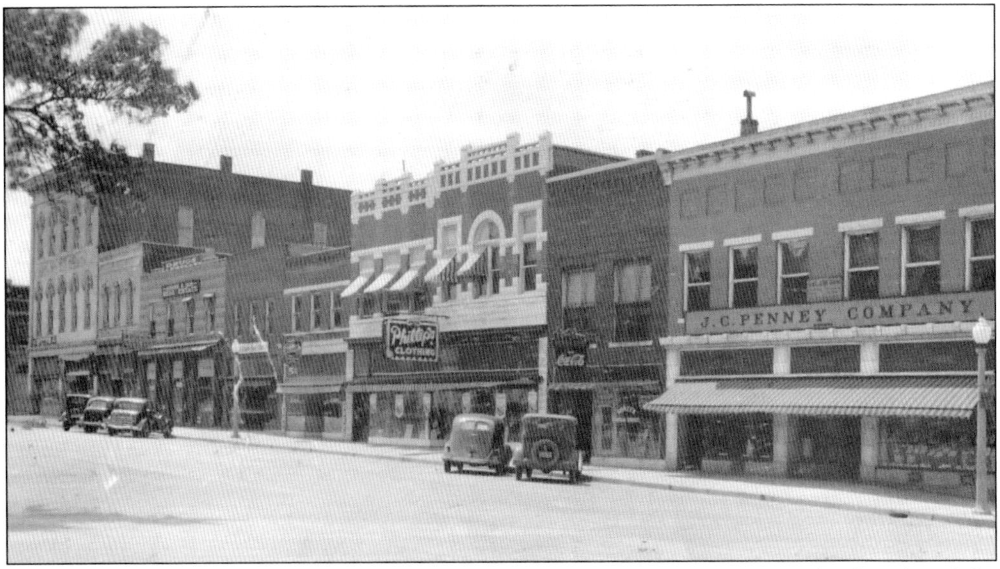

The J. C. Penney Company store graced the west side of the square in 1938. The founder of the chain, James Cash Penney, was a Missouri native.

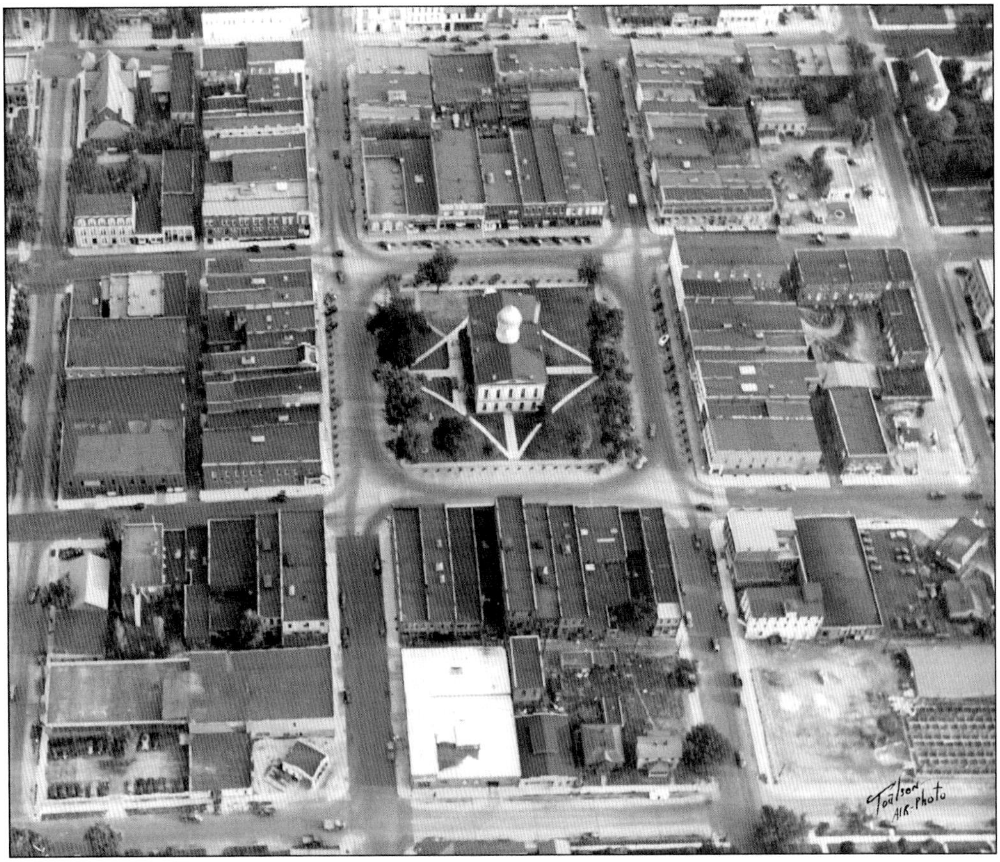

This aerial view of downtown Mexico shows the Courthouse Square in the late 1930s. The third Audrain County Courthouse sits prominently in the center of this 1939 photograph.

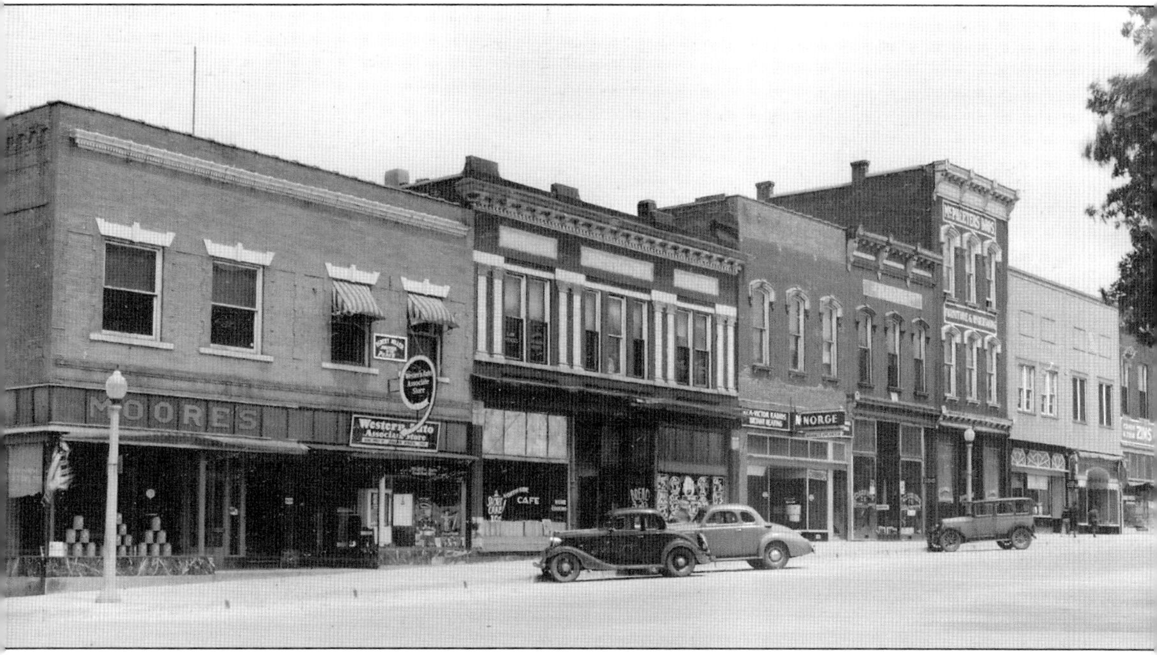

Seen here in 1938, grocery and appliance businesses operated along with others on the north side of the square.

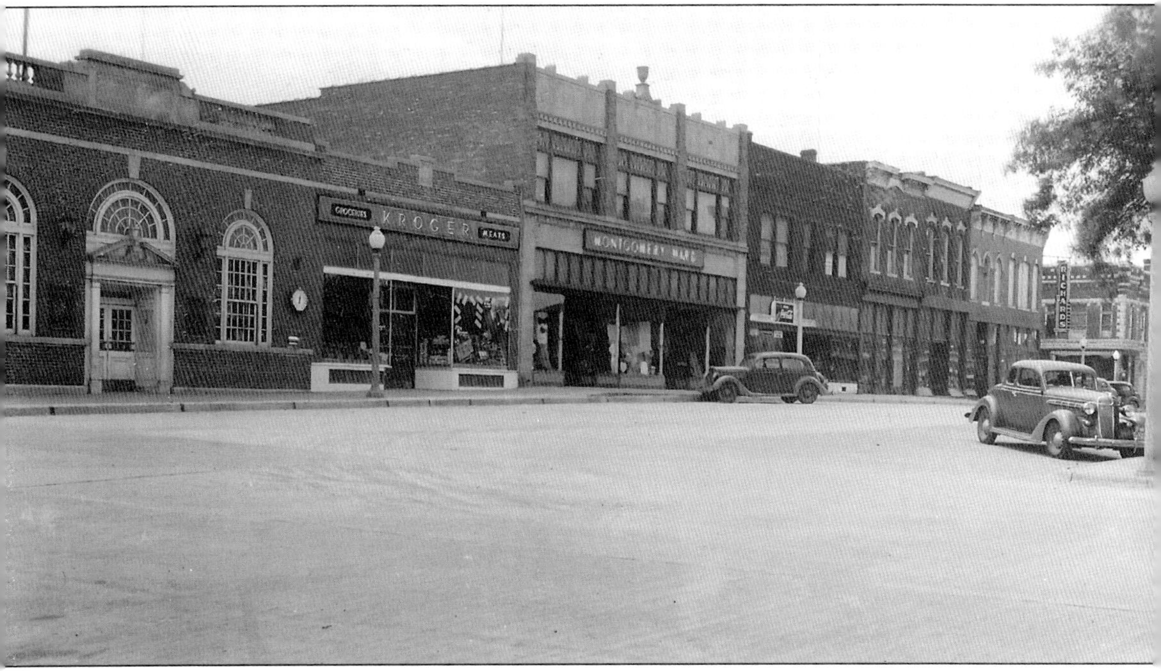

Banks, grocery stores, and department stores worked together to serve the citizens of Mexico on the streets of the square. The south side is pictured here in 1938.

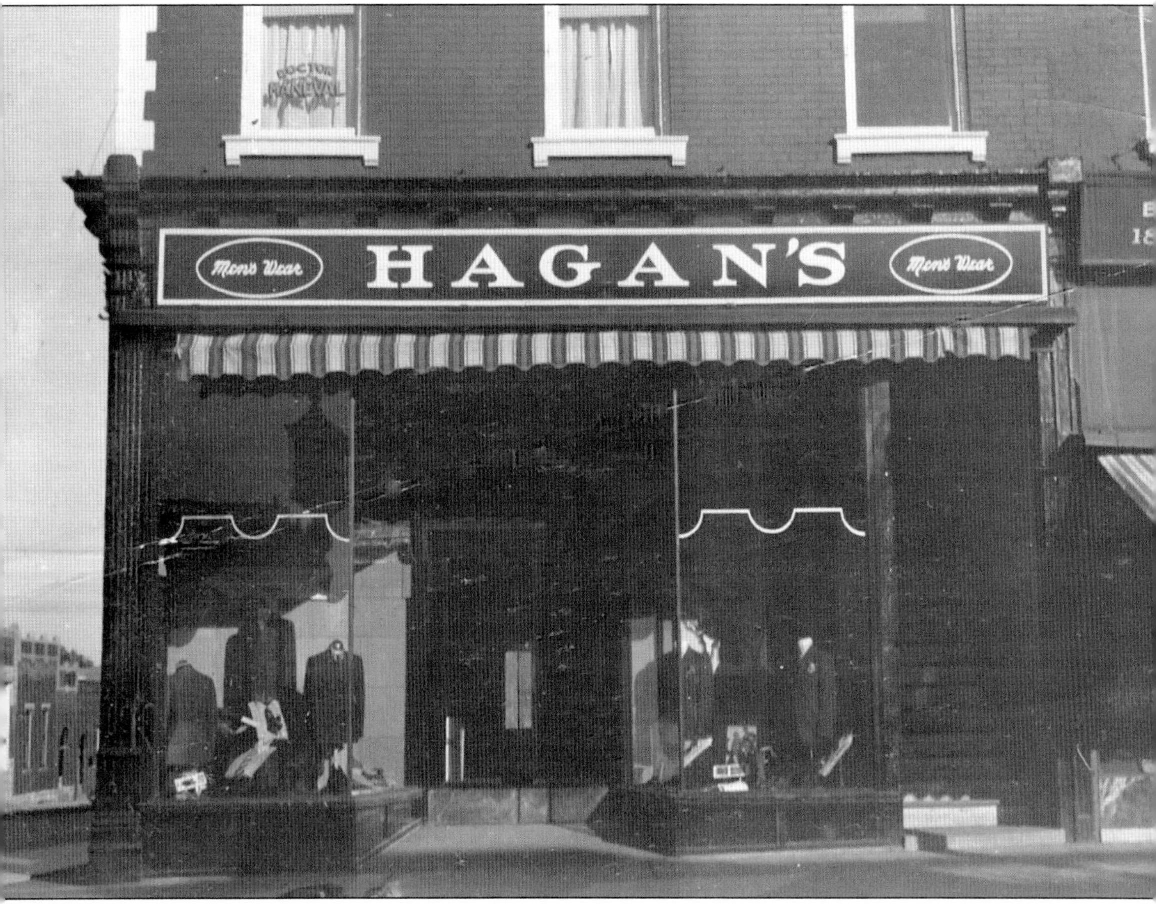

Pictured here in 1936, Hagan's was a popular men's clothing store that operated at several locations around the square from its opening in 1934.

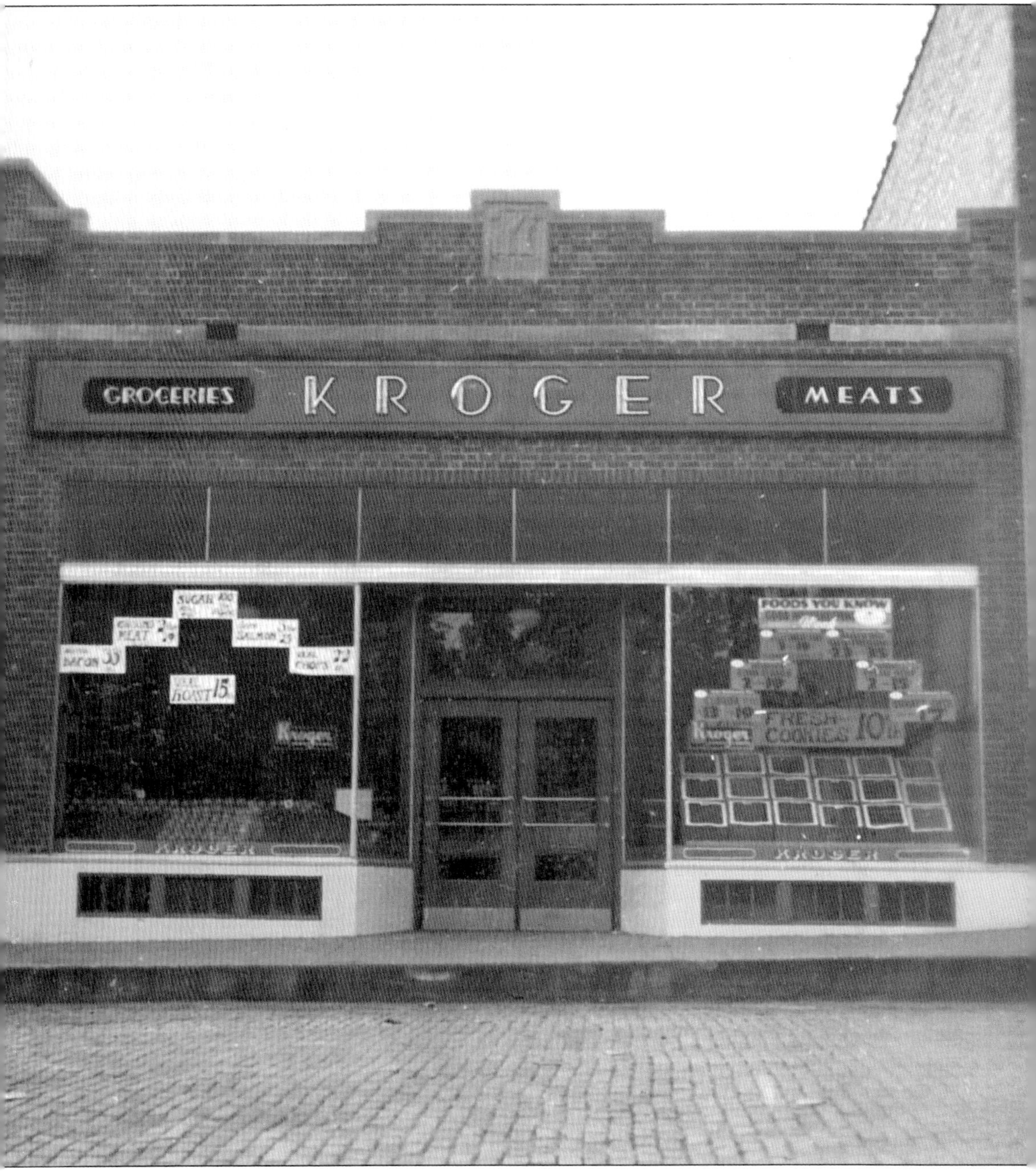

Seen here in 1938, the Kroger grocery store operated on the south side of the square, close to the spot where the first courthouse was located.

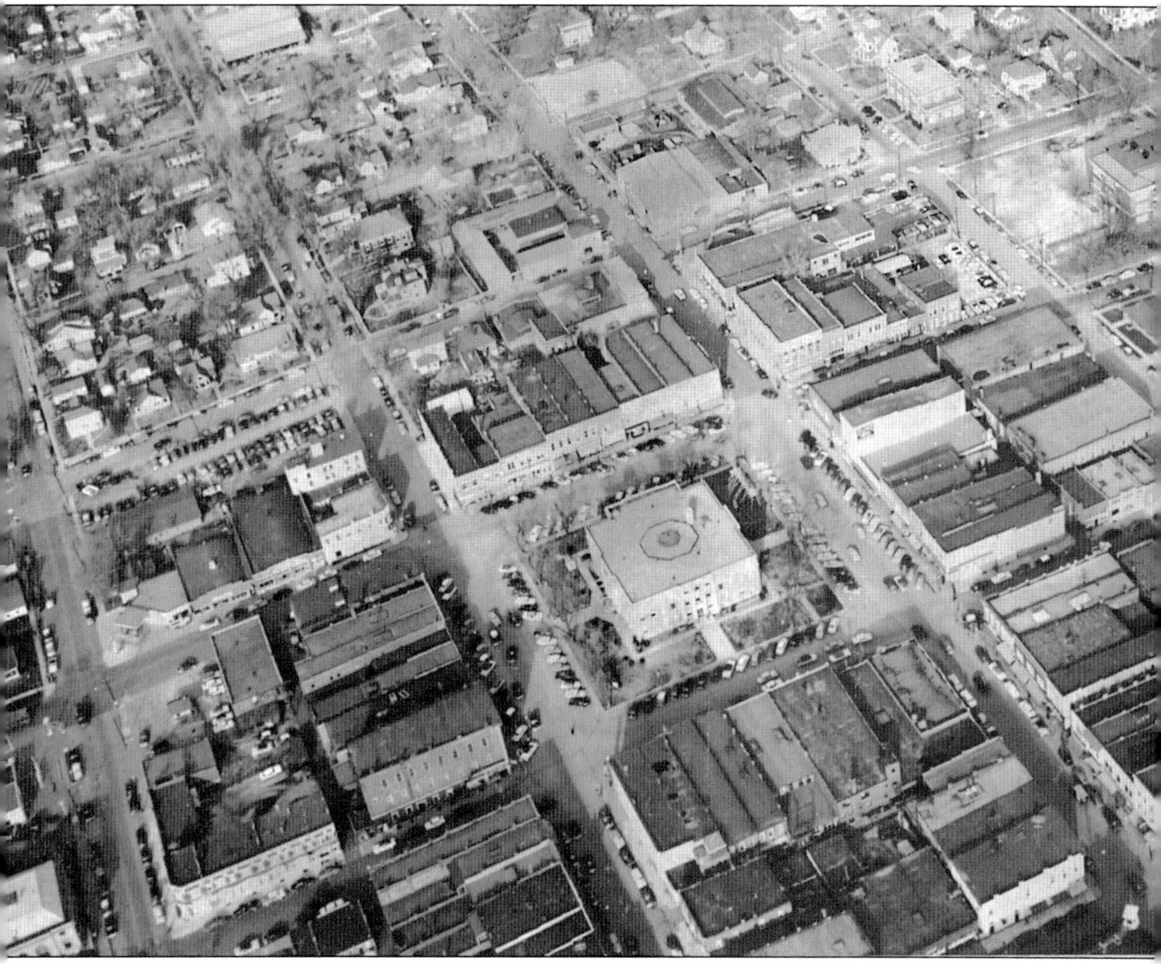

What a difference a handful of years can make. In this 1952 aerial view, the fourth Audrain County courthouse dominates the square.

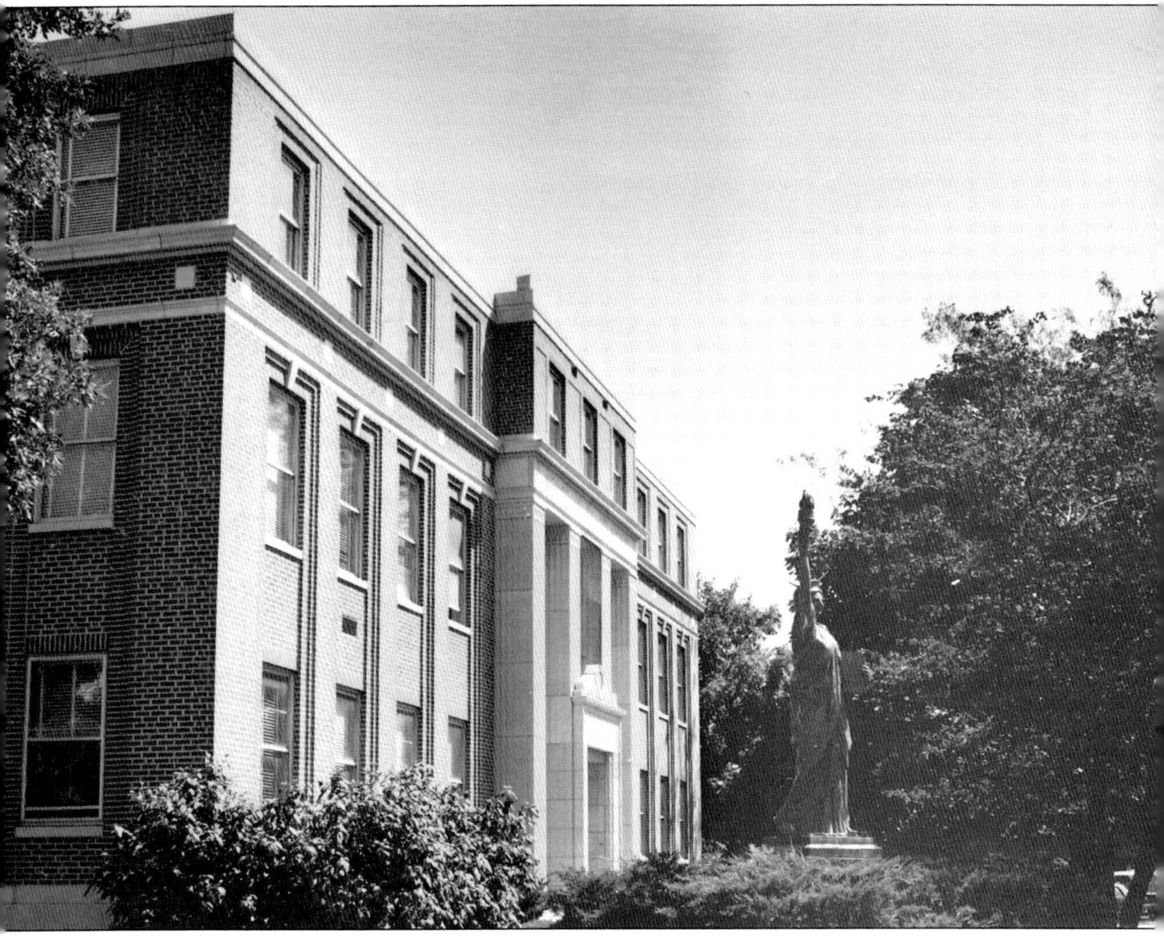

In 1950, the domed courthouse was demolished and replaced by a sleeker, modern three-story brick structure. A replica of the Statue of Liberty is featured on the grounds of the present county building.

The clock on the southwest corner of the square in this late 1950s image was originally part of Mexico Savings Bank, founded by local businessman A. R. Ringo in 1861. The bank building now houses the Mexico Chamber of Commerce.

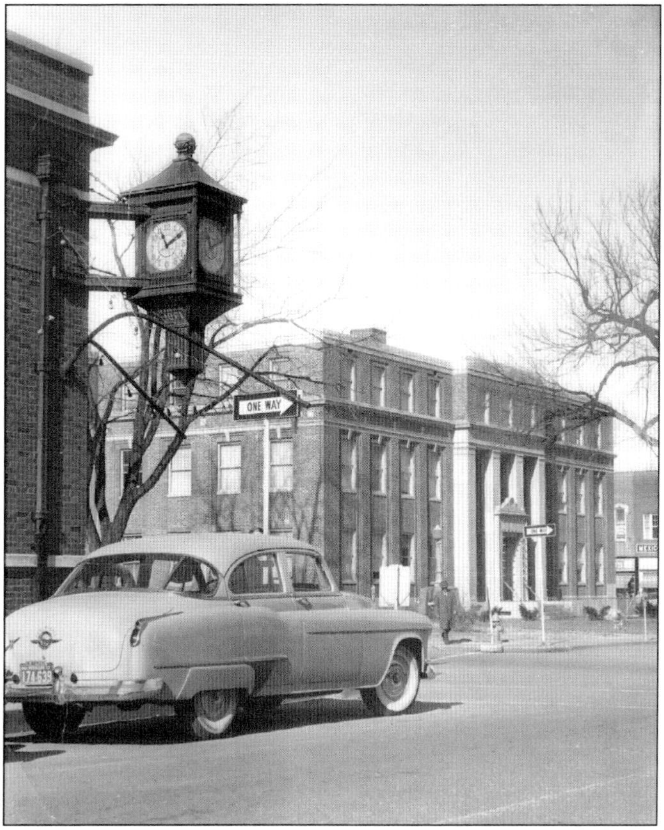

Shown here around 1983, J. C. Penney was a longtime anchor store on the northwest corner of the square. The company no longer has a location in Mexico.

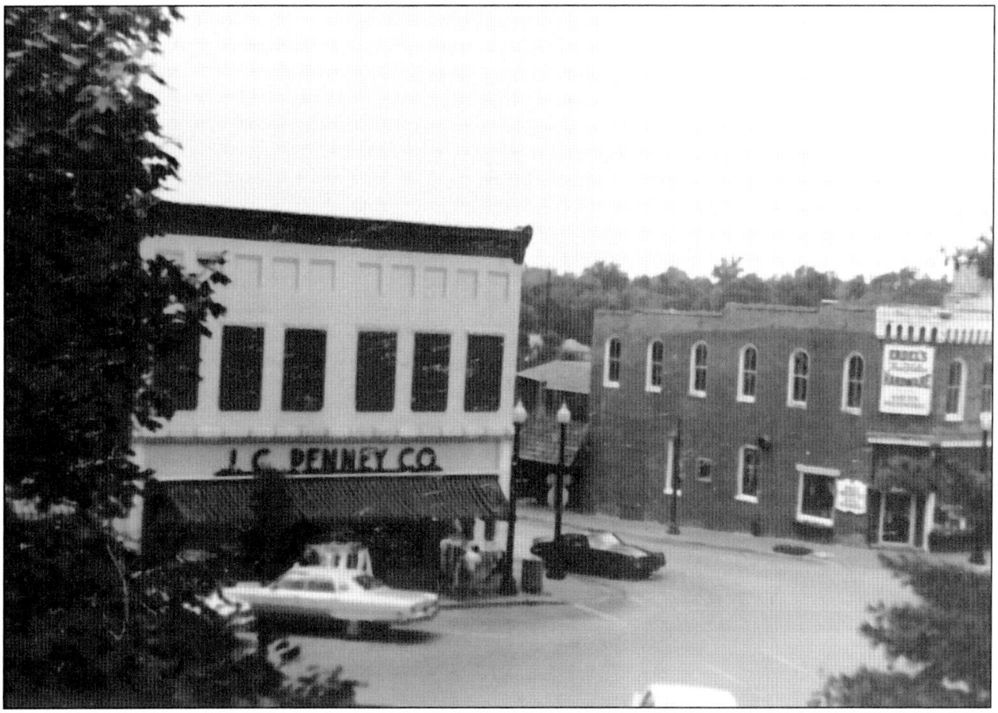

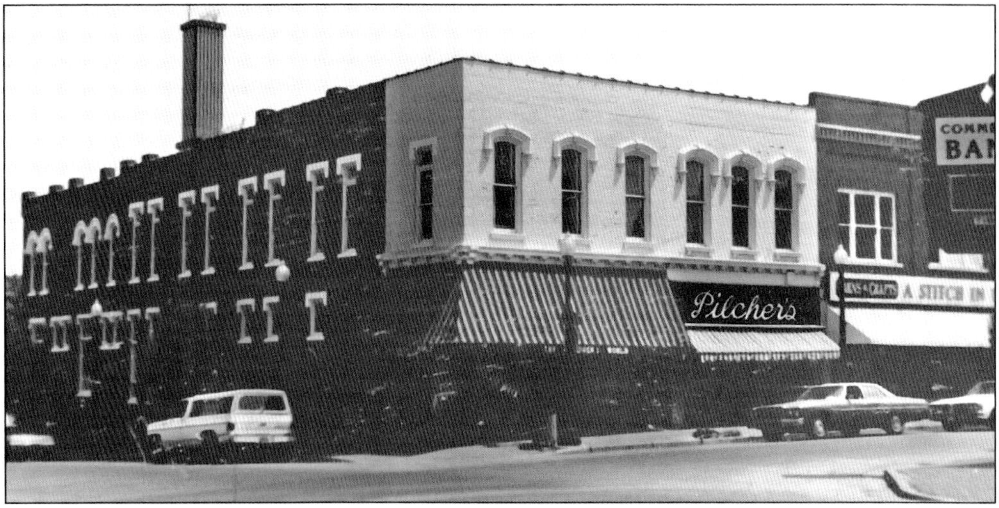

Pilcher's Jewelry has been located in downtown Mexico since 1867 and continues to serve citizens today. This photograph is undated.

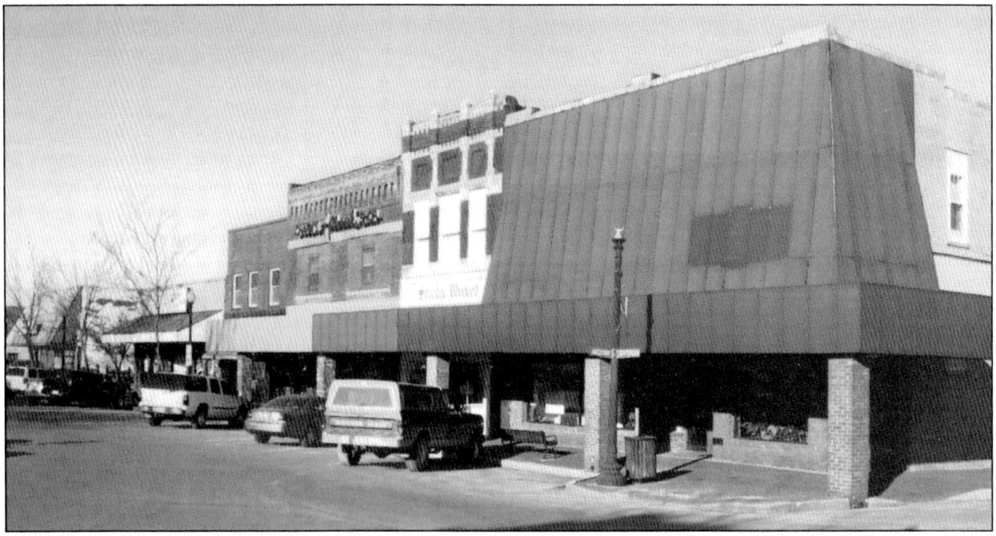
Changing shopping patterns brought big changes to the square. Retail shifted to big box stores located at the edge of town and to shopping plazas with plentiful parking located away from the center of town. Offices and professional establishments replaced retail around the courthouse. This is the east side of the square in February 2010. (Author's collection.)

Two

Saddle Horse Capital of the World

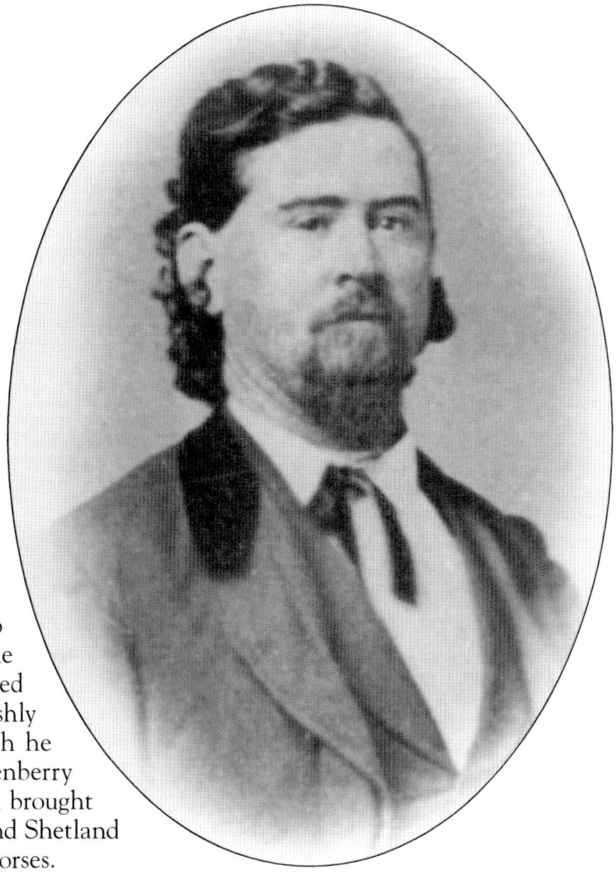

Colby T. Quisenberry moved to Mexico after the Civil War and made his mark on the city and county by bringing in purebred and pedigreed saddle horses from Kentucky. He is credited with raising the quality of Audrain horses from good to the best. Quisenberry was also the second owner of Graceland, the present site of the American Saddlebred Horse Museum, where he lived lavishly and entertained grandly. Although he had his fingers in many pots, Quisenberry considered himself a stockman and brought in the area's first shorthorn cattle and Shetland ponies, as well as many fine saddle horses.

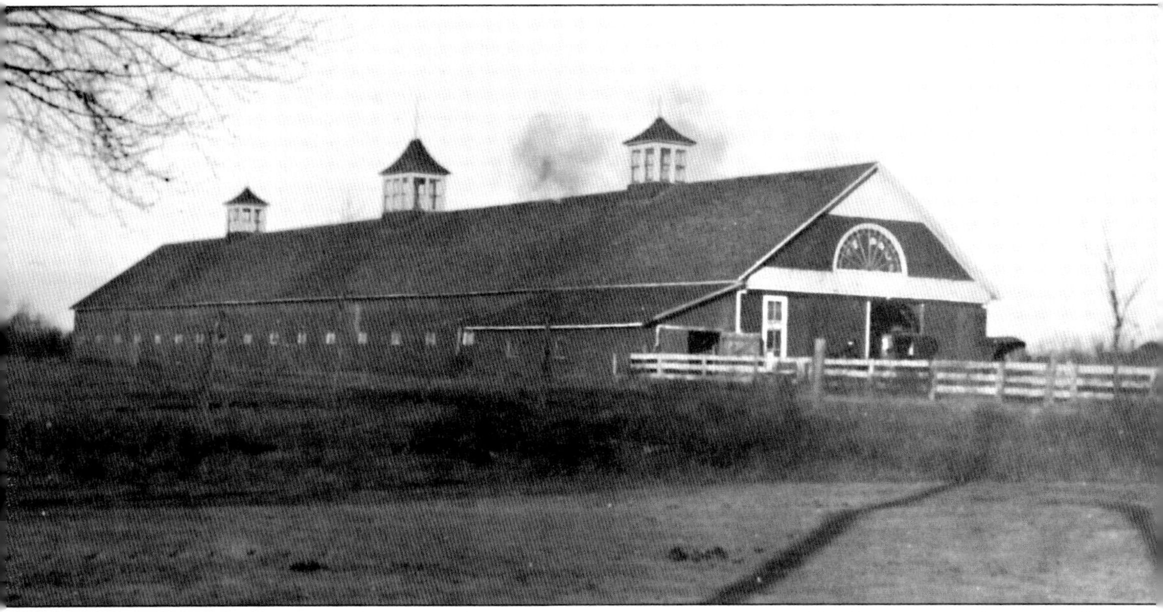

Mexico was home not only to great horses, but to great trainers as well. The door to George and Will Lee's Lee Brothers Stable on West Boulevard is said to have had more champion show horses (and trainers) pass through it than any other barn in the country. Seen here in the early 1900s, the barn was built in 1892 by C. F. Clark and Fred Panhorst, and in the course of its life as a barn it was also owned by Bill Cunningham, Robert Stewart, B. B. Tucker, and Art Simmons.

George Lee is seen in this undated image. He and brother Will learned about horses from their grandfather David Hubble, one of Mexico's pioneer residents. The brothers worked together nearly their whole lives. Horses trained at their facility won many national honors, including at Madison Square Garden, the Chicago International, and the American Royal at Kansas City.

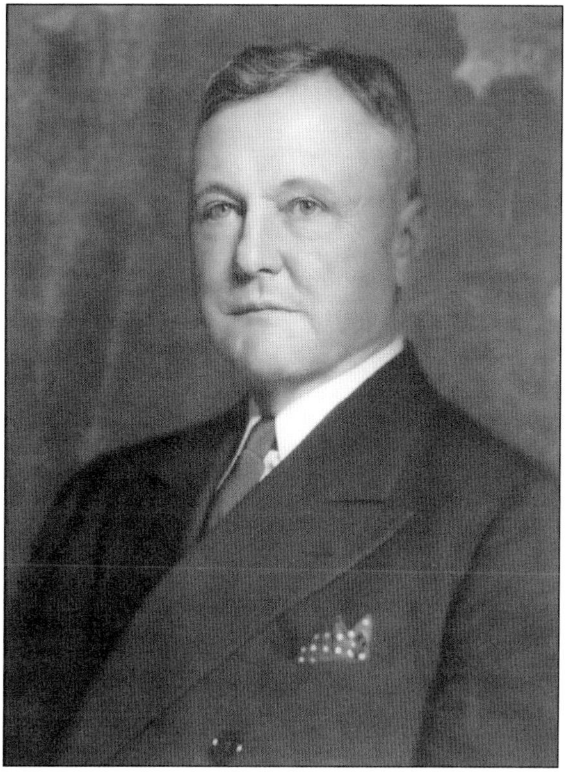

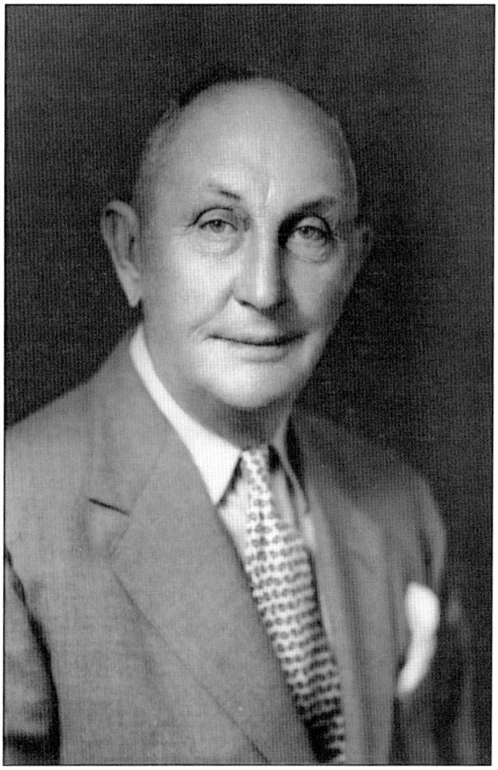

Before he went into business with his brother, W. D. "Will" Lee (seen here in this undated photograph) worked for Macon, Missouri, millionaire Col. F. W. V. Blees and purchased Rex McDonald for him for $5,000 (sometimes reported as $6,000) from a Kentucky horseman. He showed Rex for three years without defeat. The Lees also purchased horses for Pres. William H. Taft and Pres. Franklin D. Roosevelt.

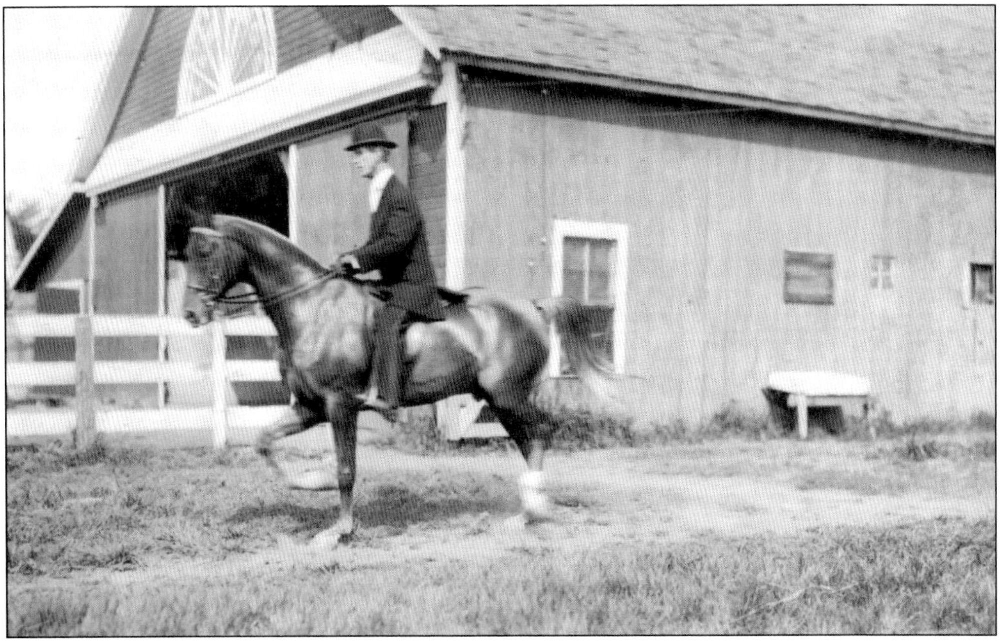

At age 16, Luther B. "Splint" Barnett (1875–1935) started his career as a horse trainer with Lee Brothers Stable. He was an expert rider and trainer and exhibited many of the nation's champion horses, including Rex McDonald.

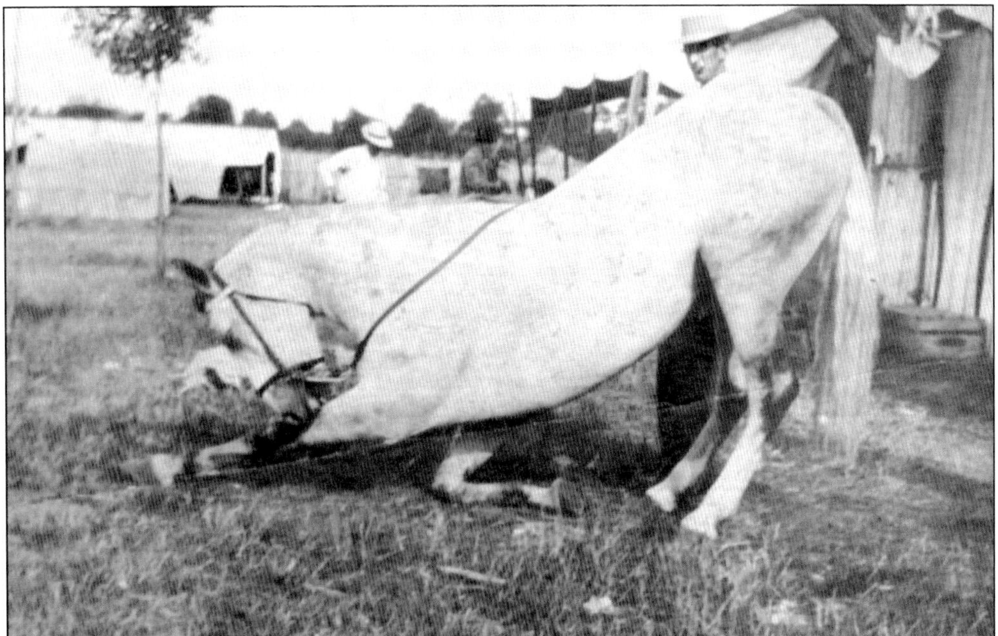

Although Mexico is known for its saddle horses and gaited champions, a number of high school mounts were also trained here. Splint Barnett trained and showed high school horses, such as the one in this photograph.

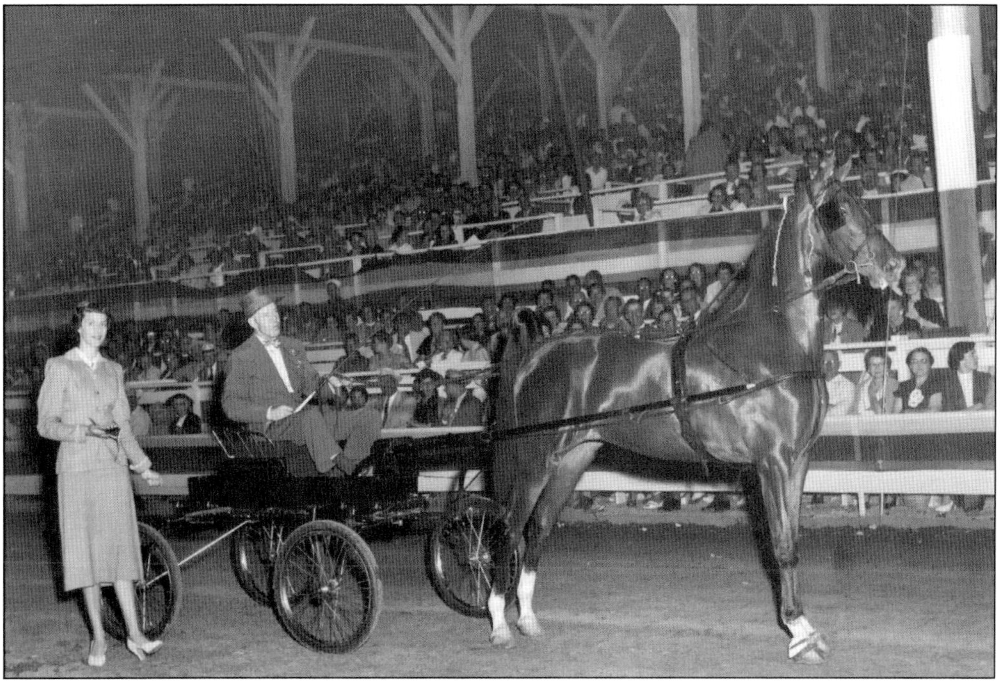

Bill Cunningham fell in love with horses while working at a livery stable in his teens. Cunningham moved to Mexico in 1944 to work with R. G. Stewart, who owned the former Lee Brothers Stable. Cunningham later had his own farm, where he bred horses. He is pictured here at the Audrain County Fair in 1953, winning fine harness with Sports Japonica.

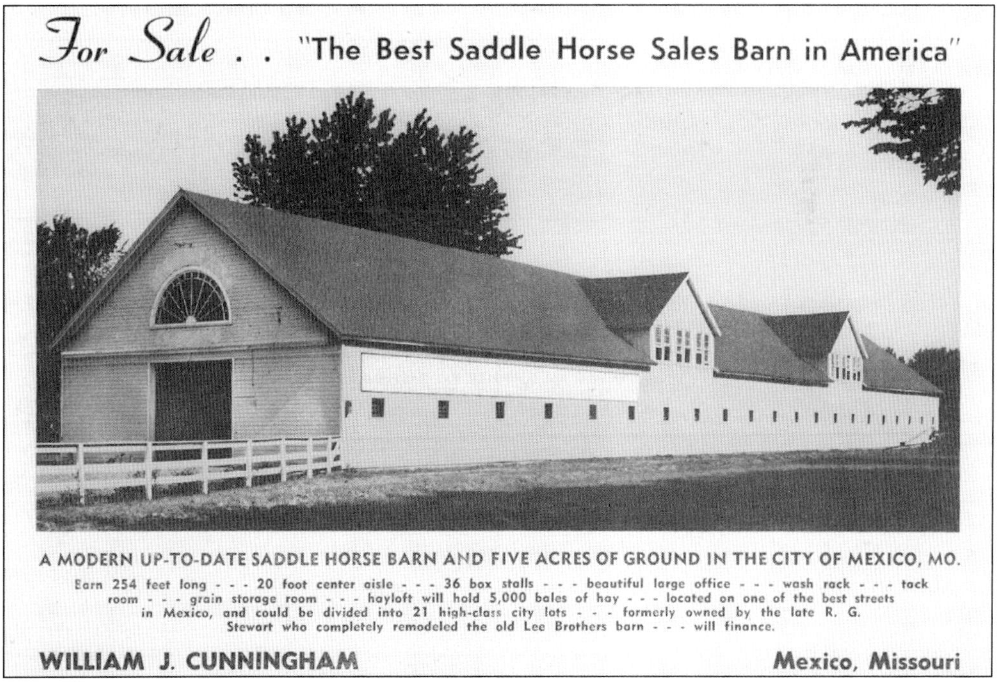

In 1948, the old Lee Brothers Stable went back on the block. A real estate ad lists the features of the barn and 5-acre lot. Fortunately the offering sold as a barn and found its way to Art Simmons.

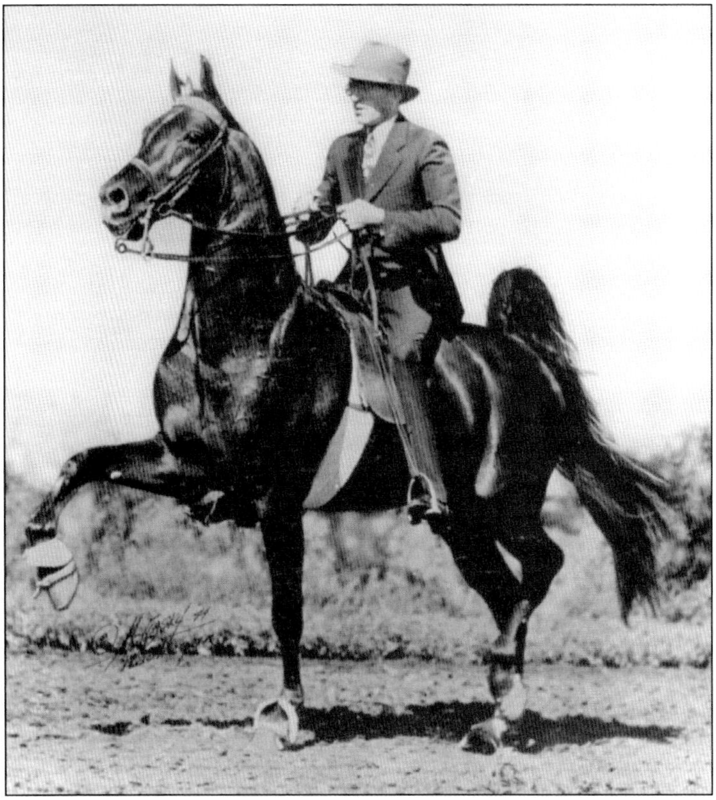

Art Simmons had a 60-year career in horses, winning most major honors. He opened Simmons Stables on West Boulevard (former Lee Brothers Stable) in 1949. Here Simmons rides Faustiana Genius.

Simmons was a show ring legend. Here he is driving Irish Lullaby to a third-place win in junior fine harness in the 1950s.

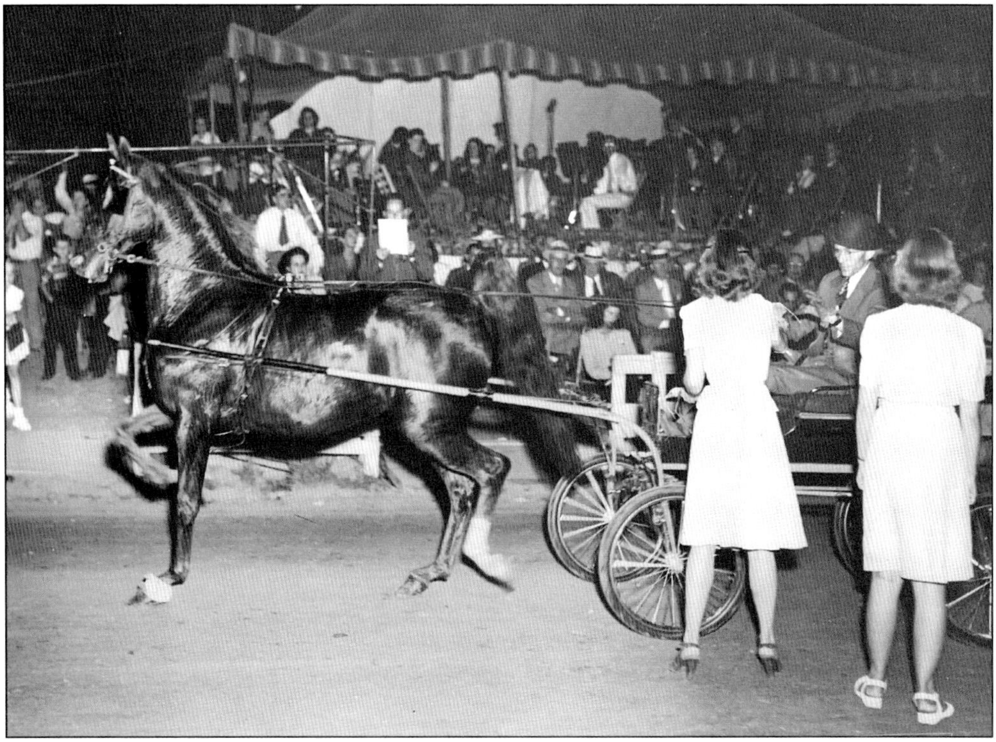

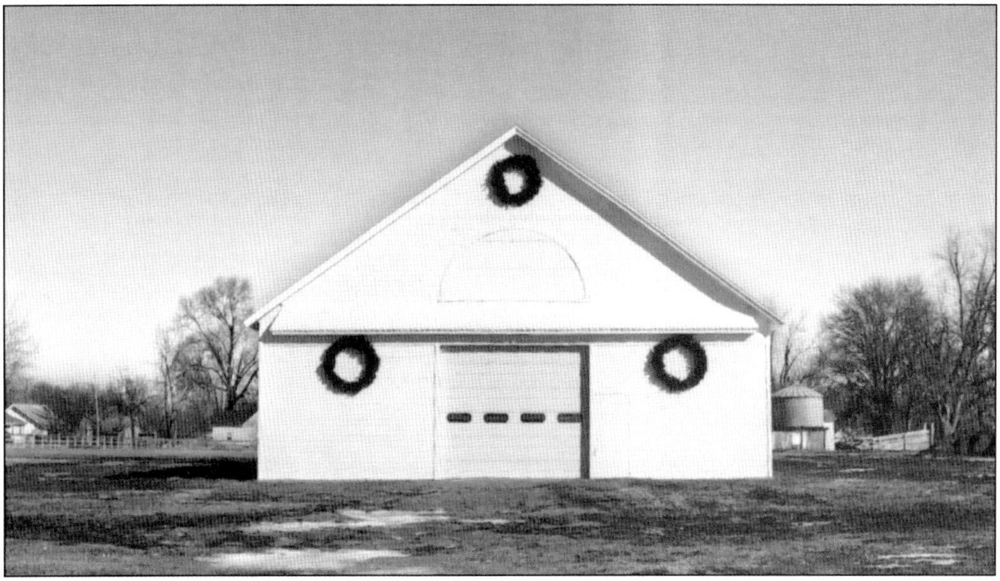

Seen here in 2010, Arthur Simmons Stables was occupied until 2001 by a long line of stellar trainers and riders, making it the oldest and largest public stable in the United States in continual use as a horse stable. (Author's collection.)

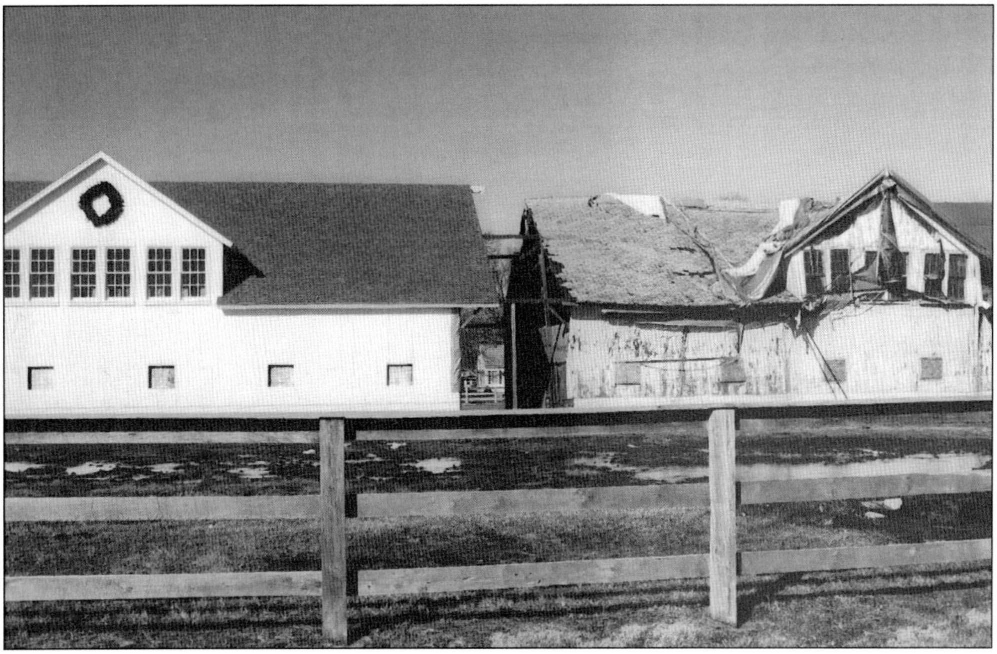

In 2002, a group of Mexico citizens formed the Simmons Stables Preservation Fund. The purpose of the fund is to protect history, to renovate and preserve the stable, and to establish the International Saddlebred Hall of Fame. The group has restored a portion of the stable at this time (mid-2010). (Author's collection.)

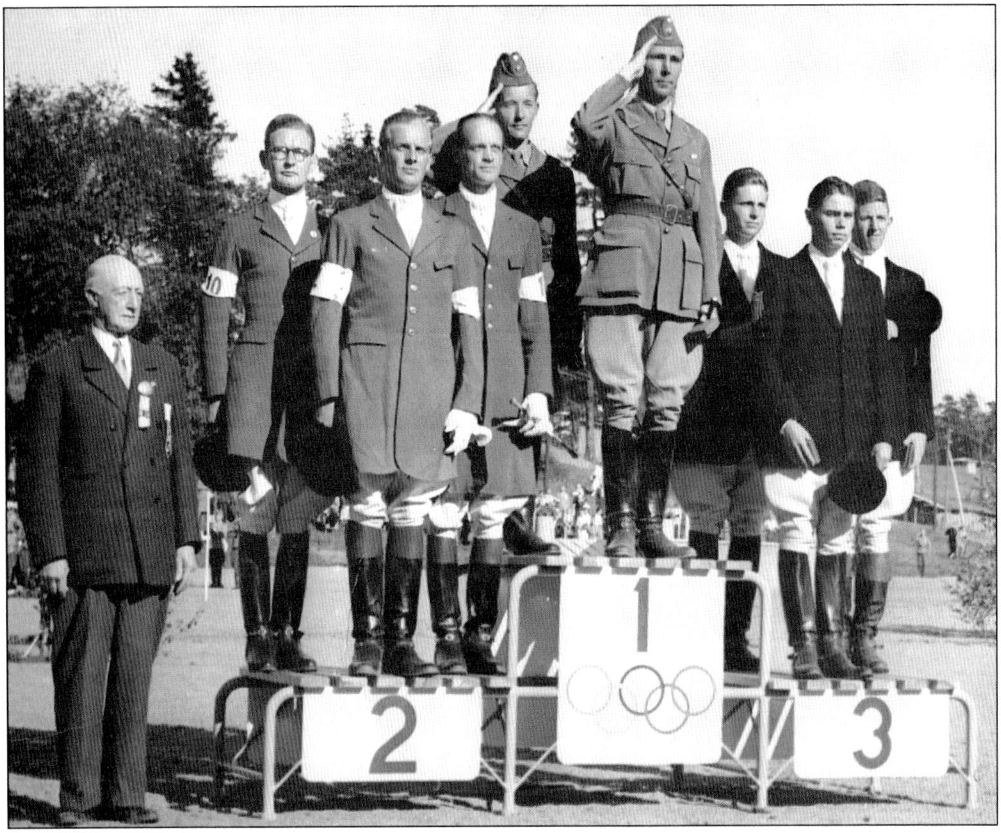

In 1952, A. P. Green's grandson Walter Staley Jr. was a member of the American team that won the bronze medal in equestrian events at the Helsinki Olympics, continuing the tradition of horse-riding champions from Mexico. The winning teams are shown here at the medal ceremony. The U.S. team, on the right, includes, from left to right, Walter Staley Jr., Champ Hough, and John B. Wofford.

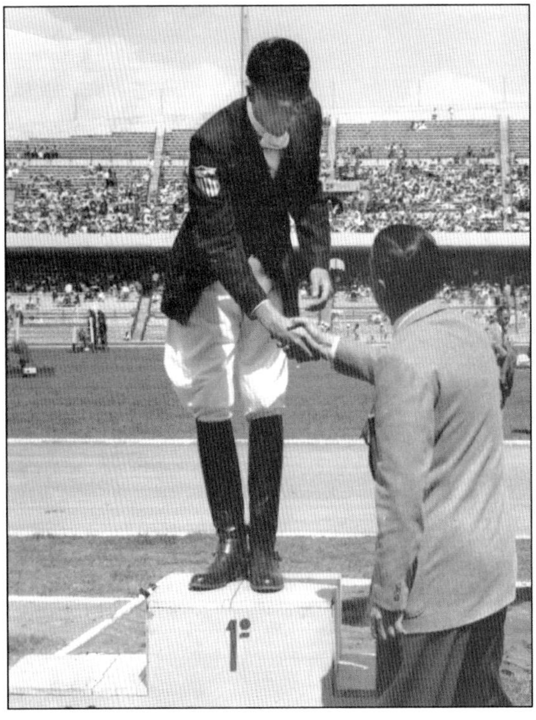

Continuing as a champion, Walter Staley Jr. is seen here receiving a gold medal at the Pan American Games in Mexico City in 1955.

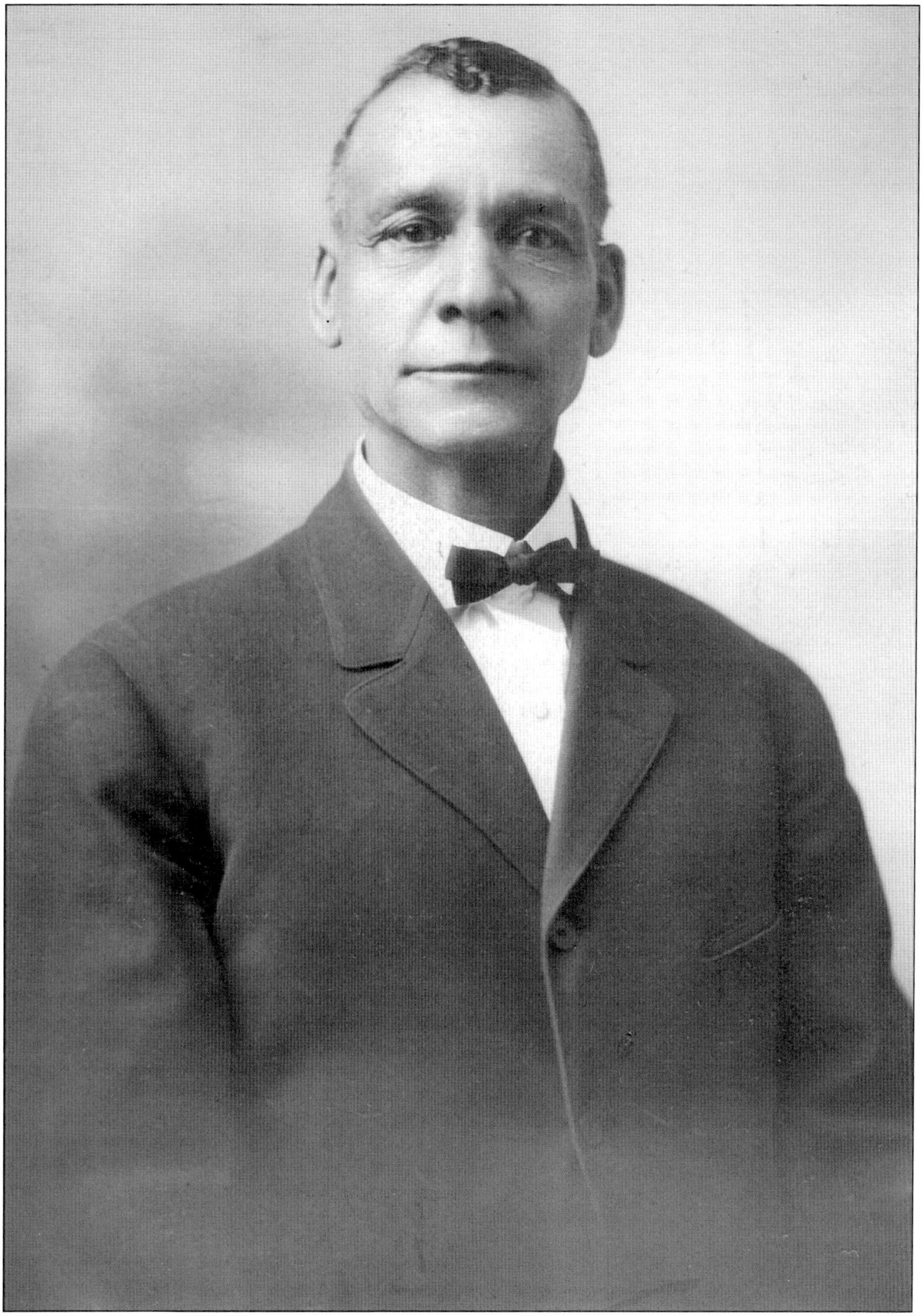

At the beginning of the 20th century, Mexico was recognized as the saddle horse capital of the world due to the quality of the horses raised and sold in the city and county and the quality of the trainers and riders working here. A friend to presidents and royalty, and perhaps the most famous Mexicoan of his time, former slave Tom Bass trained many champion horses.

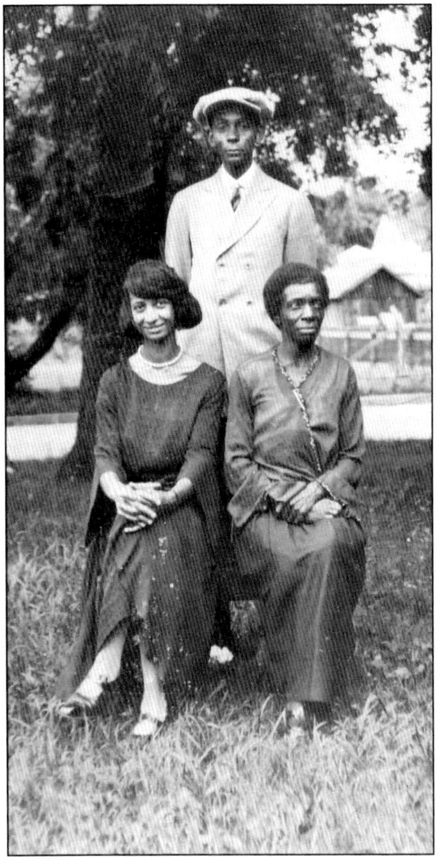

Bass was born a slave in Callaway County in 1859, the son of a planter and Cornelia Gray (seated at right). After he was freed, Bass remained on the Bass plantation for a while before coming to Mexico, where he drove the Hotel Ringo buggy to pick up passengers at the train station. His talent with horses did not go unnoticed, and soon he was working as a trainer for Joe Potts.

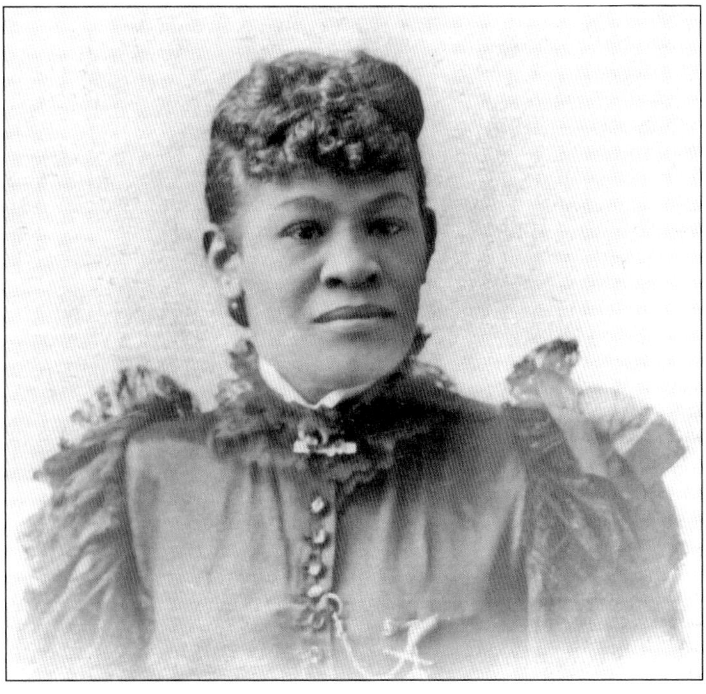

Tom Bass married schoolteacher Angia "Angie" on September 20, 1882. Angie was well educated and passed learning along to Tom, teaching him to read and helping him with math and spelling. She handled many of her husband's business affairs. Bass fathered twin sons with a woman he did not marry and was not involved in their upbringing.

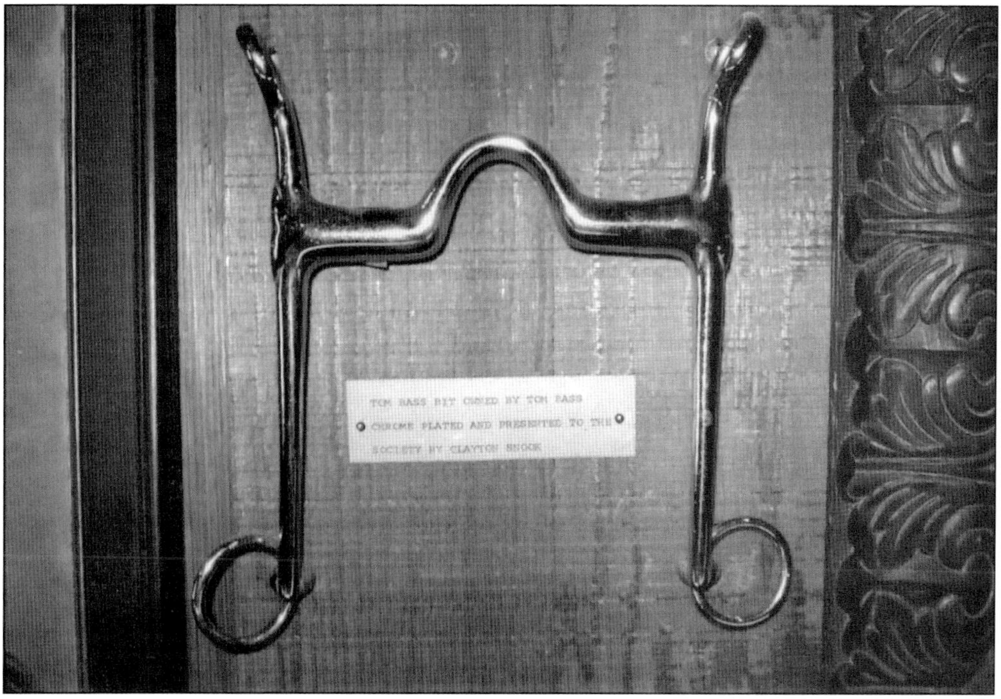

For 50 years, Tom Bass trained, bought, sold, and showed horses across the country. One of his accomplishments was the Bass Bit, which was never patented by him. This equipment made training the horse more comfortable for the animal. Bass considered it his contribution to the world he so loved. (Author's collection.)

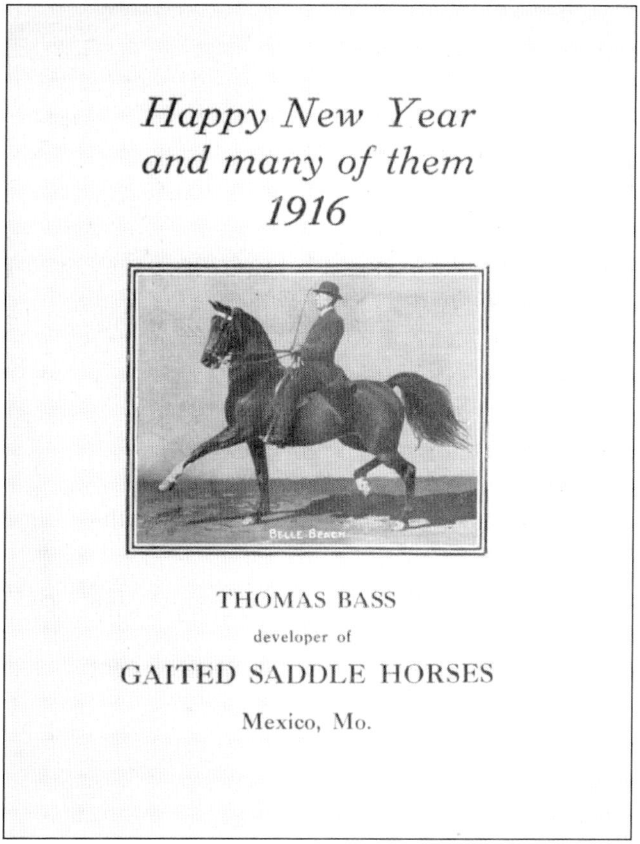
Happy New Year
and many of them
1916

THOMAS BASS
developer of
GAITED SADDLE HORSES
Mexico, Mo.

In his first show, Bass broke the color barrier in the horse ring when he won second place with Blazing Black, a horse others considered not trainable. Although he was met with prejudice, Tom never responded to the slurs shouted at him. His philosophy was that his winning was a great antidote to others' negative behavior.

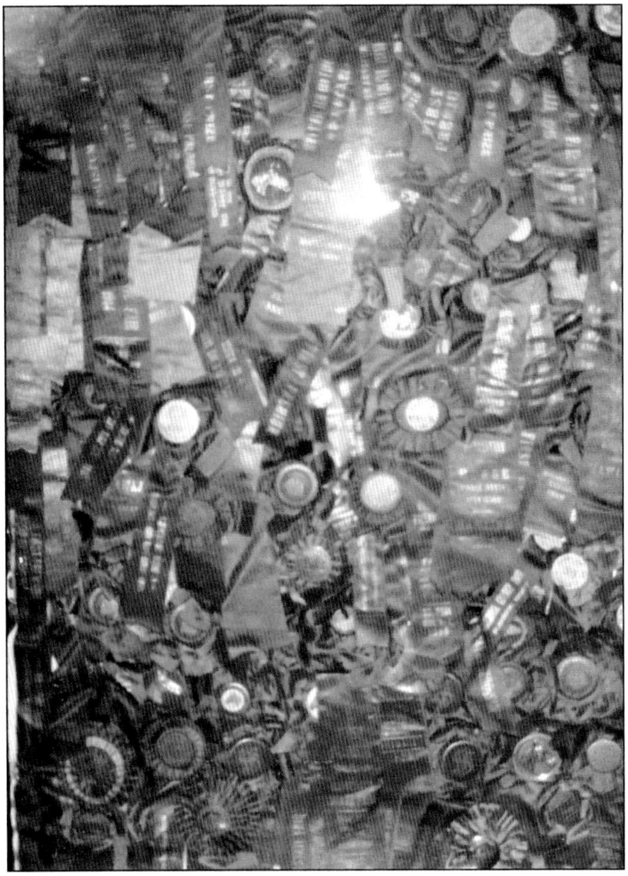

Tom Bass won innumerable blue ribbons, cups, and awards in his day; they spilled over in his home and barn. Today many are displayed at the American Saddlebred Horse Museum.

Although he trained many horses in his day, Tom Bass's favorite was a champion mare named Belle Beach. She was considered by many to be one of the most accomplished high school horses of all time. The two of them often performed rather than competed in horse shows, including Kansas City's American Royal and at Madison Square Garden. After Belle Beach retired, Bass sometimes rode her to the square in Mexico and put her through her paces to the delight of onlookers.

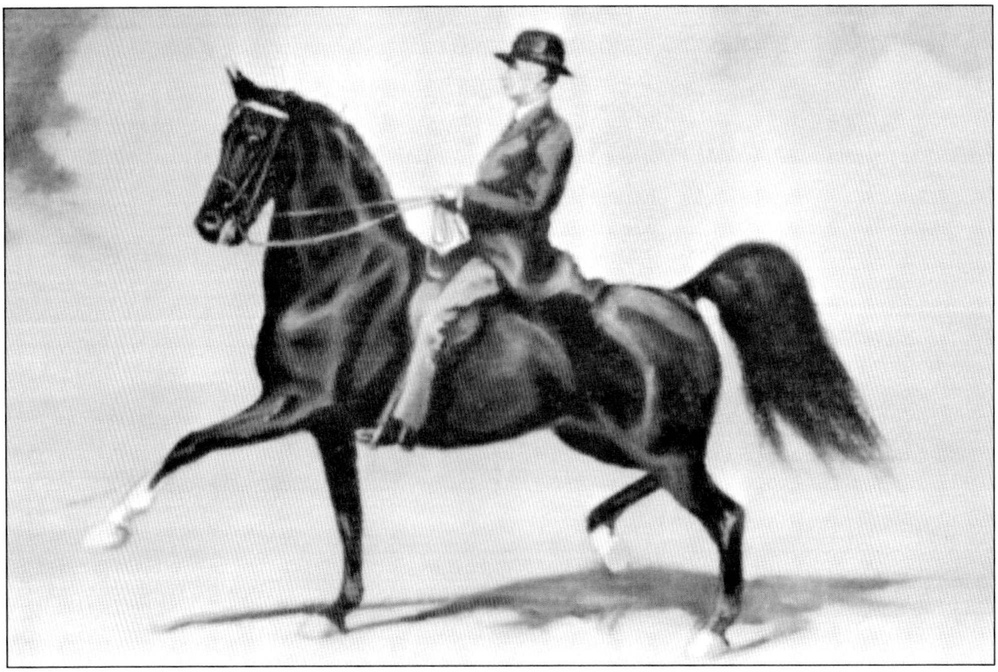

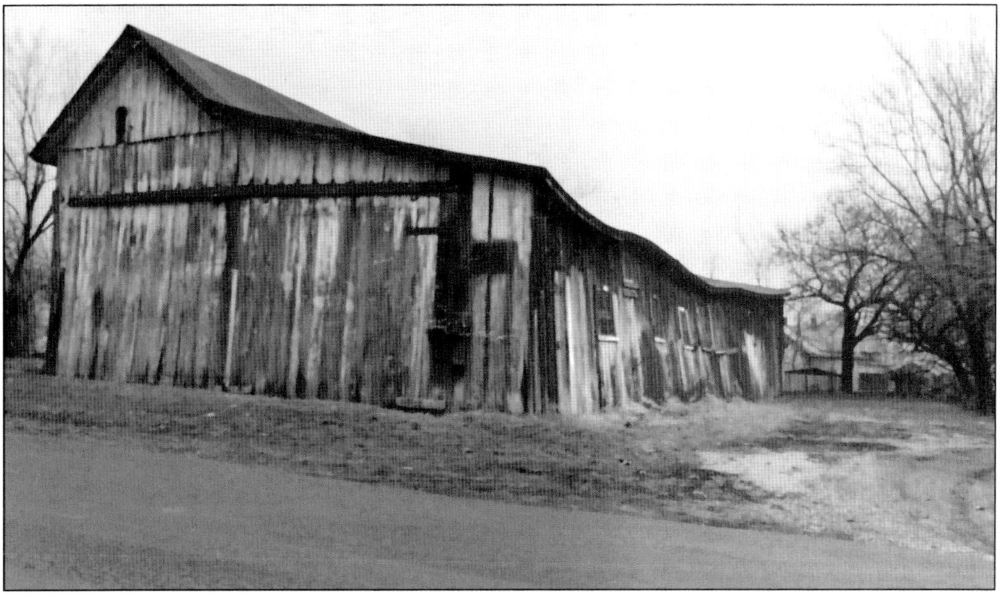

Tom Bass ran his own horse barn in Mexico for over 50 years, where he taught riding, boarding, training, and showing horses in the ring. After his death, Bass's barn slowly fell into disrepair. Several people voiced interest in saving it until it was destroyed by arson.

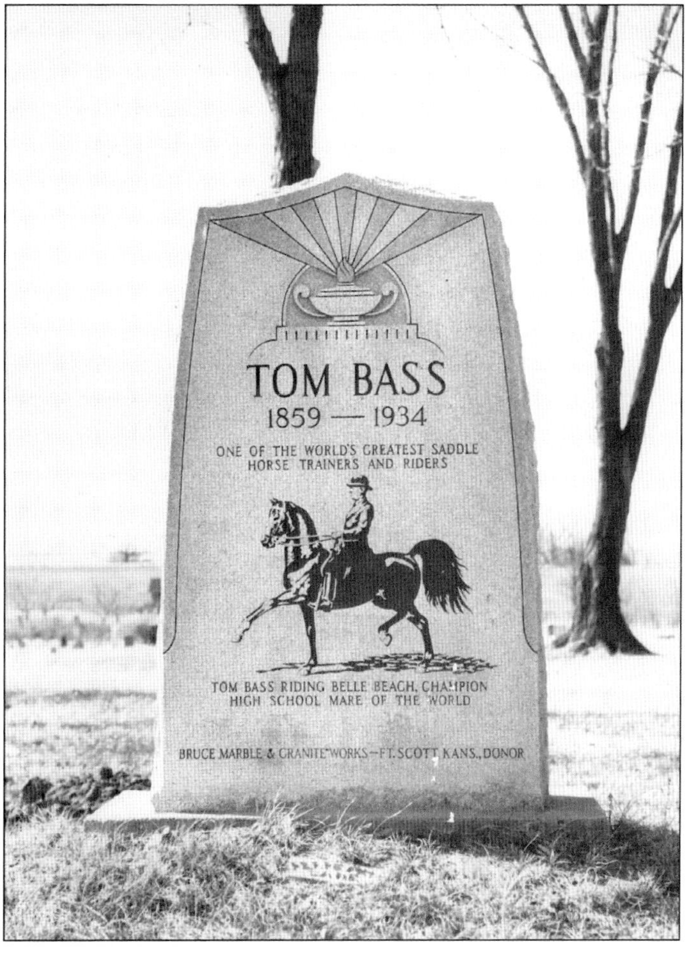

Tom Bass died in 1934 at age 75. He was greatly mourned, with eulogies appearing in newspapers around the world, including one by the famous Will Rogers. Bass is buried at Elmwood Cemetery in Mexico.

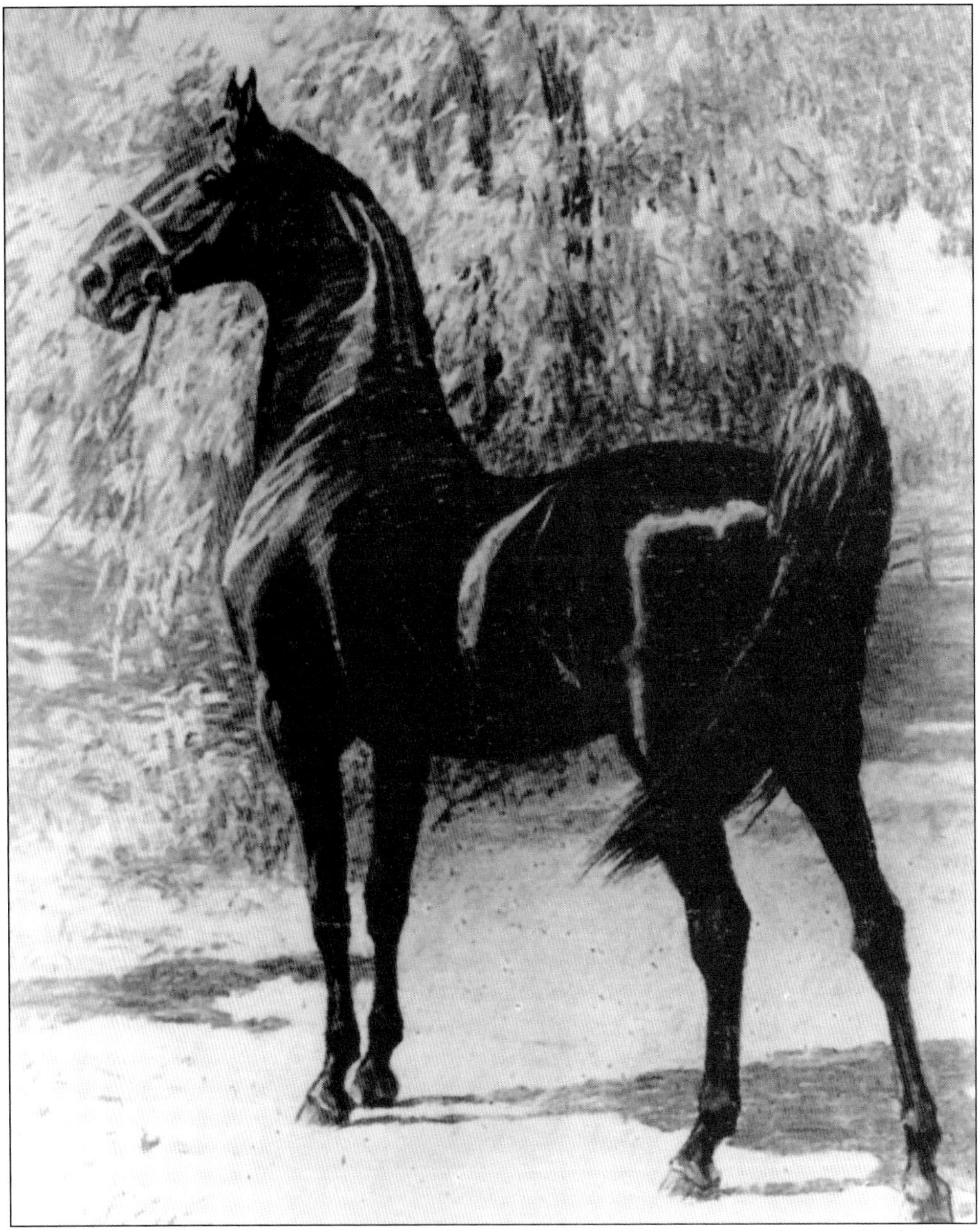

Choosing the greatest saddle horse of all time might be a problem for some but not for Audrain County residents; Rex McDonald is their choice. Rex was foaled in Callaway County, Missouri, on May 20, 1890, but (rumor has it) in a barn that straddled the Audrain County line. A jet-black, 16-hands, 1,050-pound, high-stepping five-gaiter, Rex defeated every horse he met. In his career, he was only defeated six times but later came back to win against those horses. In 1903, he was crowned Champion Saddle Horse of America.

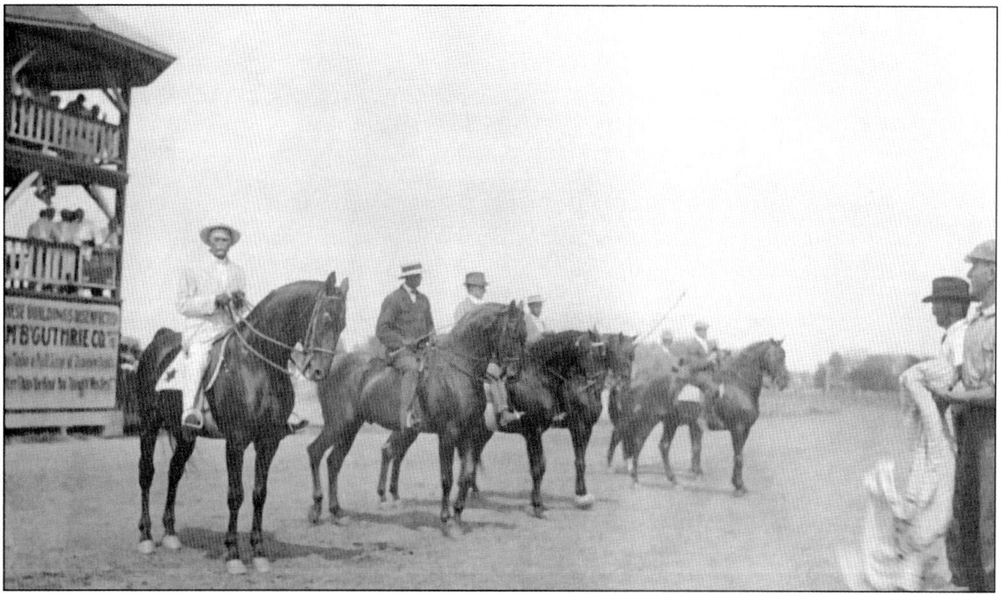

Rex McDonald (left), with Ben Middleton riding, is shown at the Mexico Horse Show with a number of his offspring. Tom Bass is up on the second horse to the right. The other horses and riders are unidentified.

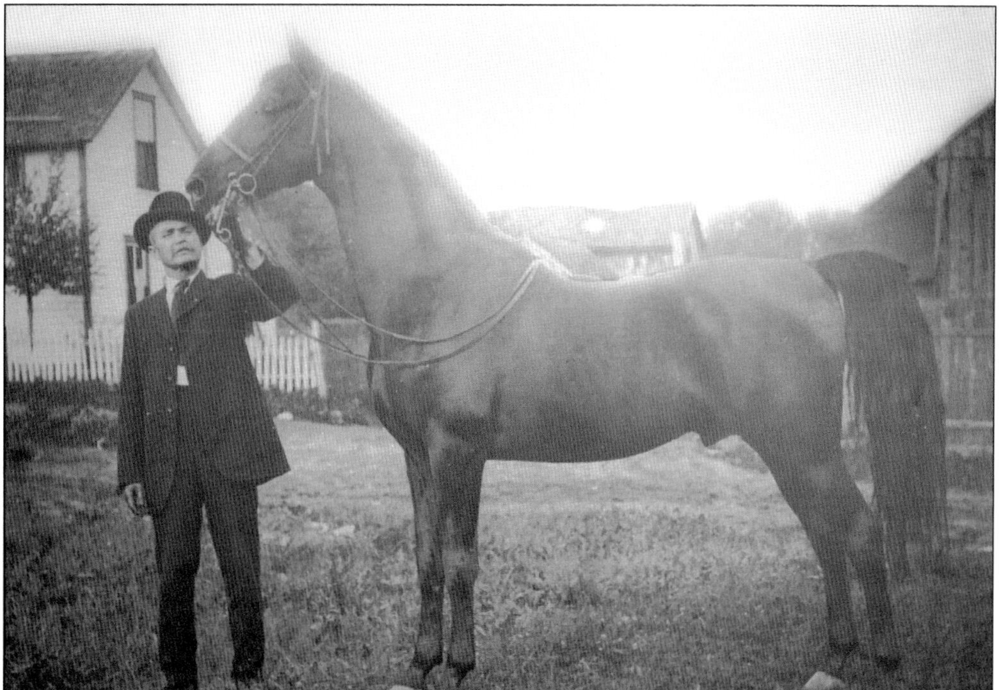

B. R. Middleton spent his life working in the world of horses. Middleton was an authority on horses and a sought-after show judge. The high point of his career was when he bought Rex McDonald when Rex was 20 years old and brought him to Mexico to use for breeding purposes. B. R. Middleton stands with Rex McDonald in this undated photograph.

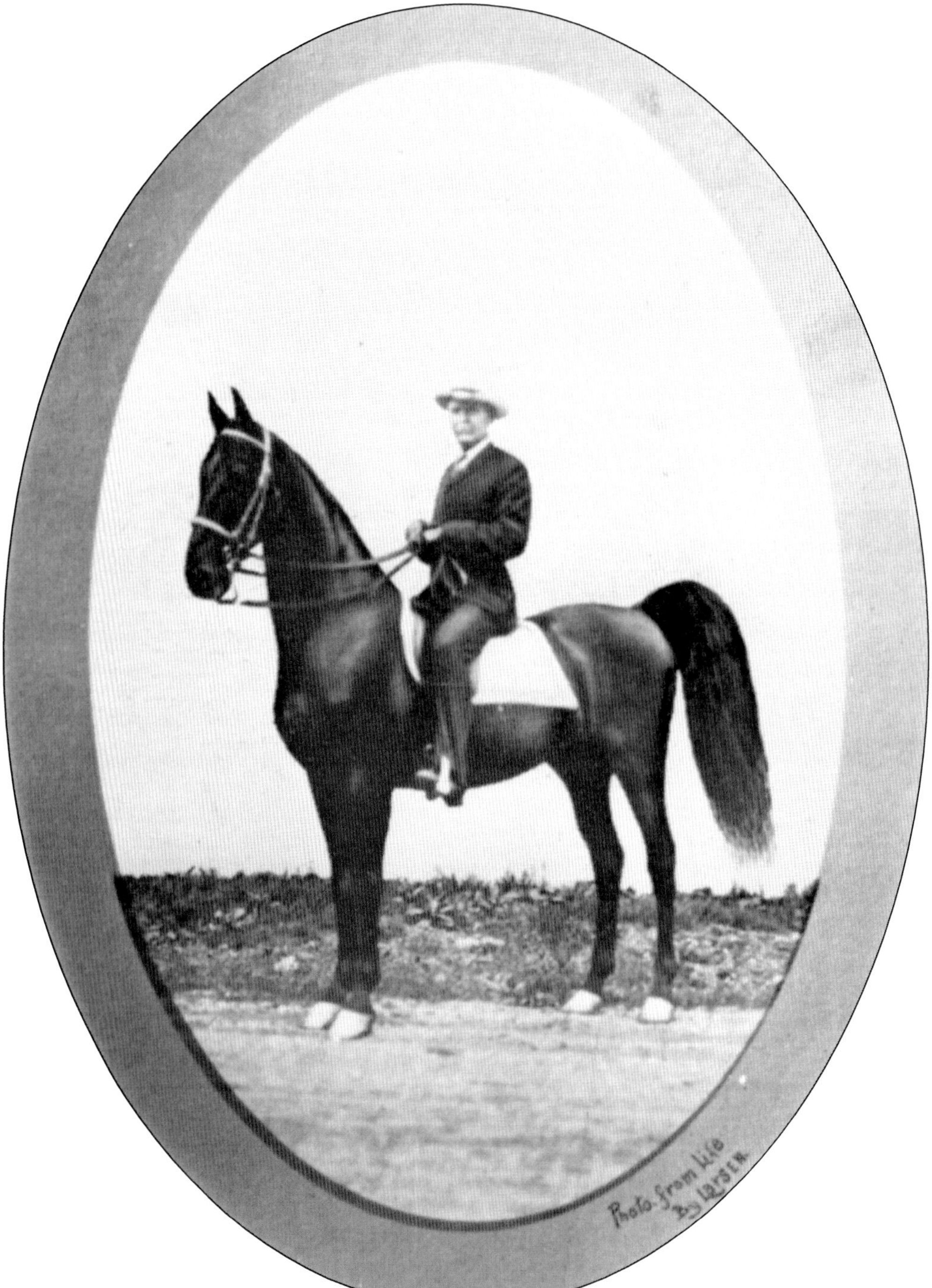

When Rex McDonald returned to Mexico, he was honored with a parade and in turn gave a grand show to the gathered crowd. Even his death did not quiet Rex's Mexicoan fans. When he died in 1913, Rex was stuffed and displayed at the Hotel Ringo. After the hotel was destroyed by fire, his stuffed body was taken to Tom Bass's barn. After two additional burials, Rex McDonald rests today at the American Saddlebred Horse Museum.

Three

The Firebrick Capital of the World

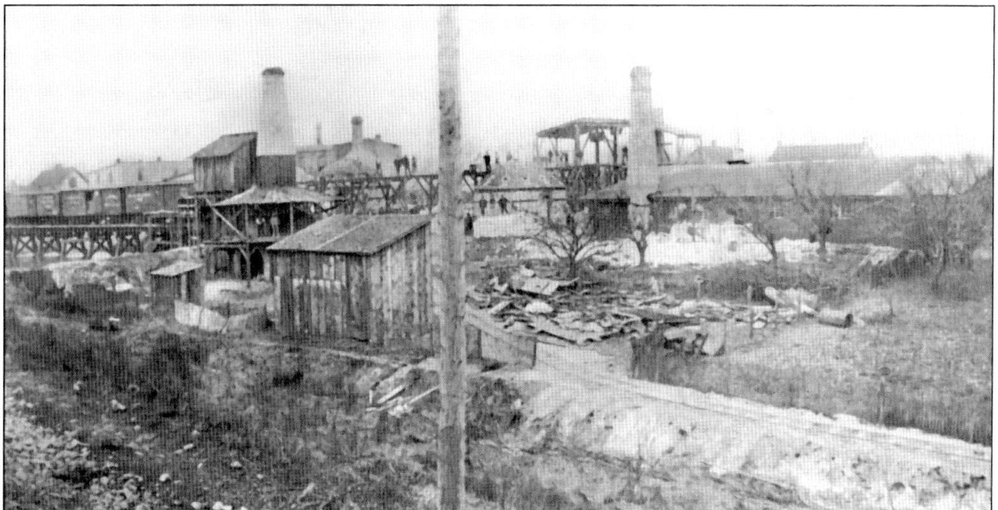

The fertile soil of Audrain County made it a leader in agriculture, but another source of industry and wealth was underfoot in fireclay deposits. Fireclay remains constant and intact even when exposed to high temperatures. Bricks made from fireclay are essential for industrial furnaces needed in manufacturing many products. One of the earliest firebrick makers in the area was the Salamander Stove Lining and Fire Brick Company, seen here at the southeast corner of West Jackson and Missouri Streets around 1890.

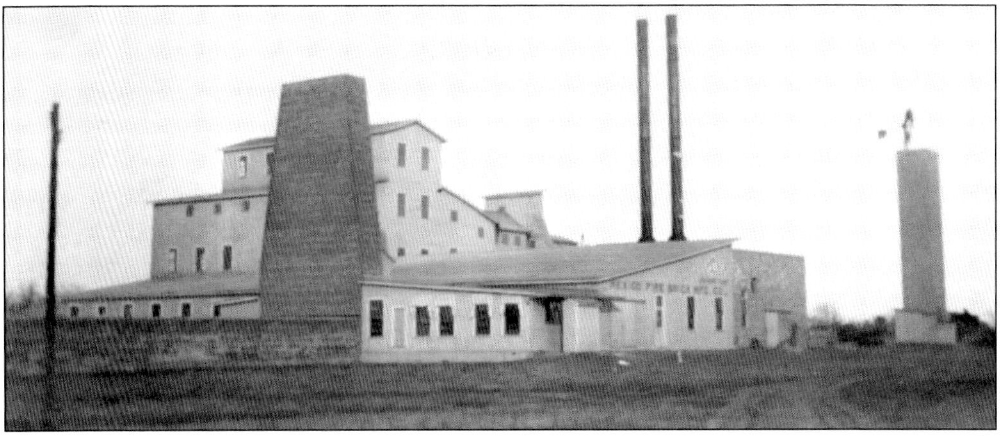

Although Salamander struggled and finally closed for good in 1895, Mexicoans were not ready to give up on this potential source of wealth lying underground ready for the taking. In 1903, J. A. Glandon, W. W. Fry, J. W. Million, R. M. White, Warren Harper, and A. K. Luckie opened Mexico Brick and Fire Clay Company. Seen here in a c. 1910 photograph, the company made both building brick and firebrick, which became its focus.

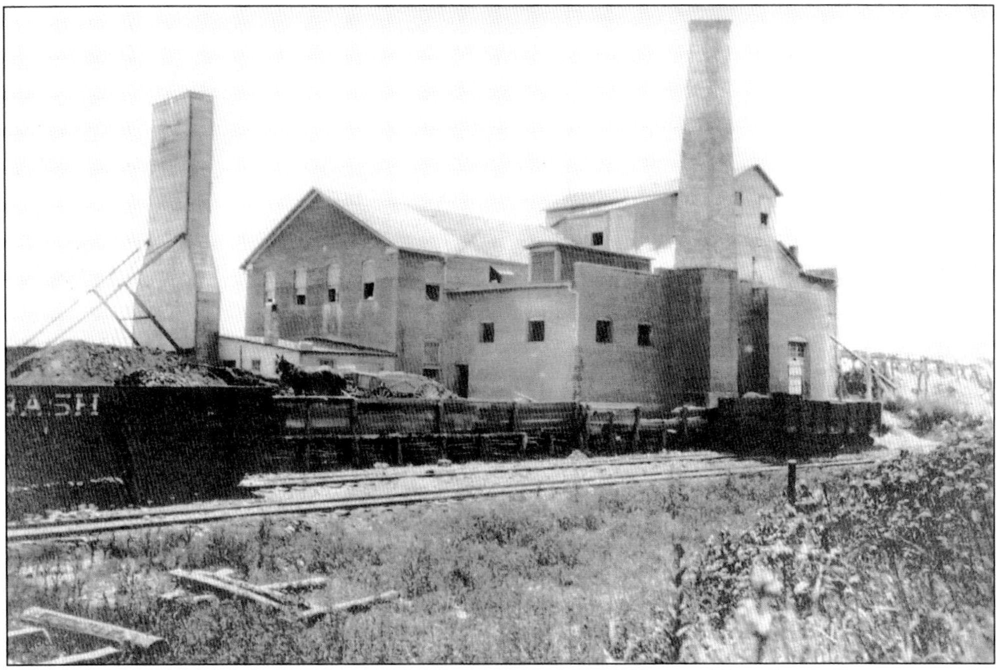

Allen P. Green was working as a manager at the Evens and Howard Fire Brick Company in St. Louis, Missouri, when he met J. A. Glandon. Green saw potential in the small, struggling Mexico operation and attempted to convince his company to buy it. When they declined, Green decided to purchase it himself. This image shows the company he bought in 1910.

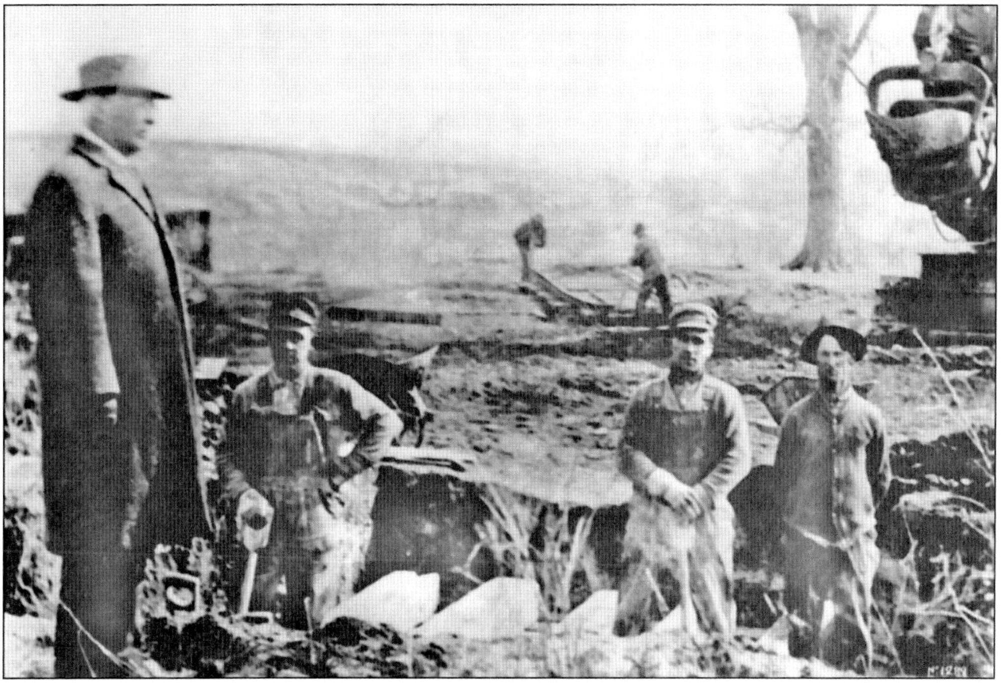

A. P. Green was 35 when he bought the brick manufacturer. He had been raised in Sedalia and Jefferson City in central Missouri and had graduated with a civil and mining engineering degree from the School of Mines and Metallurgy in Rolla. Green had a wife, five small children, and a firm belief in the potential of the firebrick industry when he made his move to Mexico. This 1912 photograph shows Green (left) and unidentified workers.

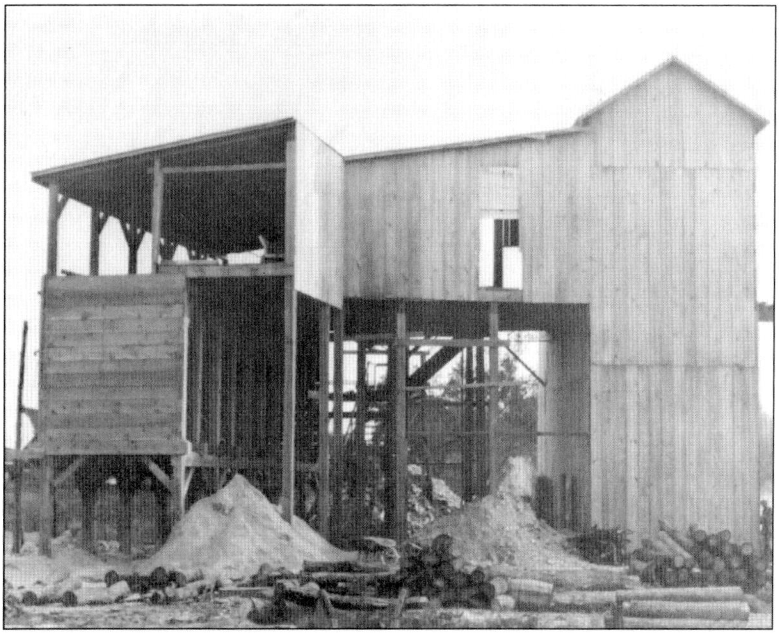

When Green took over the company, mining the fireclay was still carried out the old way; but Green had ideas to change all that. This is a mine shaft around 1912.

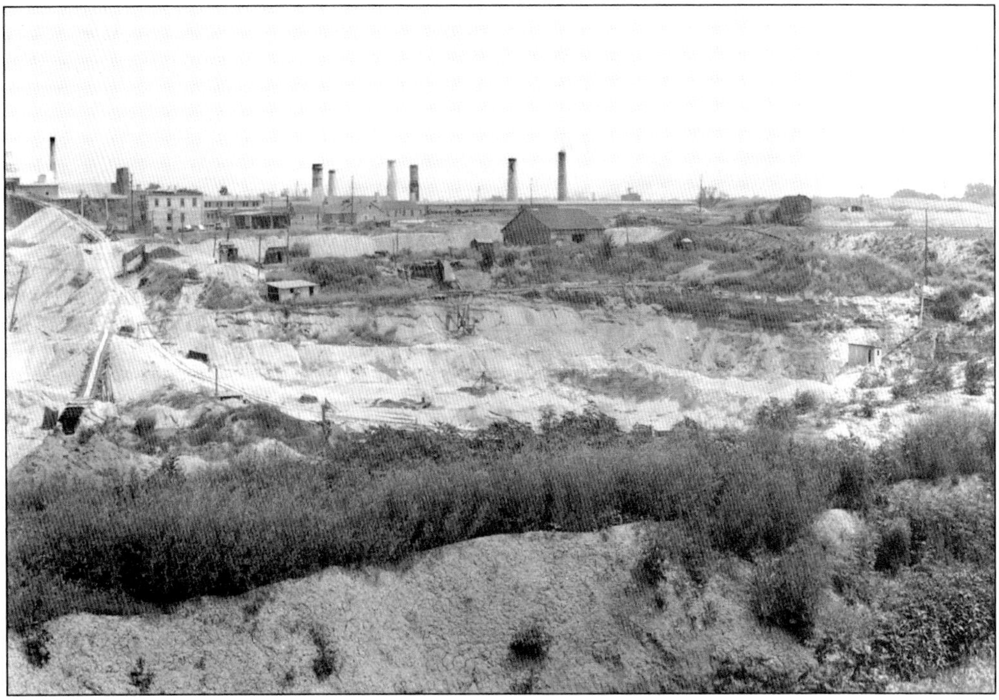

One of the ideas Green envisioned was open-pit mining. The deposits of fireclay were near enough to the surface to make this feasible. By 1915, clay was being extracted from mines like No. 1 Clay Pit, seen in this *c.* 1918 photograph.

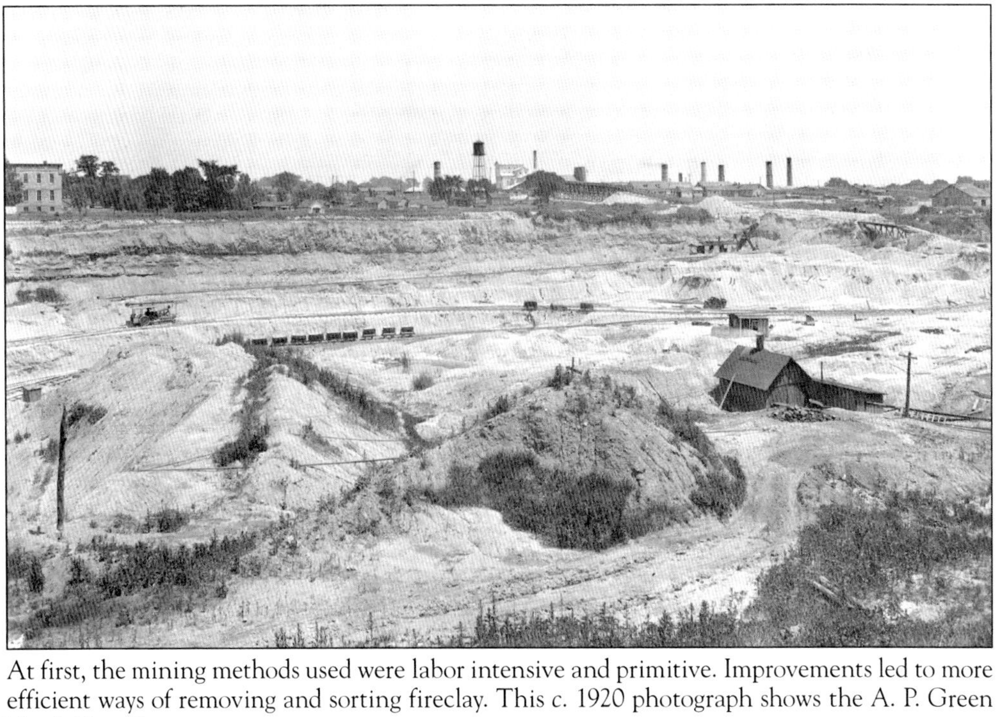

At first, the mining methods used were labor intensive and primitive. Improvements led to more efficient ways of removing and sorting fireclay. This *c.* 1920 photograph shows the A. P. Green No. 1 Clay Pit.

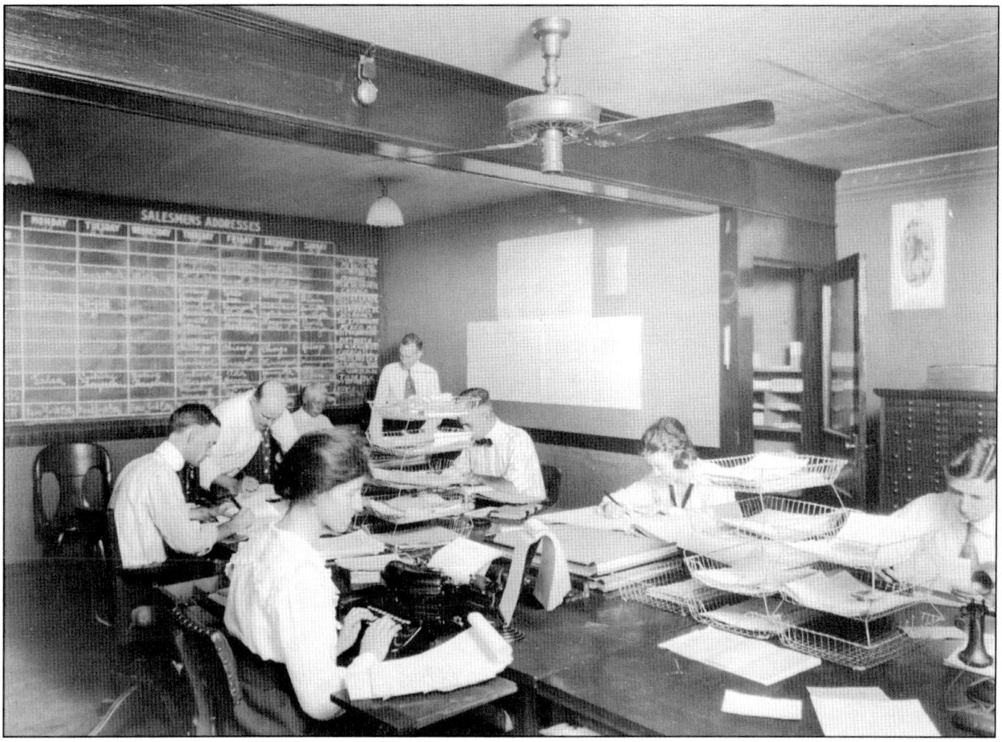

A. P. Green Company grew along with its sales. In addition to the busy main office in Mexico, Green opened branch sales offices—beginning with Tulsa, Oklahoma, and Chicago, Illinois, in 1916. Most of the plant's brick production was presold several months ahead. One of the purposes of the satellite offices was to cultivate relationships, another example of Green's business acumen.

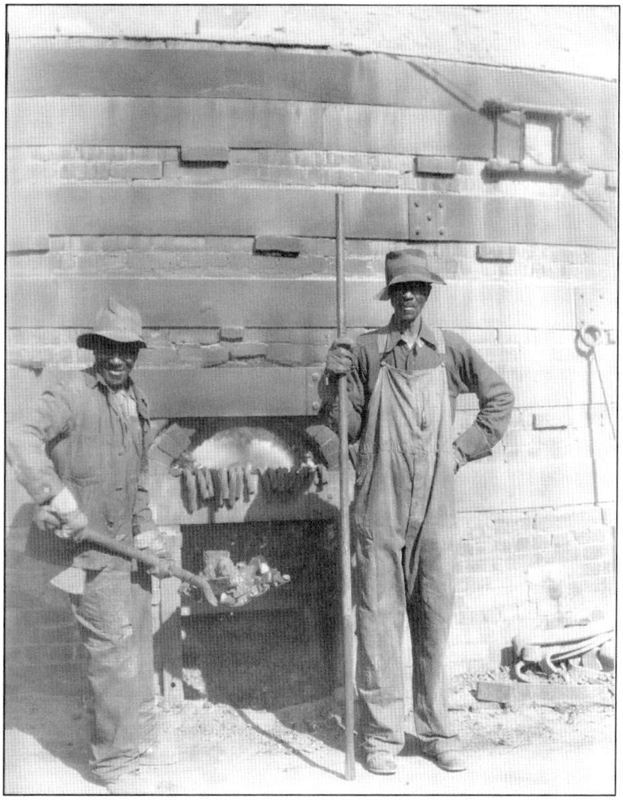

In 1925, A. P. Green Company was still using coal-fired downdraft kilns, like the one here being fed by Pops Harvey (left) and Bud Harvey. This was toward the end of an era as producing firebrick by this process was beginning to be considered slow, inefficient, and costly with inconsistent results.

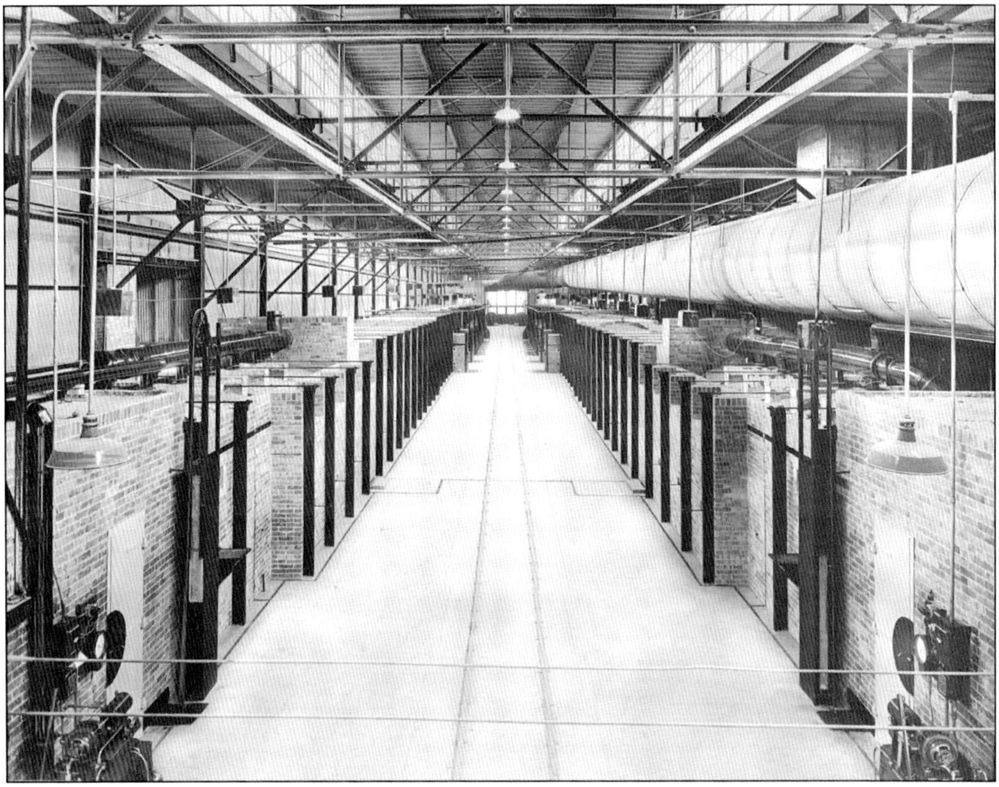

The tunnel kiln in this *c.* 1935 image was an idea whose time had come. Bricks were set directly onto flat-topped cars at the dry presses and moved through the remaining processes of drying, burning, and cooling, and then to the loading dock without further handling. The kilns were originally fired with oil but were converted to gas.

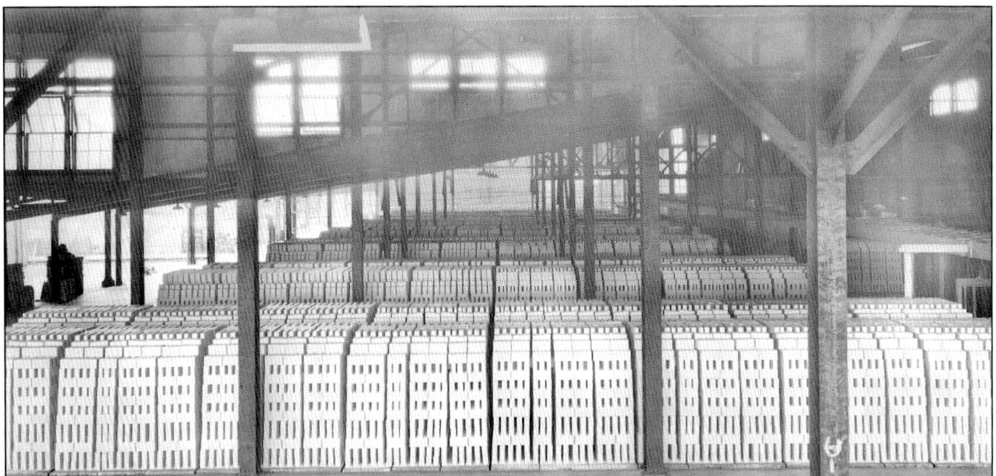

Tunnel kiln cars carried the finished brick directly to the loading dock. These bricks represent a weekend of production around 1935.

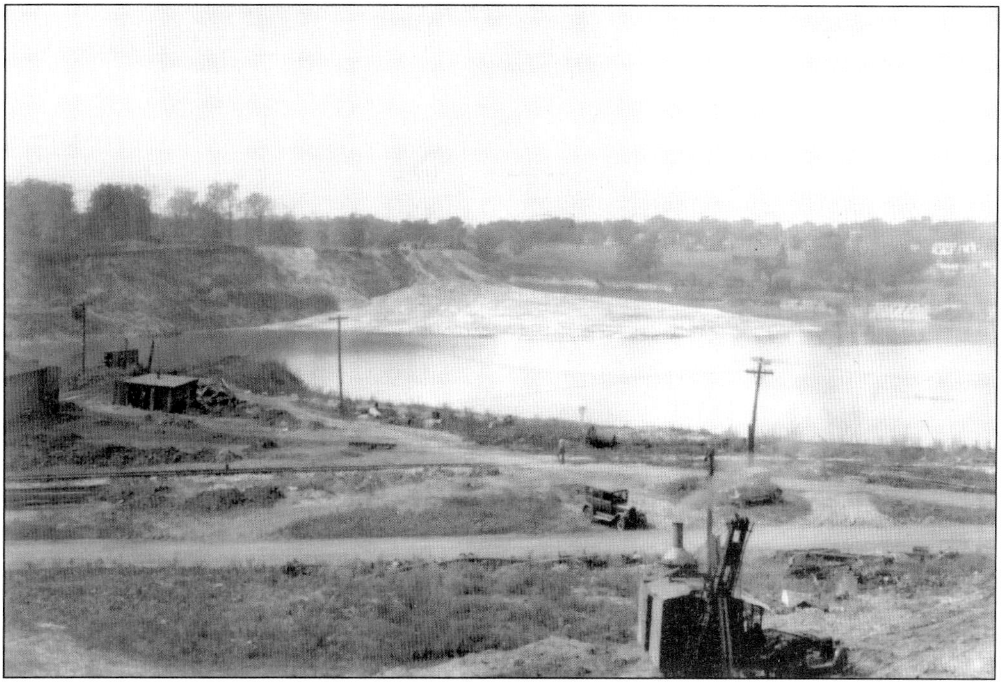

By 1925, No. 1 Clay Pit had been mined out. At that time, there were no legal requirements to tidy up the landscape. The A. P. Green Company, however, either filled in and landscaped old mines or, in the instance of Teal Lake, made them into recreational areas for employees.

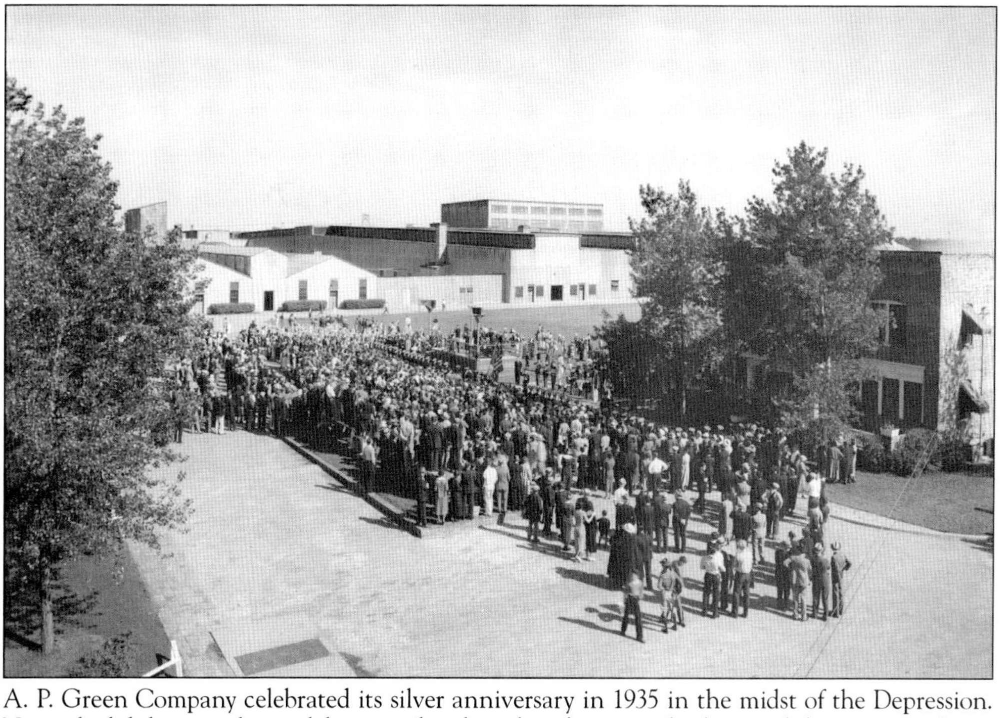

A. P. Green Company celebrated its silver anniversary in 1935 in the midst of the Depression. Not only did these workers celebrate at the plant, but the town also honored the company for its contributions to the community.

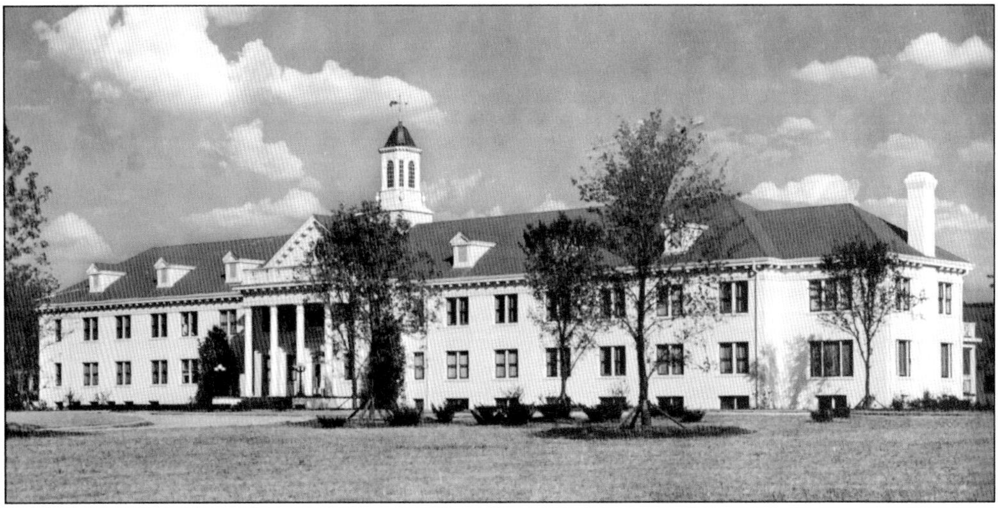

The Depression affected the A. P. Green Company as it did the entire country. During the 1930s, there were both years of cutbacks and good years when salaries and wages were increased. And in the late 1930s, new executive offices opened in a beautiful and expansive building.

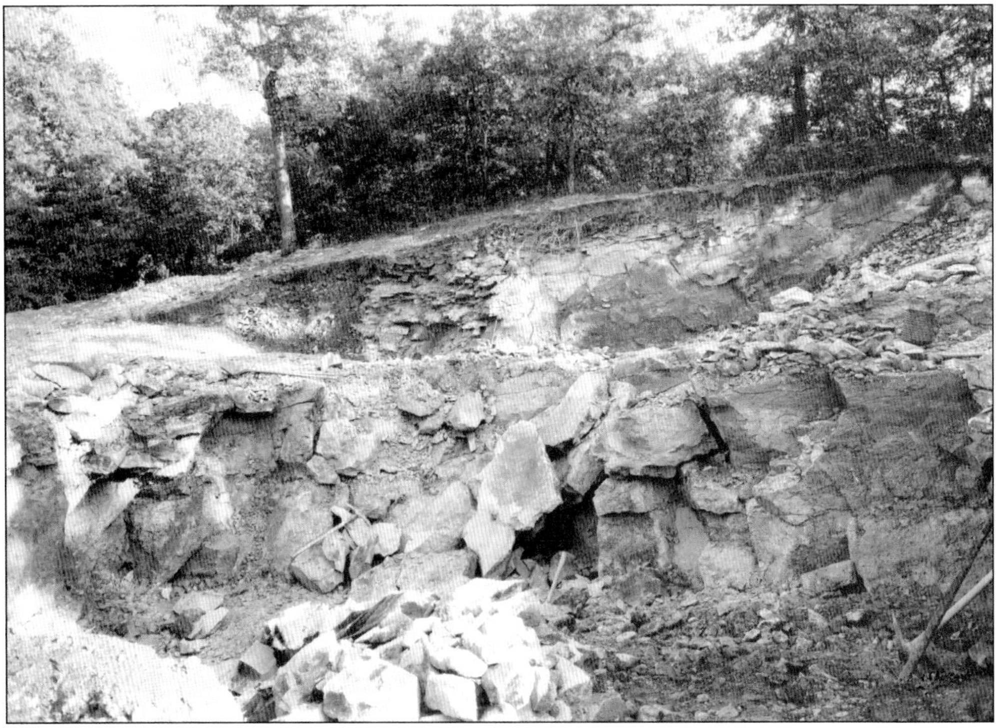

Another innovation Green instituted was the manufacture of high alumina brick made from diaspore. Local supplies of diaspore, however, were limited and were tapped out by the mid-1940s.

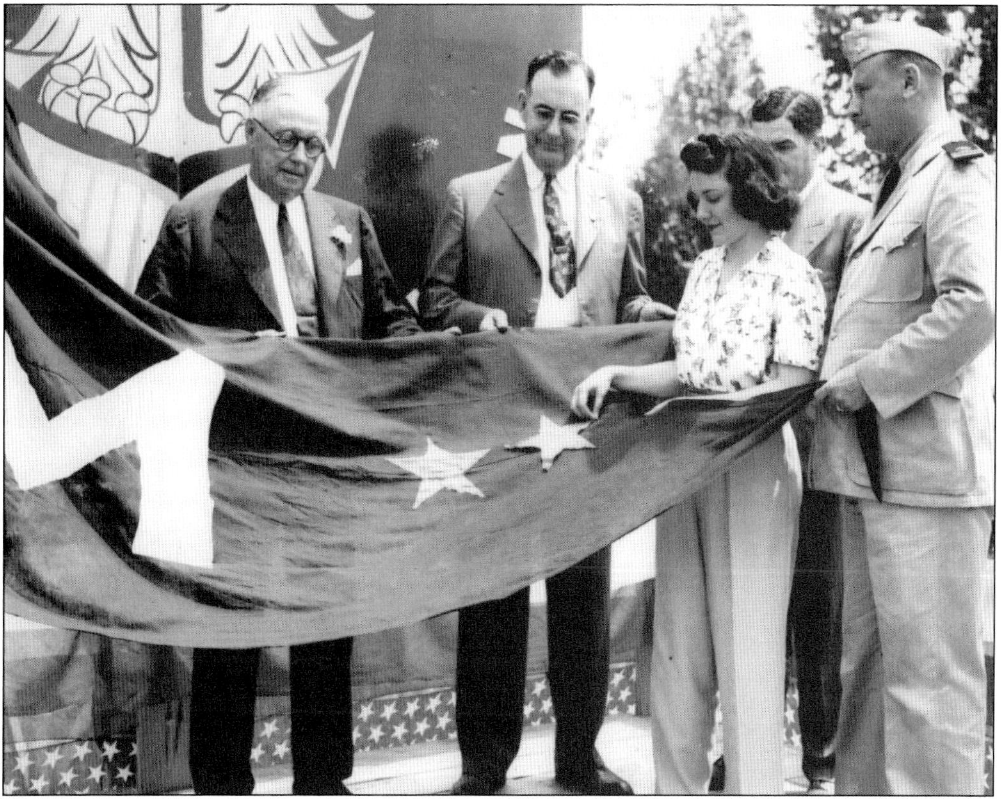

During World War II, A. P. Green Company manufactured nearly all the brick used to line the boilers of the merchant fleet and for many warships. In 1942, the Maritime "M" was awarded; a star was added in 1943 for continued excellence.

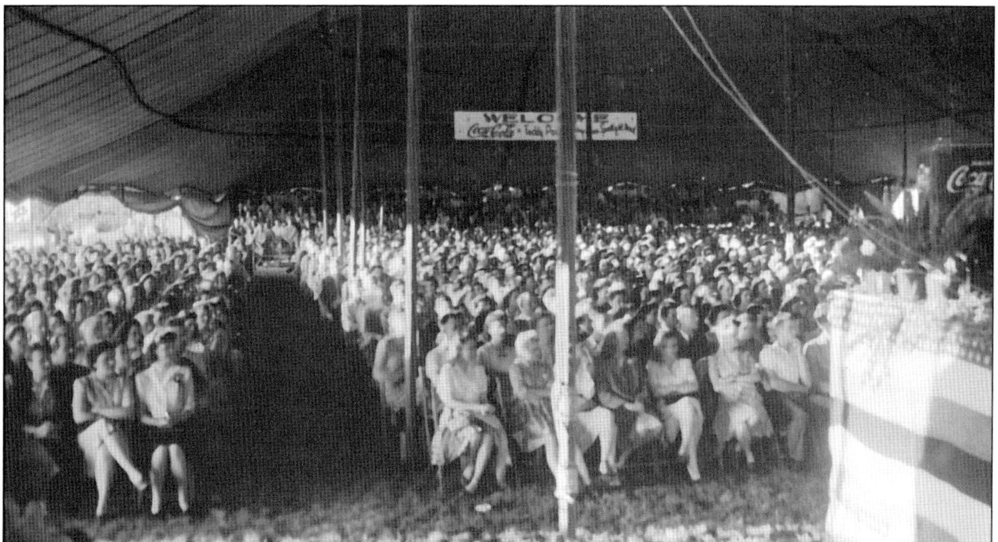

On June 14, 1944, four thousand A. P. Green Company workers (including many women) and their friends and families were saluted by the Coca-Cola Victory Parade of Spotlight Bands. The program was broadcast via radio and heard by an estimated 20 million listeners.

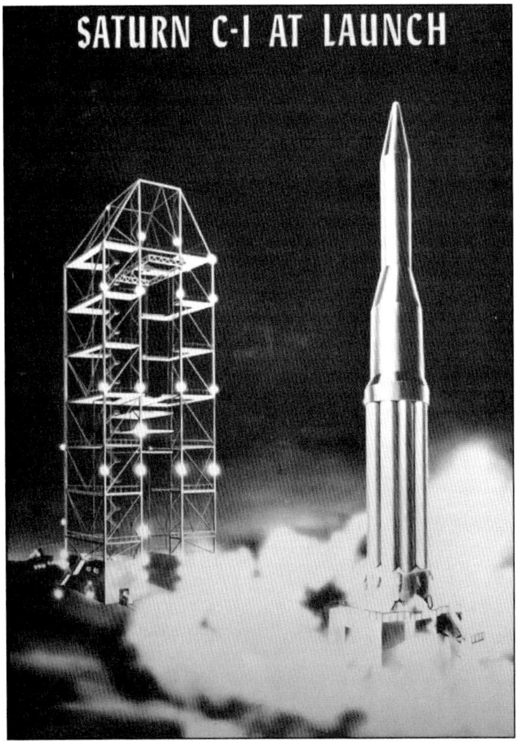

After the war, the company continued to expand, both in the United States and abroad, and develop new products. When the first American man was launched into space, it was from a launchpad of A. P. Green firebrick. It was a moment of pride for the company and the city as A. P. Green firebrick continued to be a part of the space program, providing brick, research, and installation services.

A. P. Green Fire Brick Company was the world's largest firebrick plant by 1937. The company merged in 1967 with U. S. Gypsum. In 2002, A. P. Green Fire Brick Company closed its doors. Those doors have reopened recently (2010) for production of facing brick.

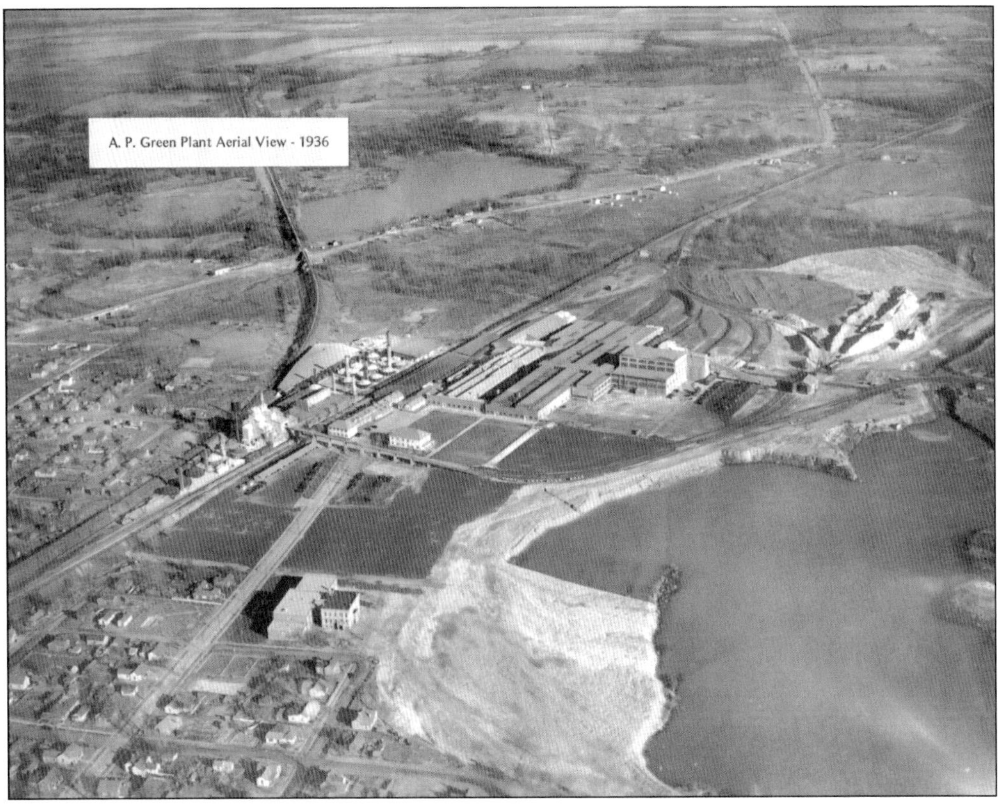

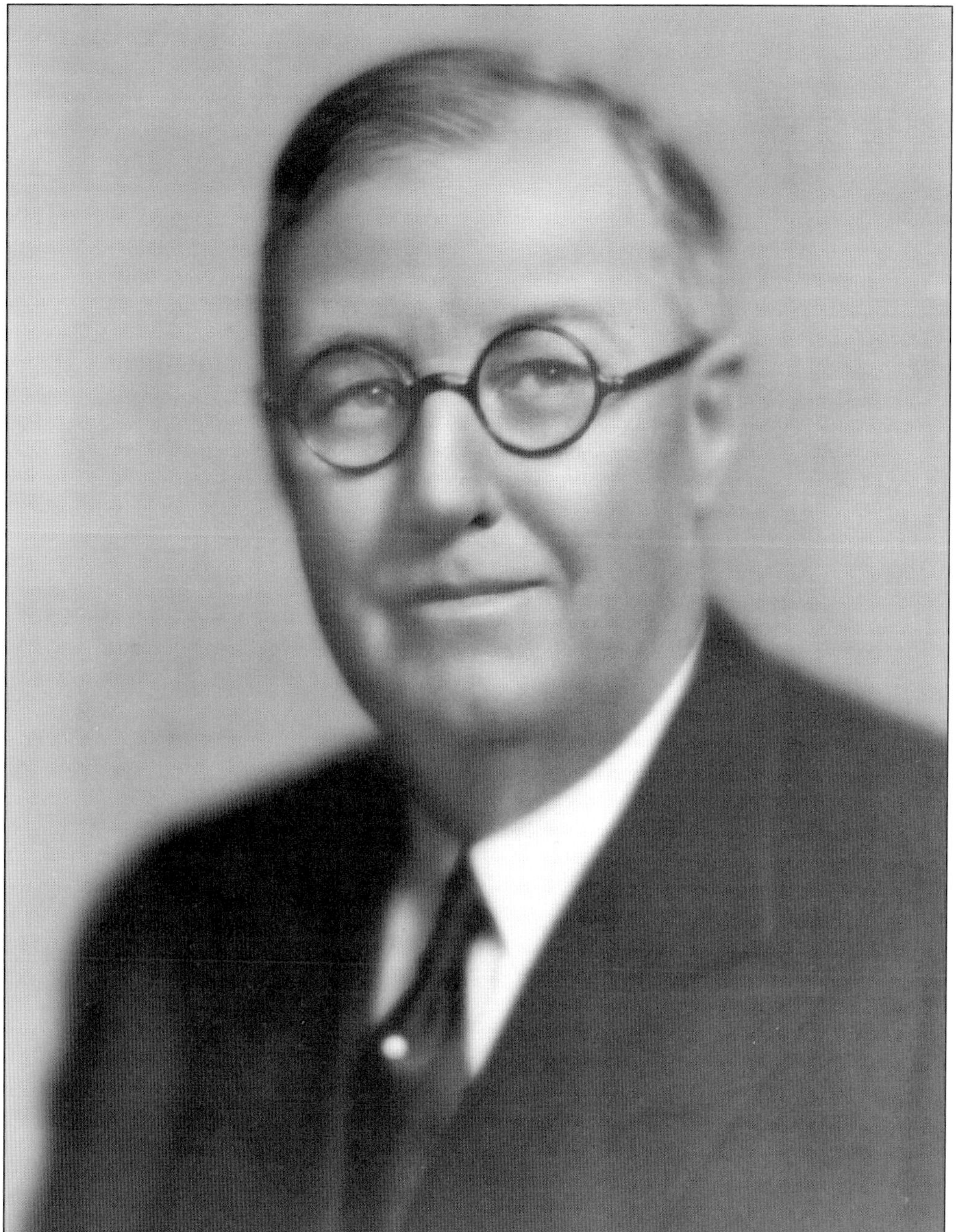

Allen Percival Green was born in Jefferson City, Missouri, on July 22, 1875. He literally fought his way through the Missouri School of Mines and Metallurgy at Rolla, Missouri, financing his education by prizefighting. He married Josephine Brown in 1903, and they had five children. A. P. Green died in 1956. He and Josephine made many financial and civic contributions to the city.

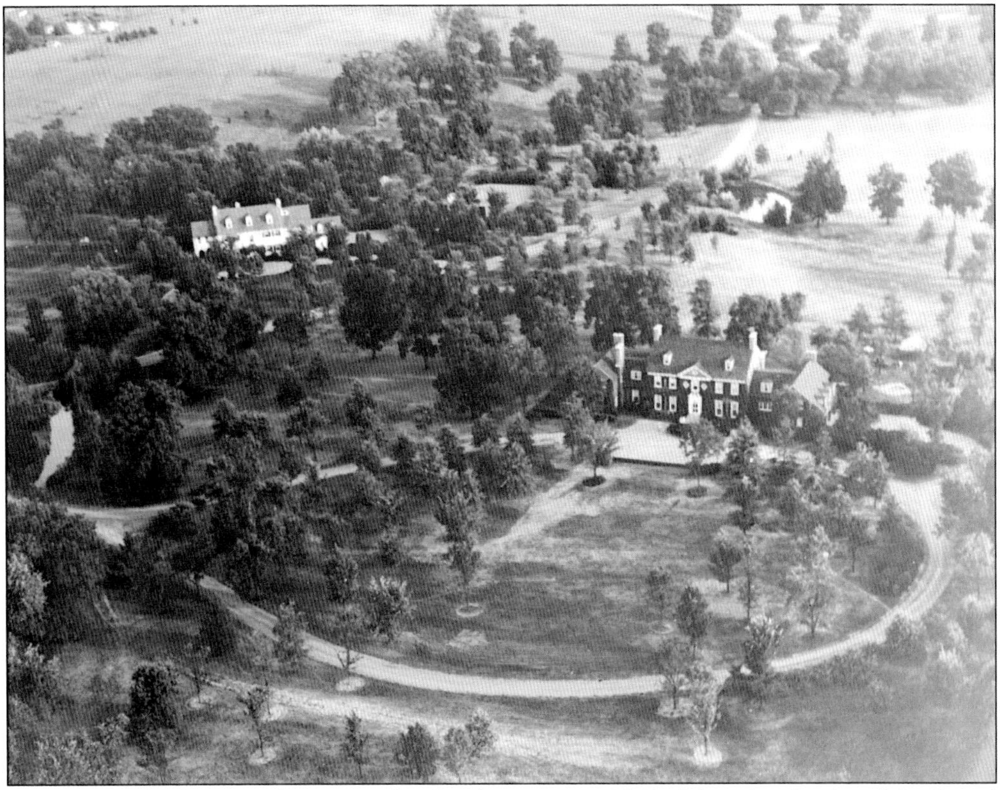

The Greens built a new house on the family estate in 1941. After the deaths of A. P. and Josephine, the company bought the home and converted it into a guesthouse. Today the house is privately owned.

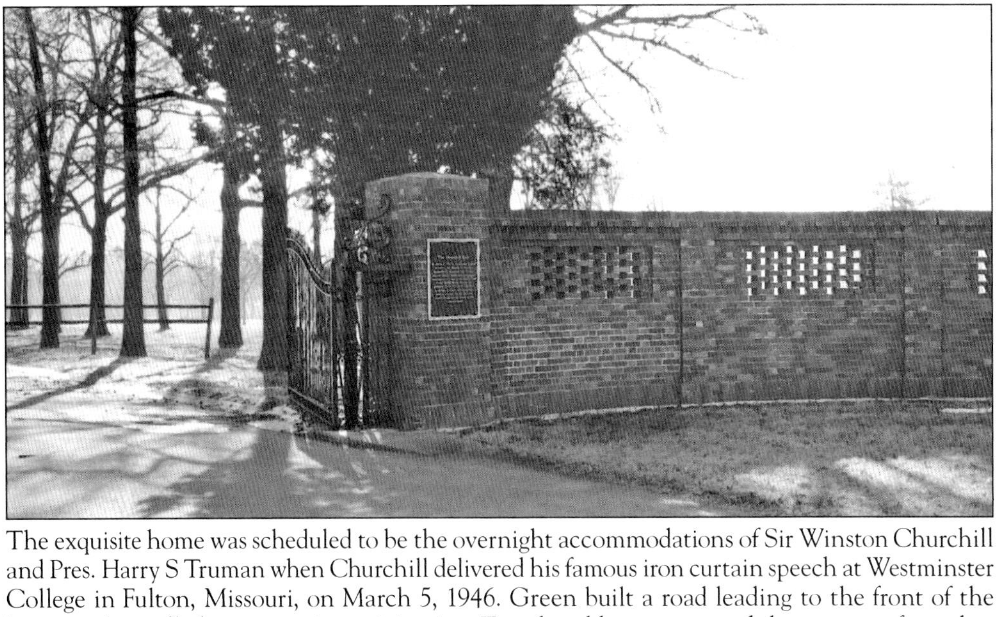

The exquisite home was scheduled to be the overnight accommodations of Sir Winston Churchill and Pres. Harry S Truman when Churchill delivered his famous iron curtain speech at Westminster College in Fulton, Missouri, on March 5, 1946. Green built a road leading to the front of the house and installed iron gates in anticipation. Travel problems prevented the two men from that visit, but the gate is now known as the Churchill Gate.

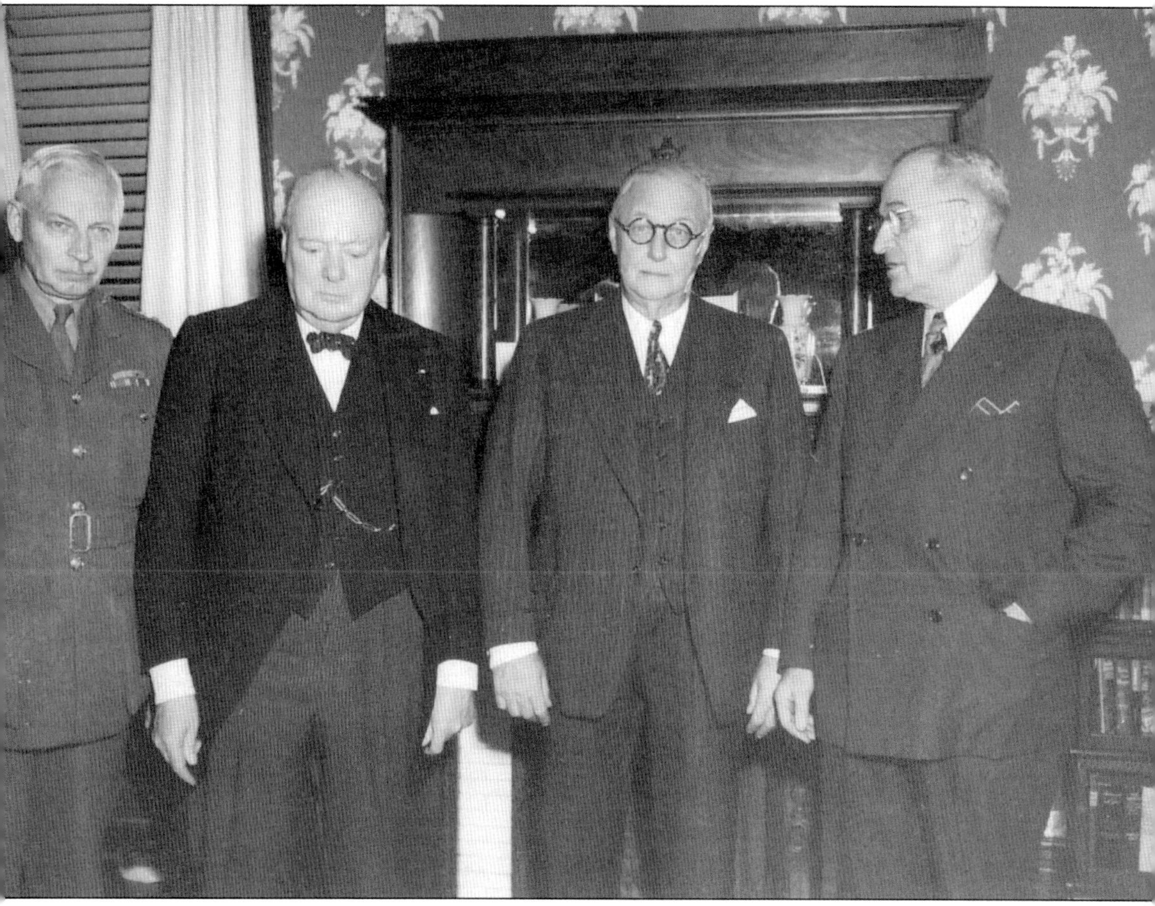

Green did join the famous men in Fulton. Pictured here, from left to right, are Truman aide Gen. Harry Vaughn, Sir Winston Churchill, A. P. Green, and Pres. Harry S. Truman.

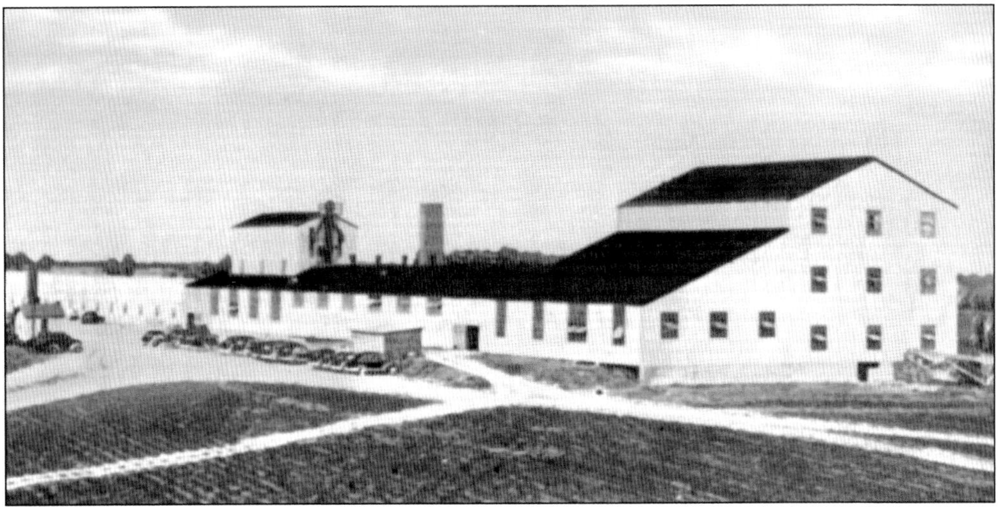

J. B. Arthur, a longtime employee of A. P. Green Fire Brick Company, left in 1929 and formed Mexico Refractories. Several key people left A.P. Green to work with Arthur right at the outset of the Depression when sales were already dwindling.

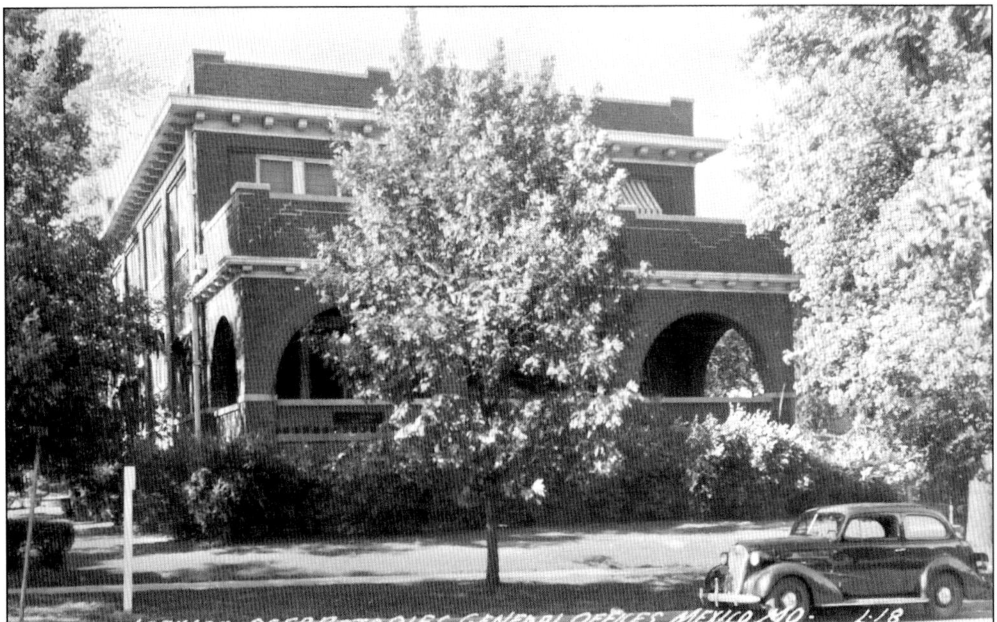

Arthur purchased the Elk's Lodge located at North Coal and East Love Streets to use as the company's offices. Today the building is Mexico City Hall.

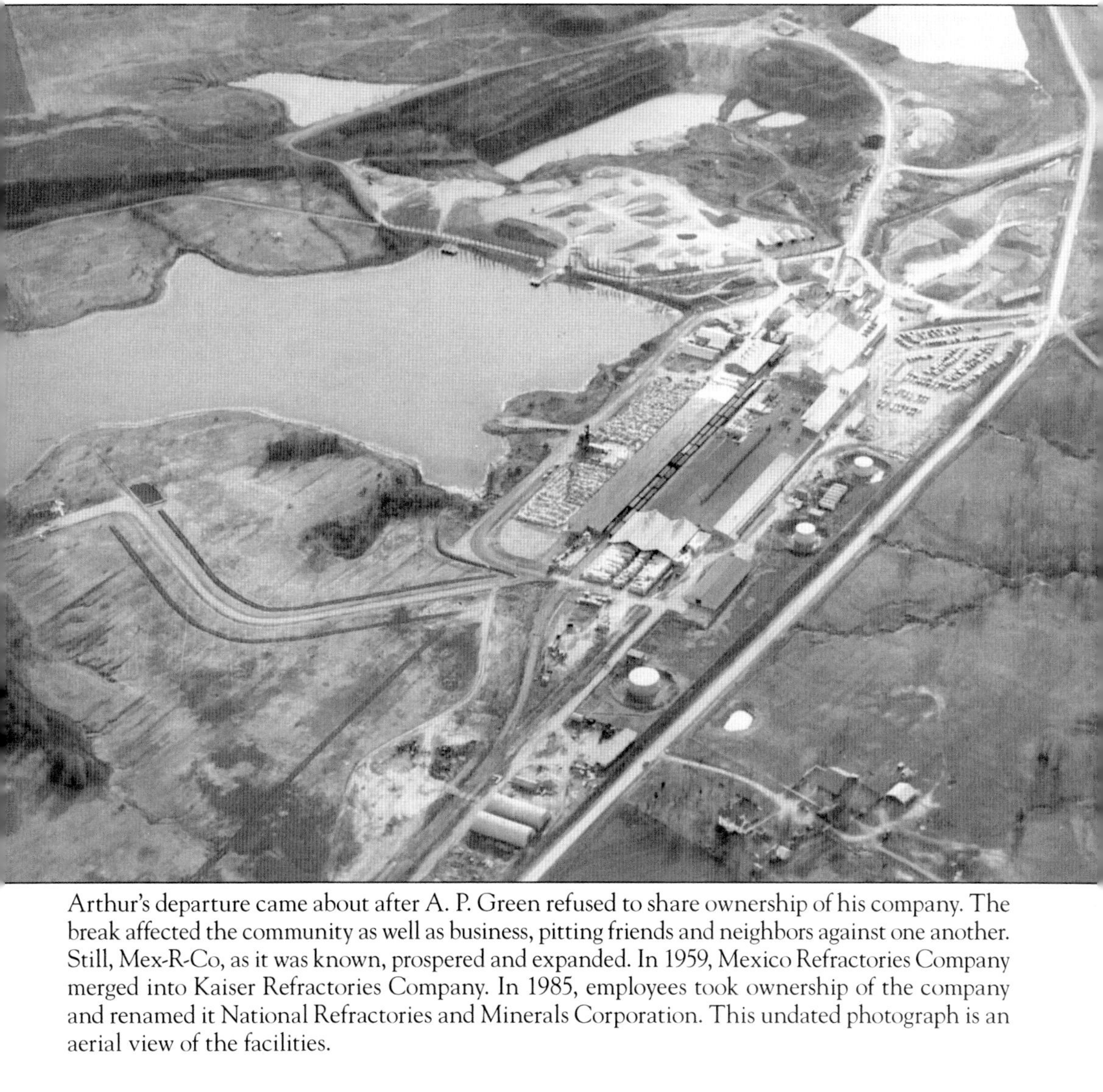

Arthur's departure came about after A. P. Green refused to share ownership of his company. The break affected the community as well as business, pitting friends and neighbors against one another. Still, Mex-R-Co, as it was known, prospered and expanded. In 1959, Mexico Refractories Company merged into Kaiser Refractories Company. In 1985, employees took ownership of the company and renamed it National Refractories and Minerals Corporation. This undated photograph is an aerial view of the facilities.

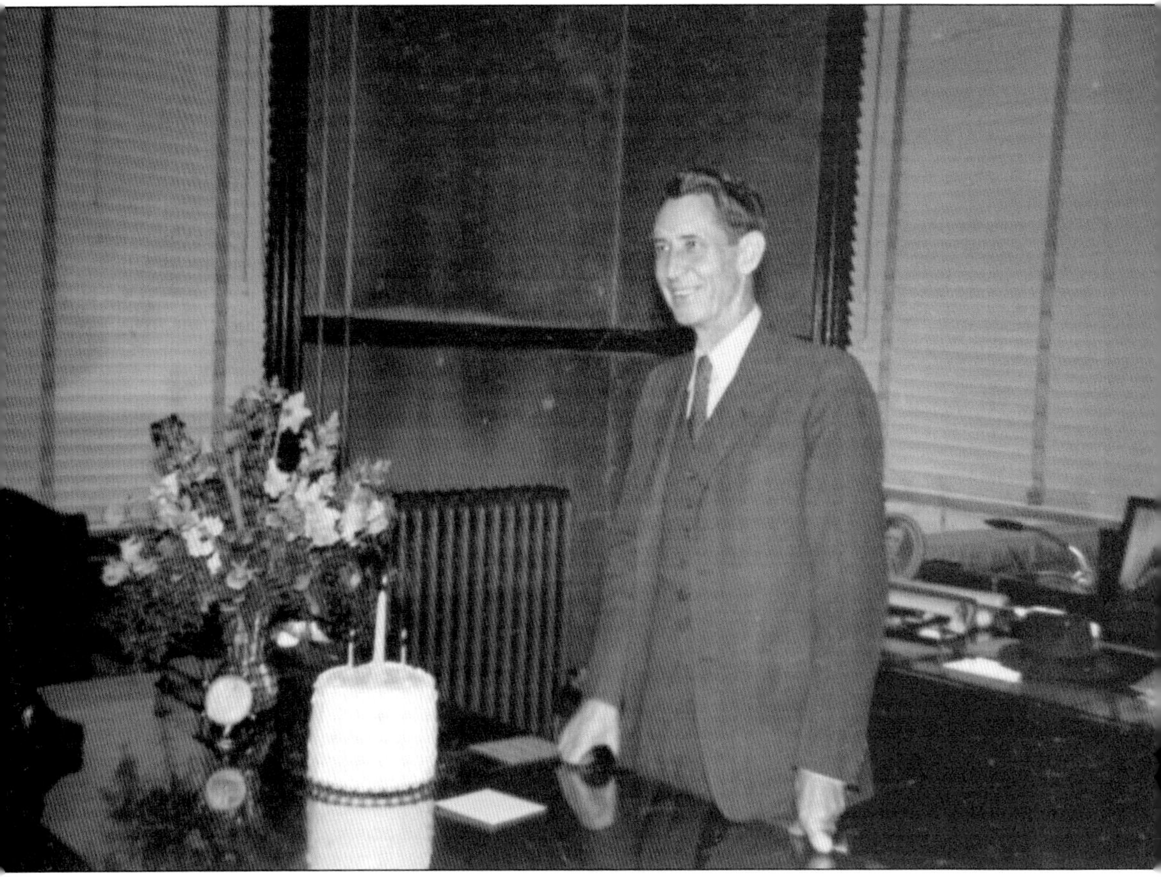

Pictured here celebrating his 50th birthday, John B. Arthur was born in Butler County, Missouri, on January 29, 1889. He attended school in Alabama, where his family moved when he was young. Arthur worked with his father in the lumber business until he returned to Missouri, where he went to work at A. P. Green Fire Brick Company as bookkeeper, rising to vice president and general manager. Arthur married Gretta Lawson in 1913, and they had two daughters.

Four

AREA BUSINESS

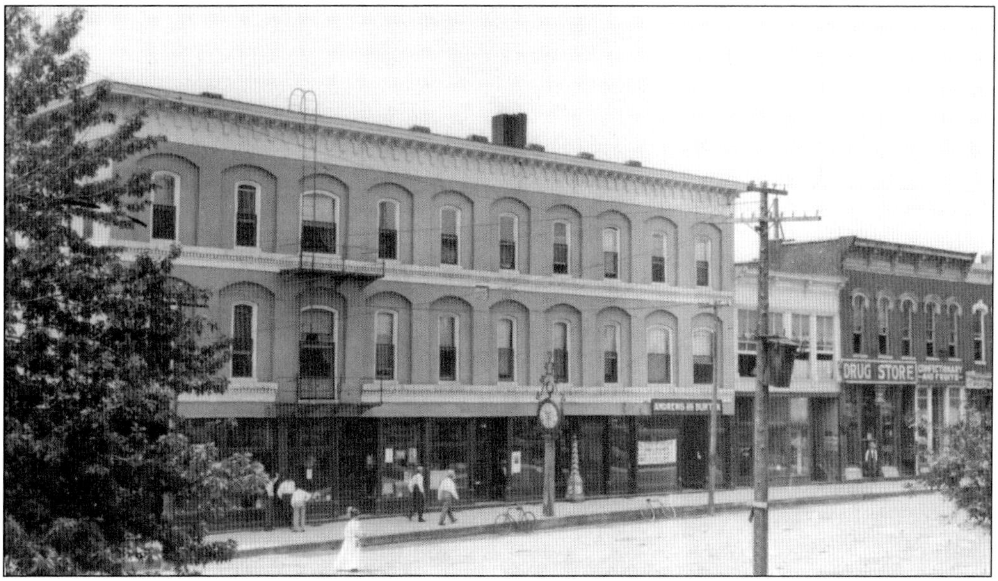

One of the jewels of the square in the late 1800s was the Hotel Ringo, seen here in 1910. It was considered one of the most elegant lodgings in Missouri. A. R. Ringo built the three-story brick hotel for $65,000 on the southeast corner of the square in 1866. The chamber of commerce now occupies the site.

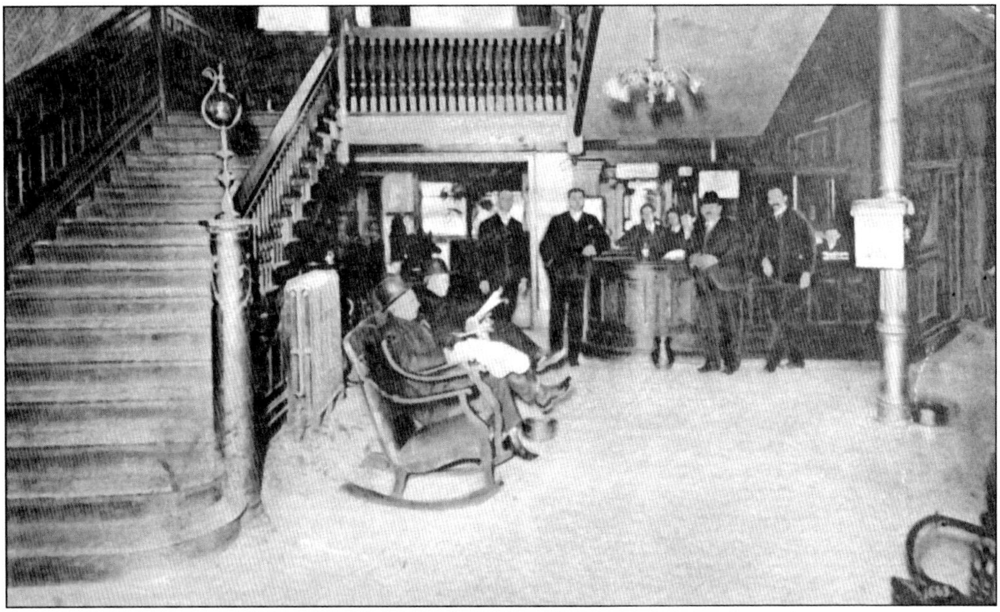

The hotel boasted a large paneled lobby, a formal parlor, a reading room, a dining room, and 60 guest rooms. The Hotel Ringo was renowned for its hospitality. A buggy (at one time driven by Tom Bass) met guests at the train station. Comfortable rocking chairs were available in the lobby as well as shops on the ground level. A bridge crossed over muddy Jefferson Street to enable ladies to make the trip without getting their skirts dirty.

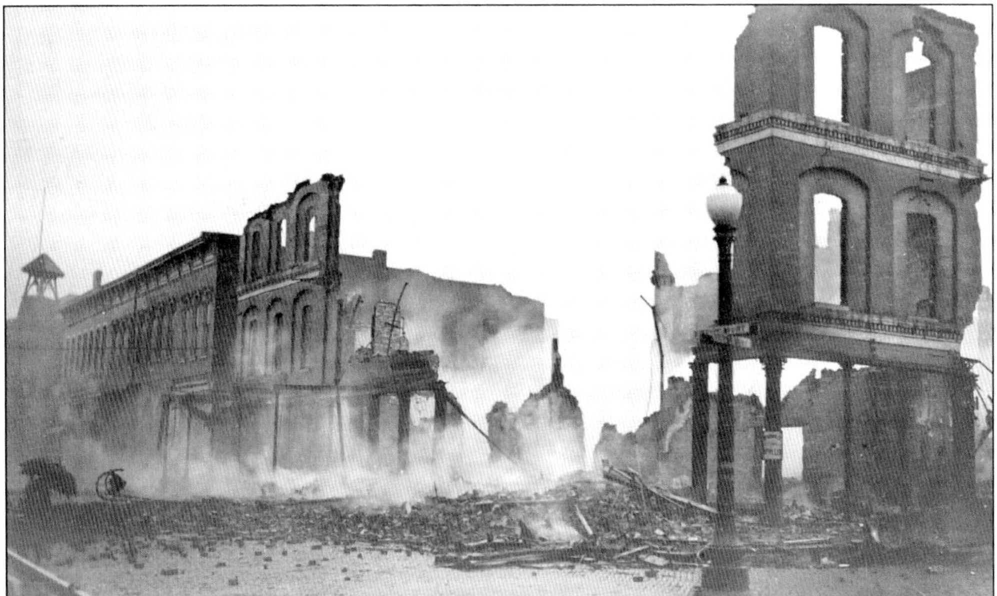

On April 19, 1918, fire blazed through the hotel causing $250,000 in damage and also destroying six adjoining buildings along West Jackson Street. Fortunately no one died, and there were no serious injuries.

From 1876 to 1986, the local White family owned the *Mexico Ledger*. Robert M. White graduated from Westminster College in 1876 and was offered a chance to play baseball for the St. Louis Browns. Instead, he bought the 21-year-old *Mexico* (originally *Missouri*) *Ledger* founded by John B. Williams 1855.

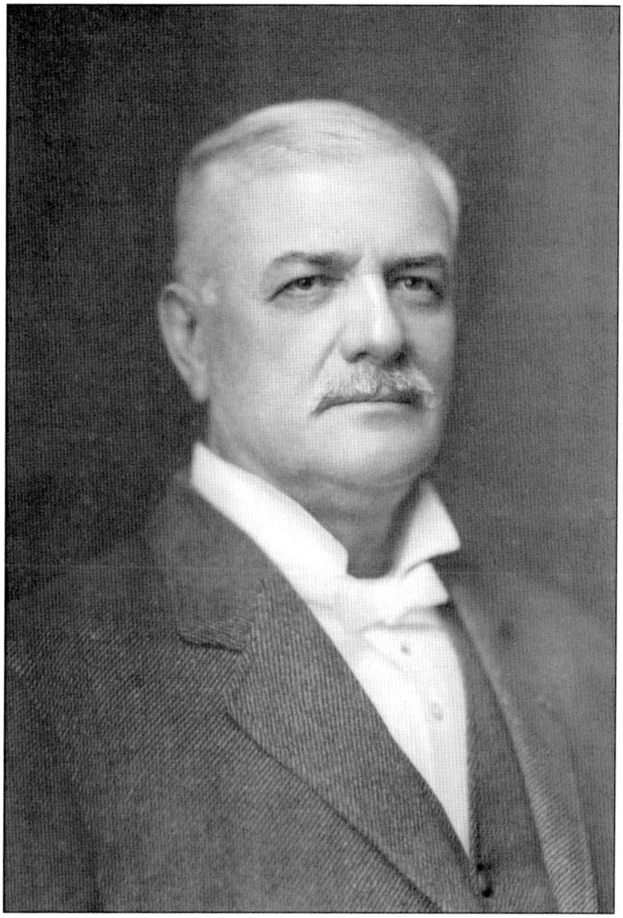

The paper was published weekly out of offices located on the northwest corner of the square until 1886, when it became a daily. The weekly edition, published on Saturday, continued until 1956 with a paper published six days per week. This *c.* 1938 photograph shows the *Ledger* offices.

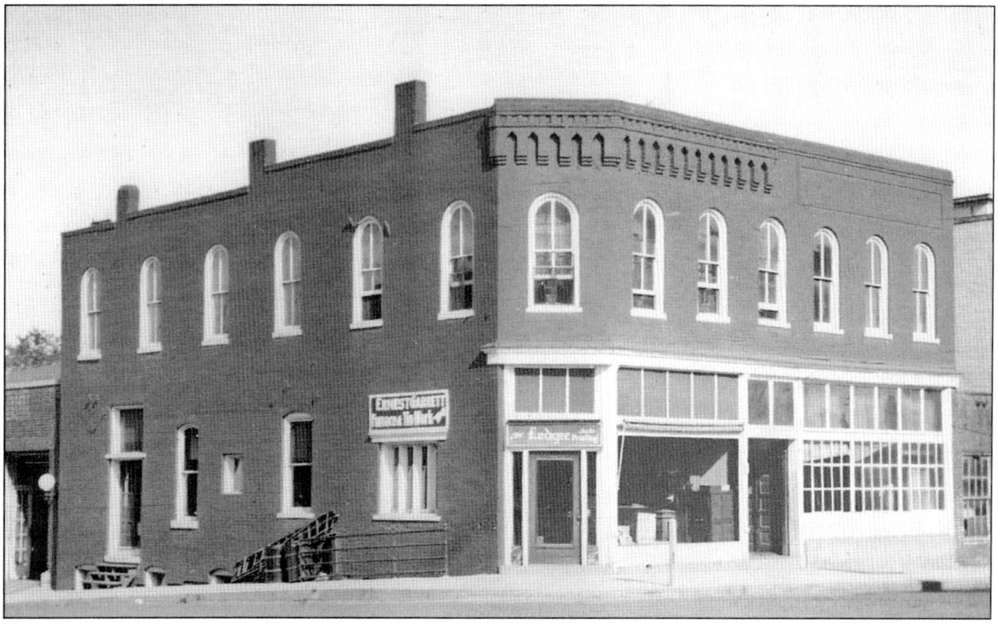

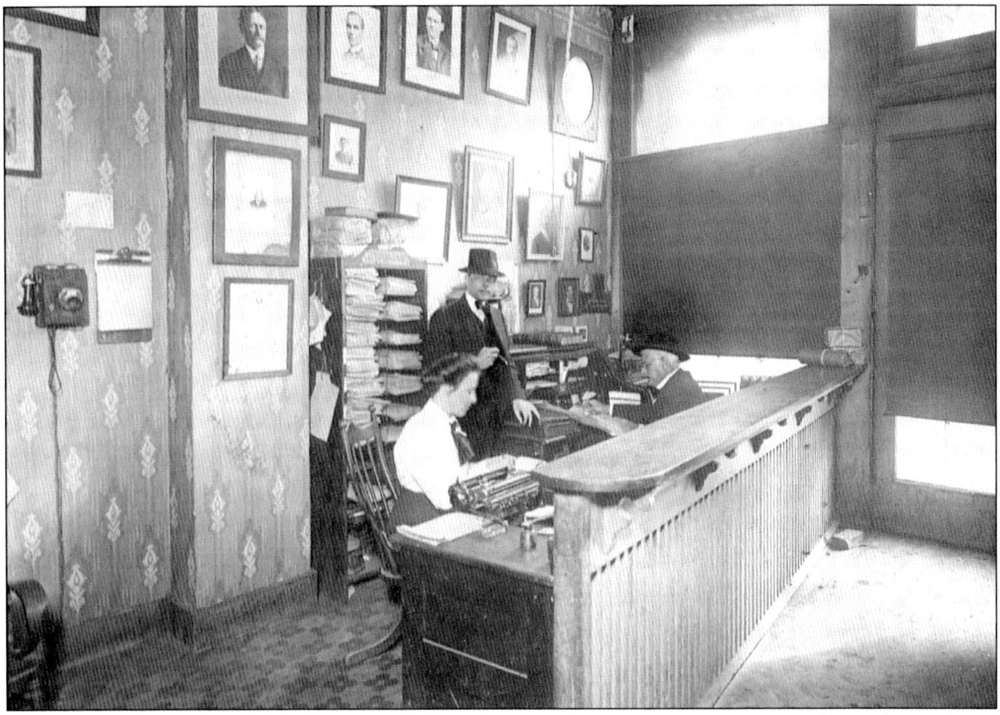

This *c.* 1916 image shows Camilla Garrett, L. M. White, and R. M. White in the *Ledger* offices. L. Mitchell White took over running the paper in 1917.

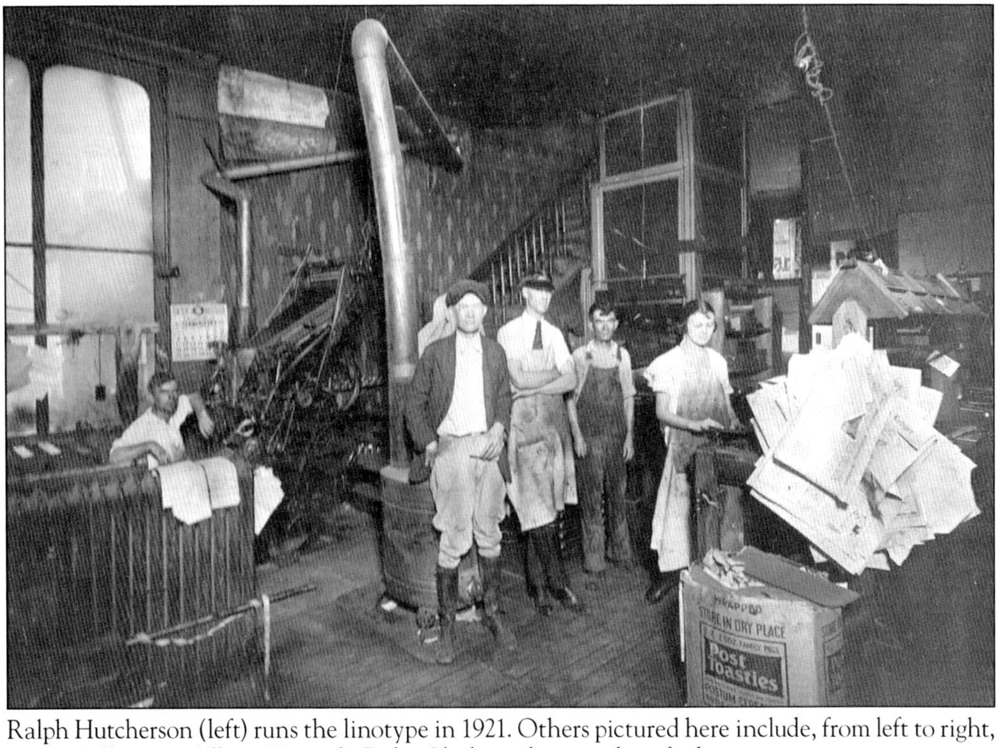

Ralph Hutcherson (left) runs the linotype in 1921. Others pictured here include, from left to right, D. C. Hallopater, Albert Nierrick, Ruby Clark, and an unidentified person.

Distance signs posted outside the Ledger Building were a familiar Mexico landmark. And the reach of the newspaper extended almost as far, as *Ledger* alumni such as Mary Margaret McBride, Herschel Schooley, Leigh Mitchell Hodges, Curtis Mitchell, and Dr. William Howard Taft made their marks on the world of journalism. The author's first published work also appeared in the *Ledger*.

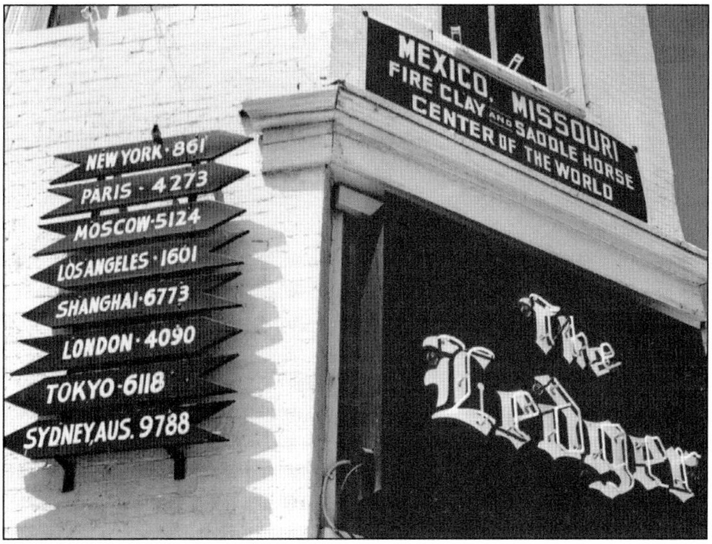

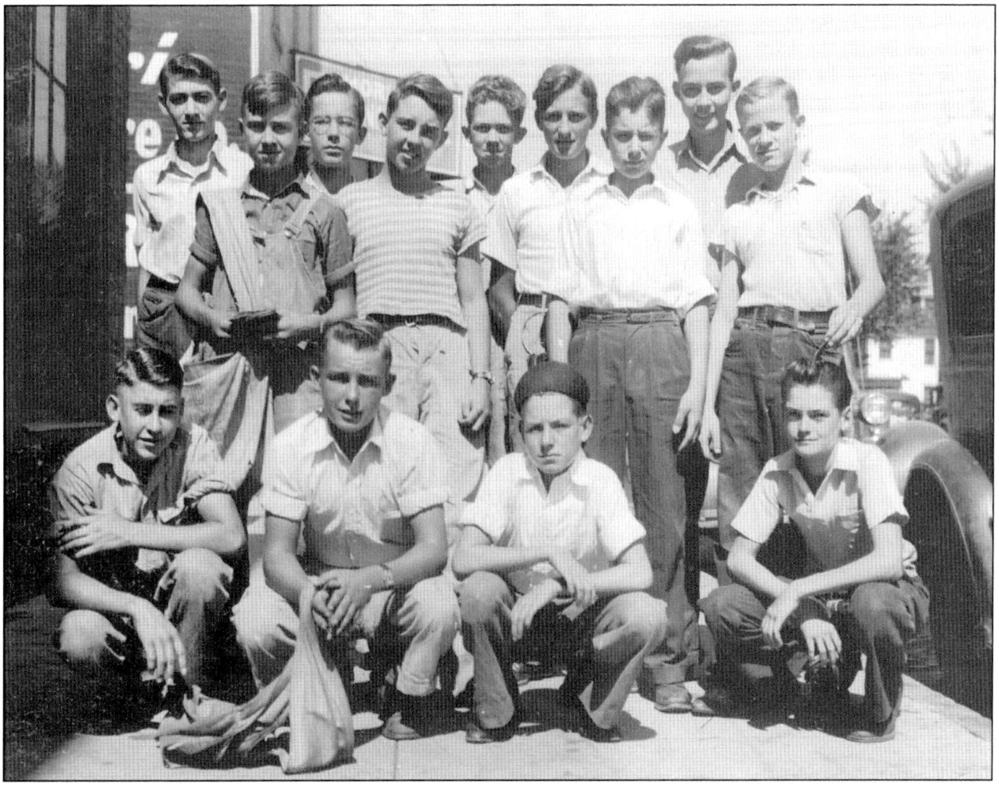

Many a Mexico boy's first job was delivering the *Mexico Ledger*. These are unidentified carriers around 1939.

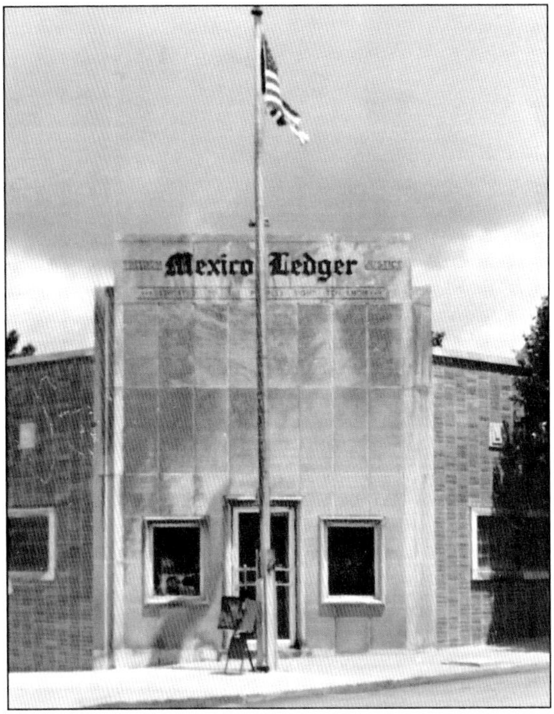

The *Ledger* moved its operations a block north of the square in 1956. Faced with a stone front page, the building (seen here in 1983) was judged by the *London Printing News* as "the most original looking newspaper building in the world." Under the masthead, the words "Dedicated to the People's Right to Know" are cut into the stone.

Robert M. White II (left) joined his father, Mitch, at the *Ledger* after World War II and took over as editor and publisher in 1965. He tripled circulation with the Ledgerland concept: expanding coverage and delivery into surrounding towns. He also introduced local access television to Mexico with See-TV. Three generations of family control ended in 1986, when White sold the paper to Thomason Newspapers, Inc. The *Mexico Ledger* is still published daily.

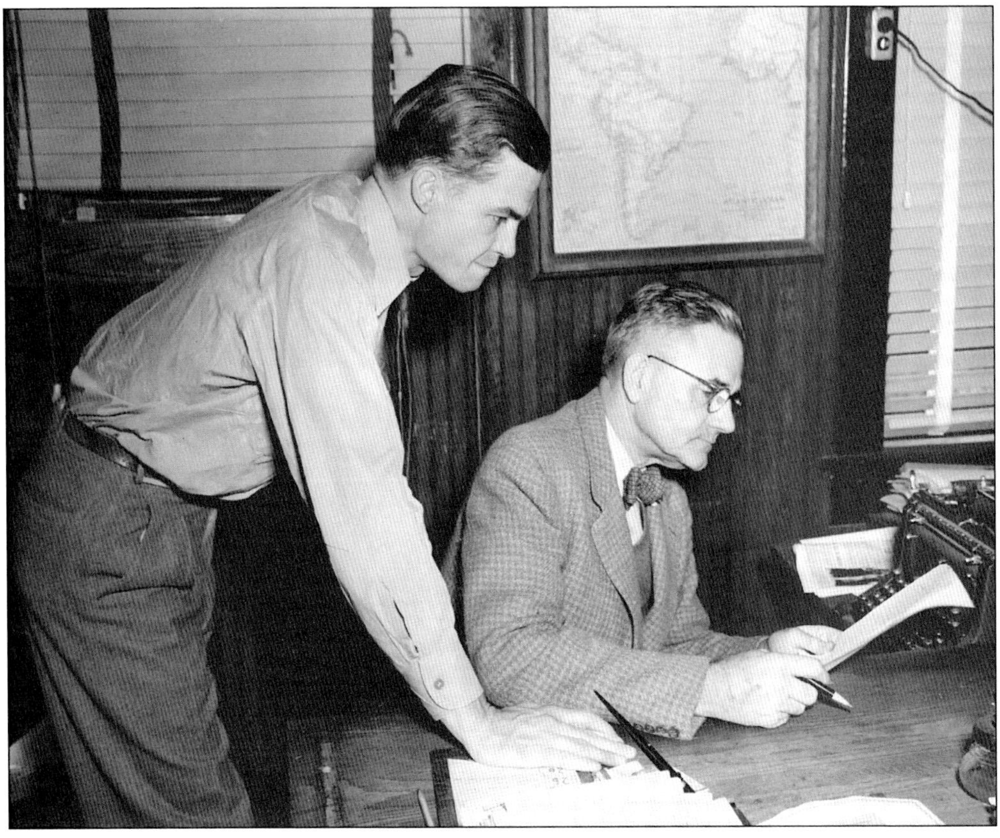

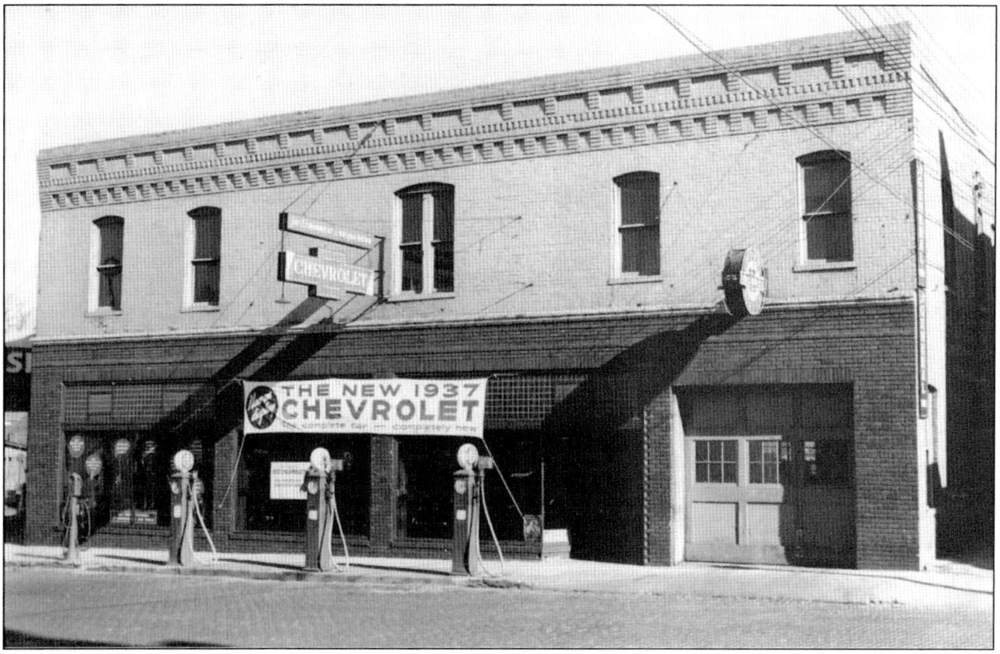

Pearl Motor Company has been in the business of selling and servicing automobiles in Mexico since 1916. This photograph gives a view of the showroom around 1937.

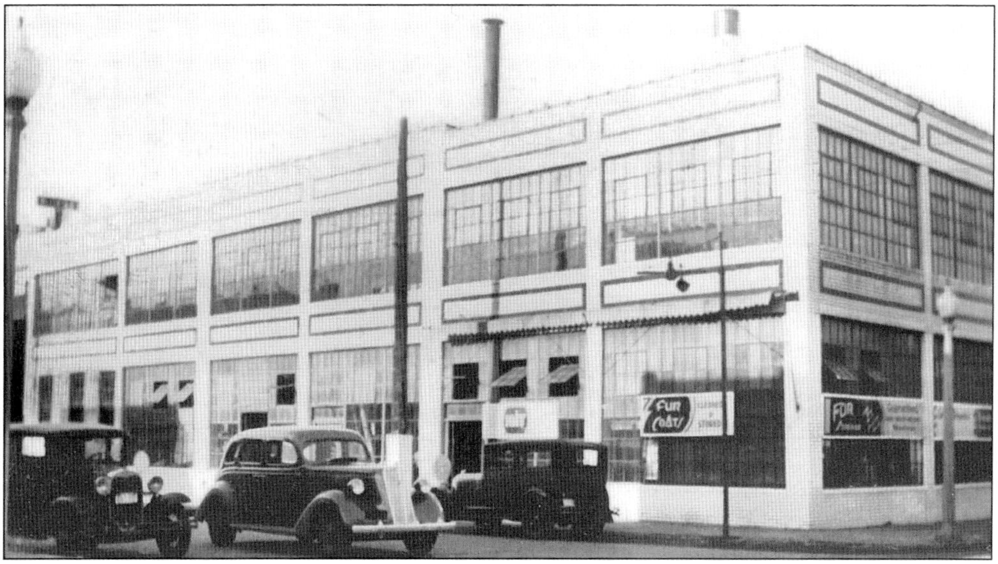

In 1891, Warner W. Williams and his father-in-law, W. H. Turner, founded Mexico Steam Laundry. The family sold the company in 1892 and moved to Chicago. Williams returned to Mexico in 1904 and created Crown Laundry, seen in this c. 1937 image. Today Crown Linen Company is solely linen and industrial supply and institutional laundry.

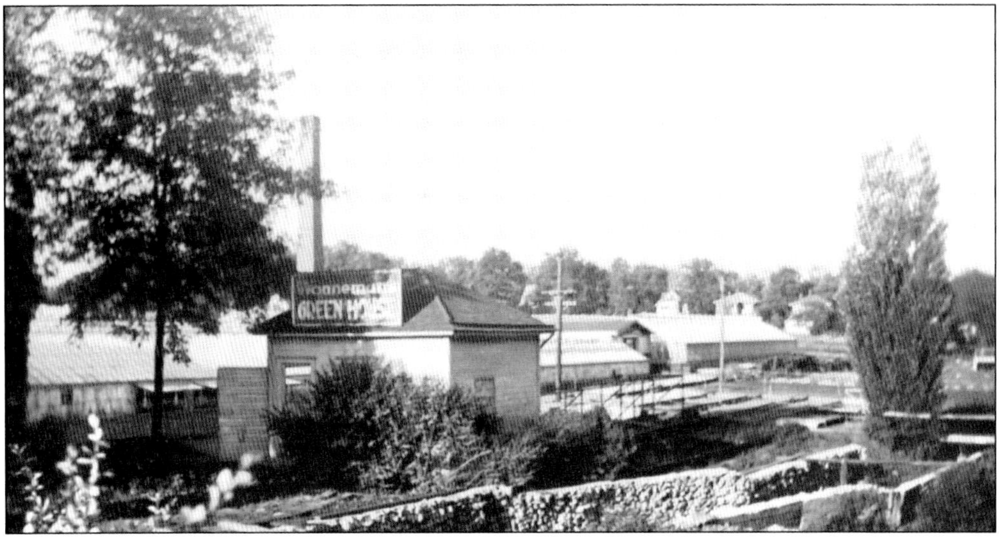

Wonneman's Florists is another longtime local business still under family control. Here are the Wonneman greenhouses as they looked around 1937.

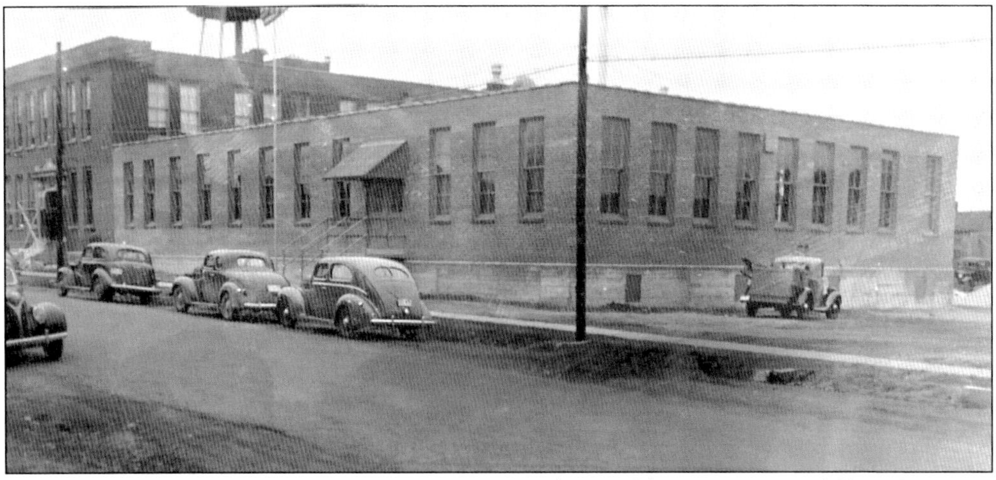

Morris Shoe Company opened in Mexico in 1905 and was sold to International Shoe Company in 1912. Shown here around 1945 in the old plant on West Liberty Street, the business moved to a more modern facility at the edge of town on Elmwood Drive in 1970. The company ceased operations in Mexico in 1981.

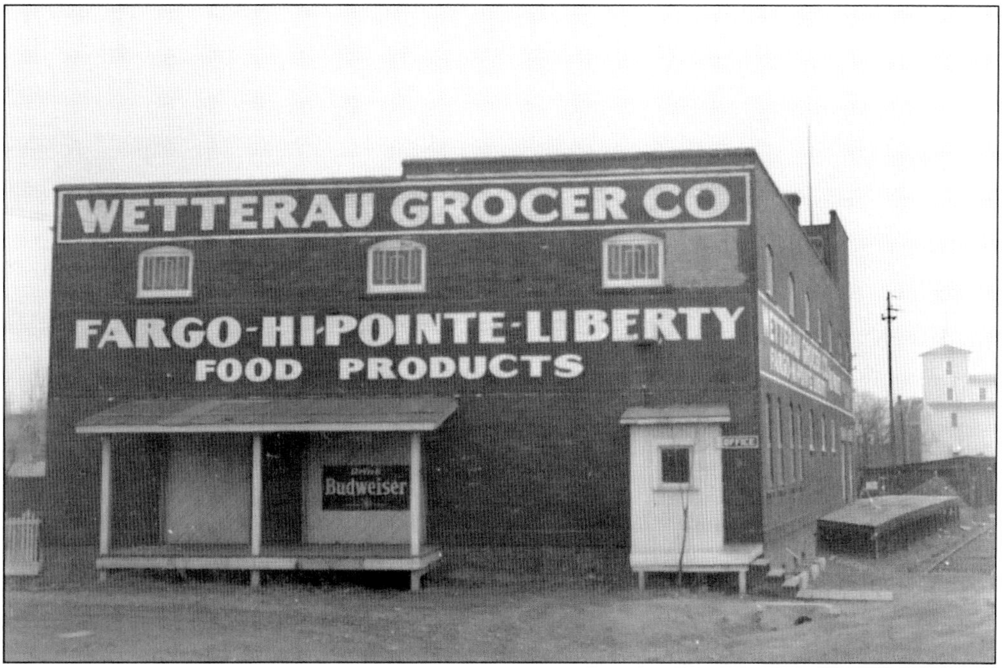

Wetterau Grocery Company moved to Mexico in 1928. The company grew and diversified, greatly expanding warehouse and office space from the original location directly east of the Gulf, Mobile and Ohio Railroad station. In 1992, Wetterau Inc. was acquired by SuperValu and subsequently moved out of Mexico. This image dates from before 1951.

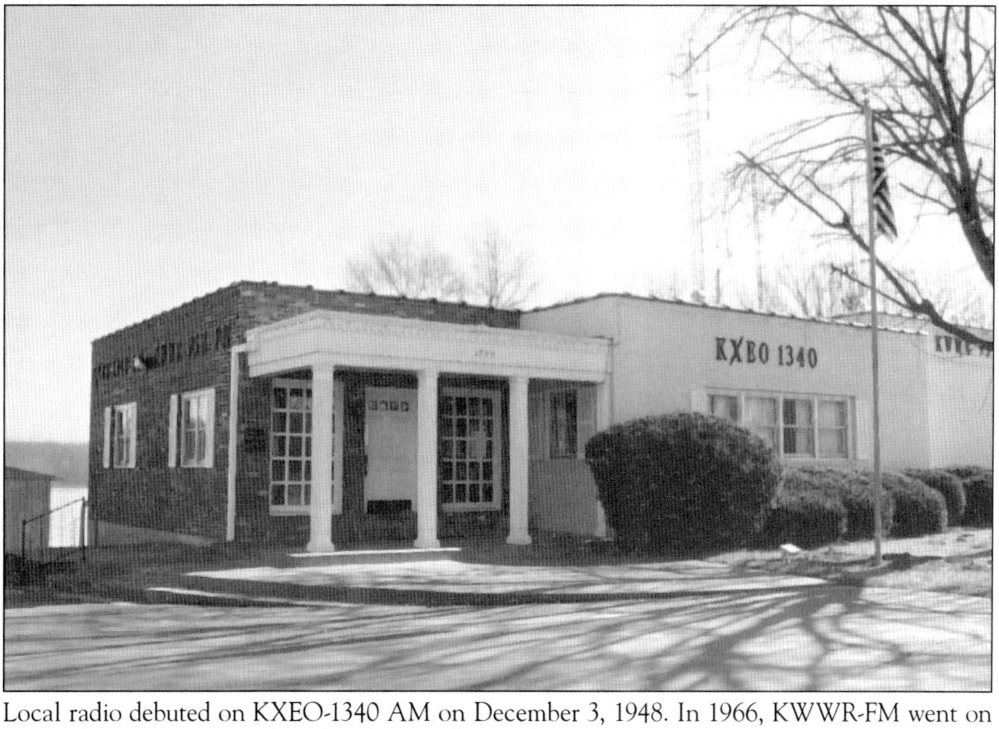

Local radio debuted on KXEO-1340 AM on December 3, 1948. In 1966, KWWR-FM went on the air from the same studios. (Author's collection.)

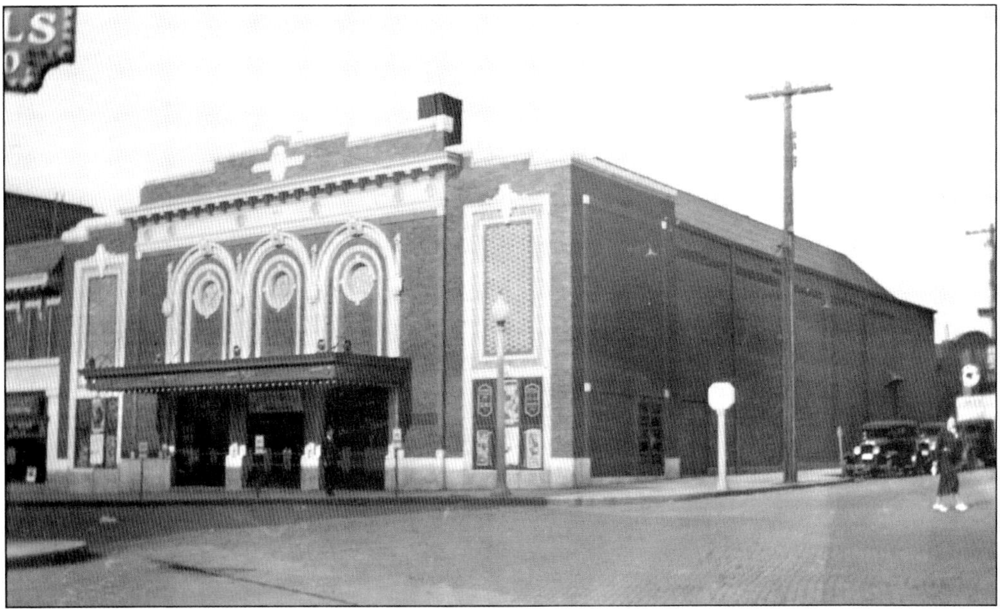

Although no longer in business or even in existence, the Liberty Theater opened in 1920 and cost $150,000 to build. Vaudeville was still in vogue, and the theater sported a stage and a $15,000 organ. Sound movies debuted here in 1929, air conditioning was added 1933, and the theater integrated in 1962.

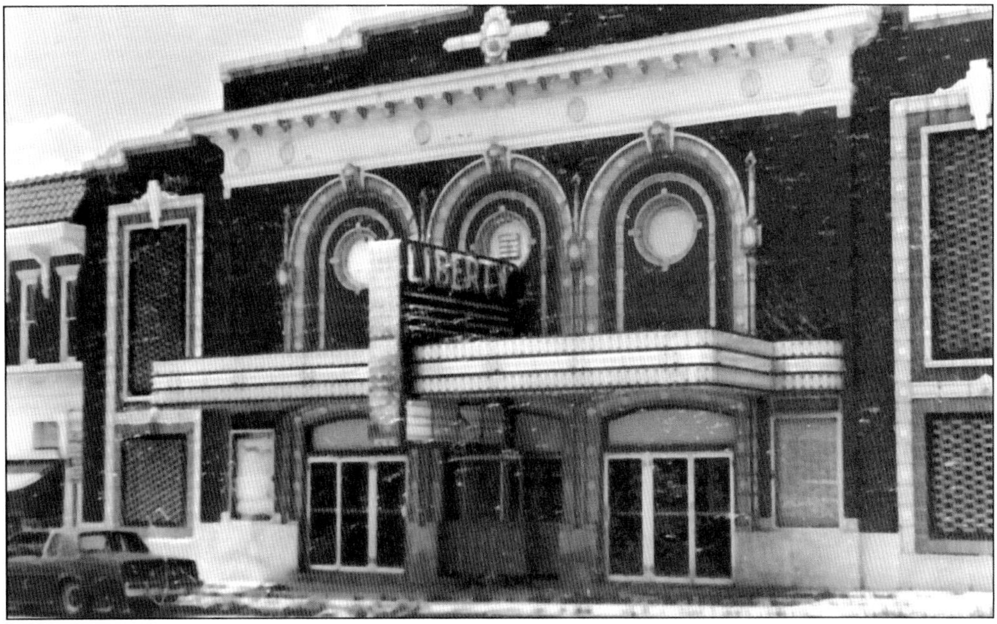

A victim to shifting shopping and entertainment tastes, the theater showed its last film, *Night Shift*, on September 30, 1982. This is how it appeared around 1983, with the addition of a light marquee. The building no longer exists.

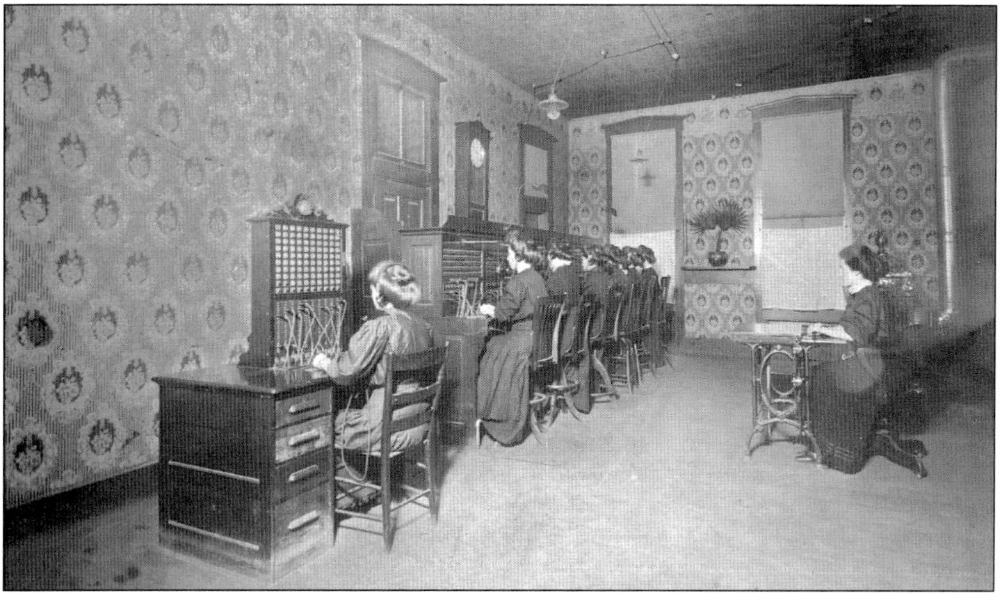

J. A. Glandon introduced telephone service to the city in 1884, but a lack of subscribers led to failure. In 1892, E. D. Graham opened a second telephone exchange that had 48 subscribers. Households paid $18 per year for a one-party phone and cheaper rates for party lines. Operators shown here are probably in the original office on South Washington Street in the late 1890s. Women were preferred as operators and worked at an average salary of $2 per week.

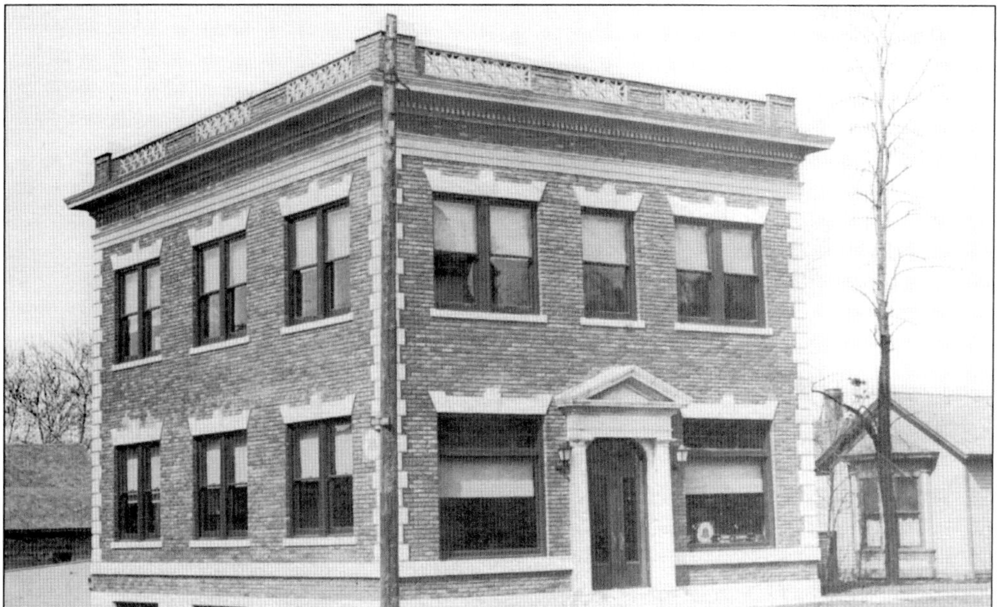

In 1911, the Mexico Telephone Company was taken over by the Bell System and became the Missouri and Kansas Telephone Company. Service and equipment moved to a new building on the northeast corner of Coal and Promenade Streets, shown in c. 1913 photograph. Telephone numbers were originally two digits before expanding to the first letters of the exchange name, "Justice," plus four digits; later the exchange became a numbered code, 581.

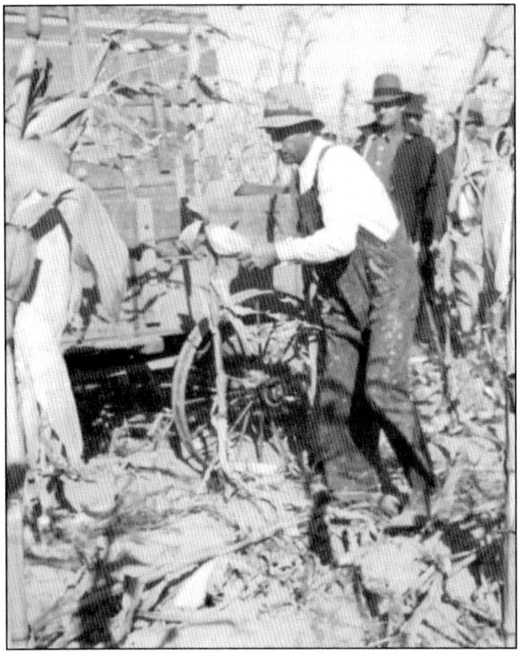

Agriculture has always been an integral part of the life of Mexico and Audrain County. Roy Cox harvests corn in this undated photograph.

In recent years, there have been fewer but larger farms. In this 1939 image, from left to right, Ernest Lierheimer, Glen Mutti, and J. B. DeVault Jr. stand in front of stalks of Audrain County's first hybrid seed corn.

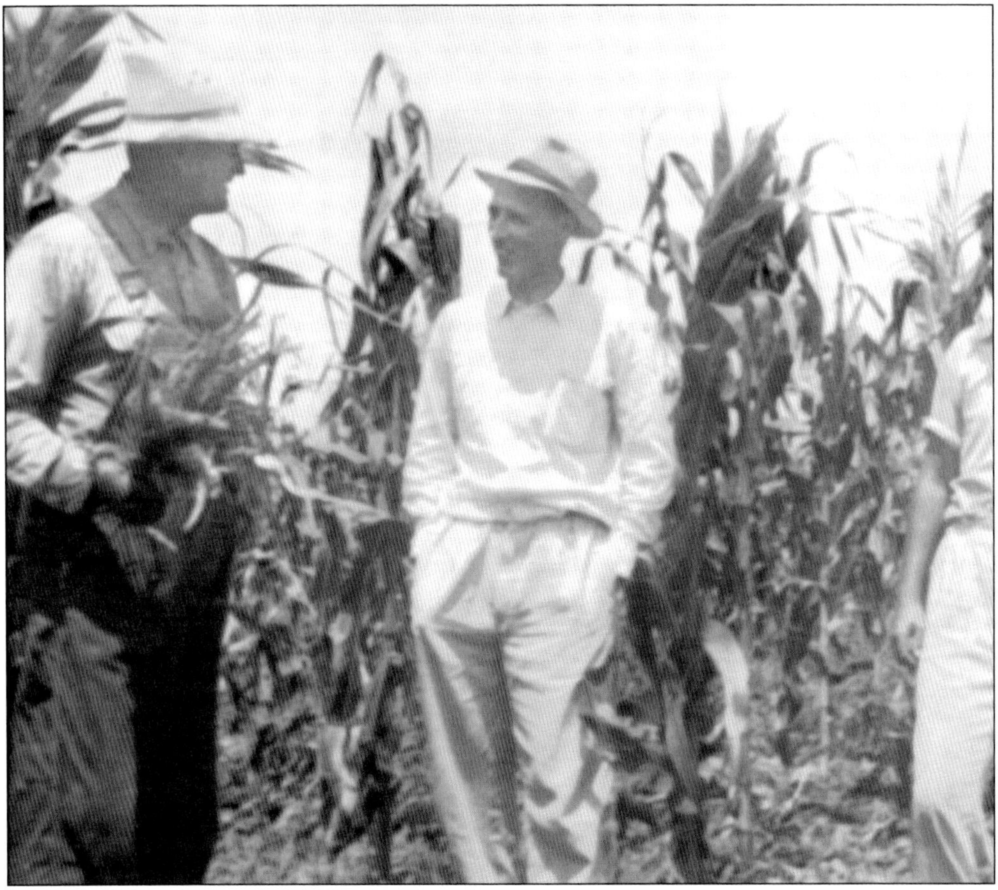

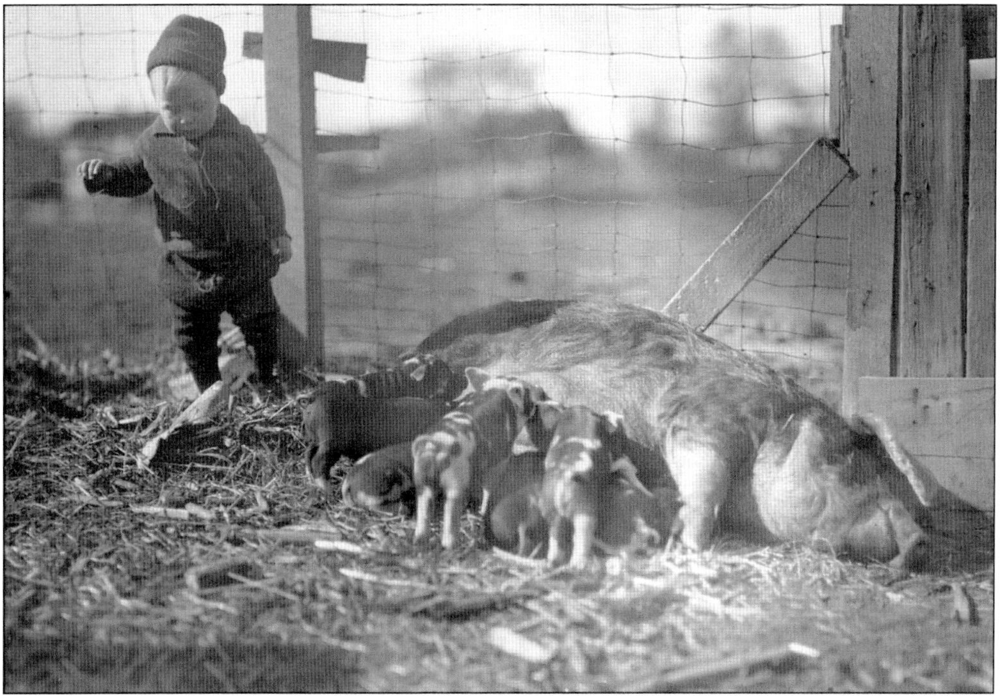
Livestock is part of farm life. This is Clark Garrett's son with a litter of pigs in 1925.

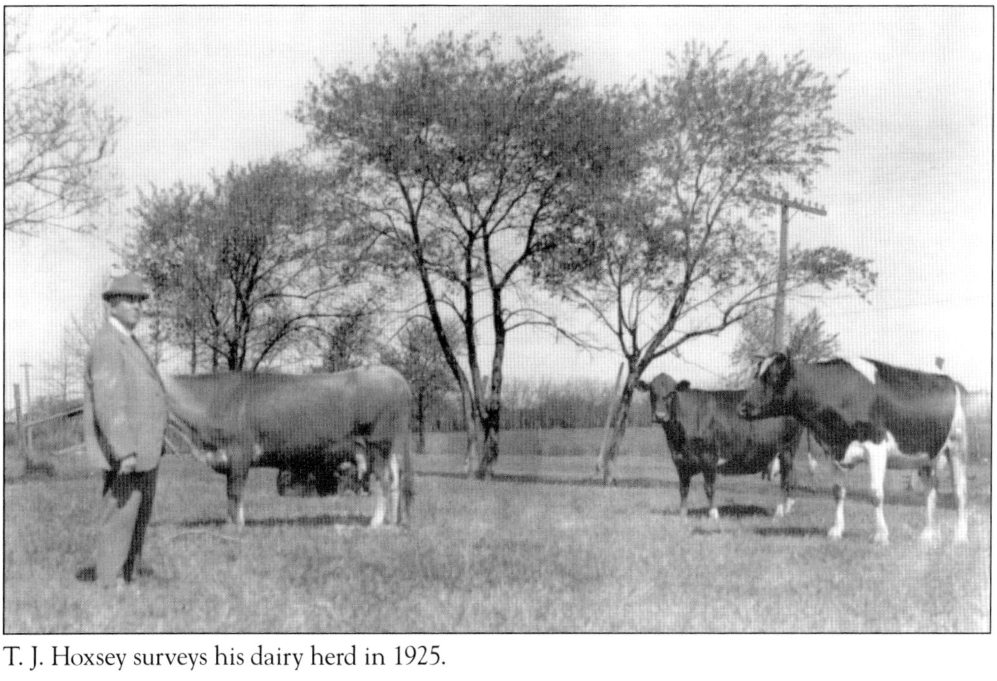
T. J. Hoxsey surveys his dairy herd in 1925.

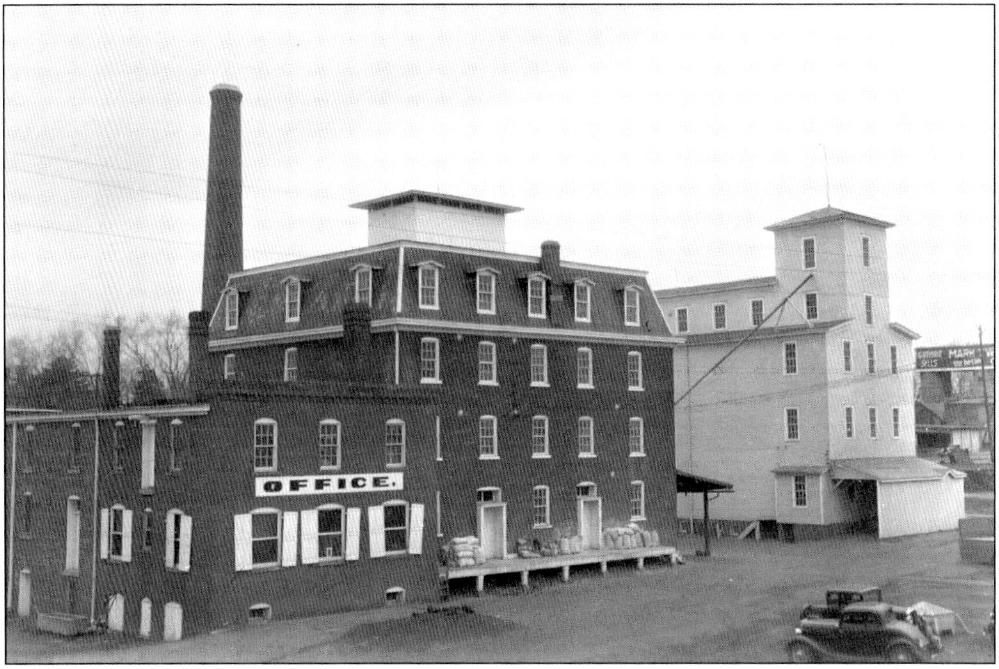

Many Mexico businesses came into existence to support agriculture. Shown here in 1937, the Pollock Milling and Elevator Company originated in 1869. The business no longer exists.

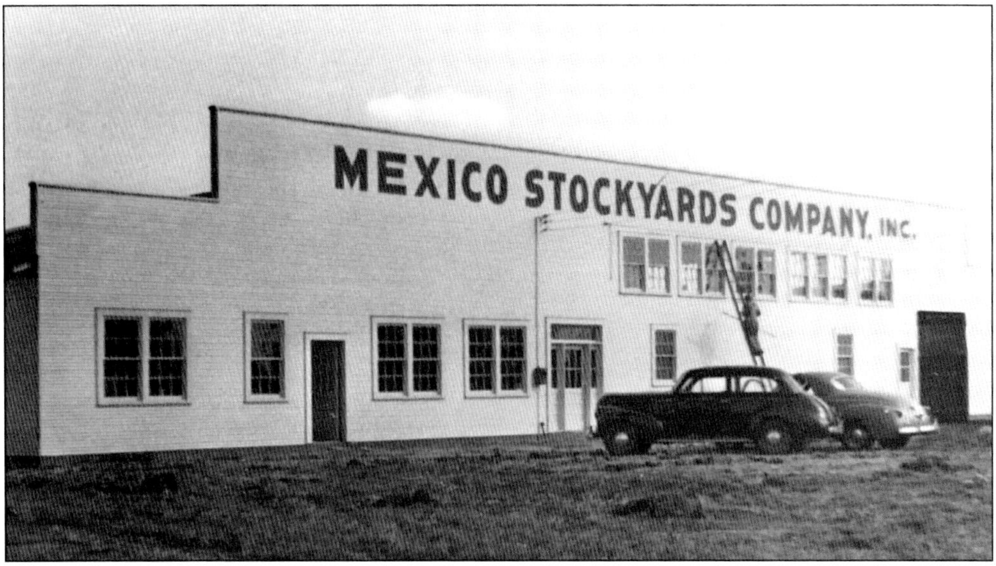

The Mexico Stockyards Company Inc., which handled sales of local livestock, is also now out of business.

Five

Transportation

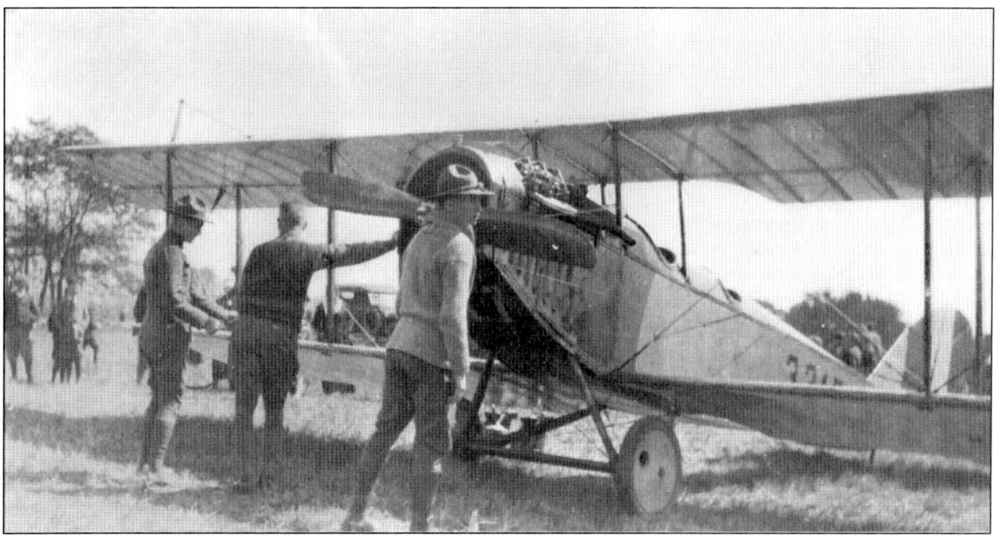

The first plane to land in Mexico was a World War I flyer that set down in a meadow on the C. W. Pease farm in 1918. This photograph shows several unidentified men with the plane.

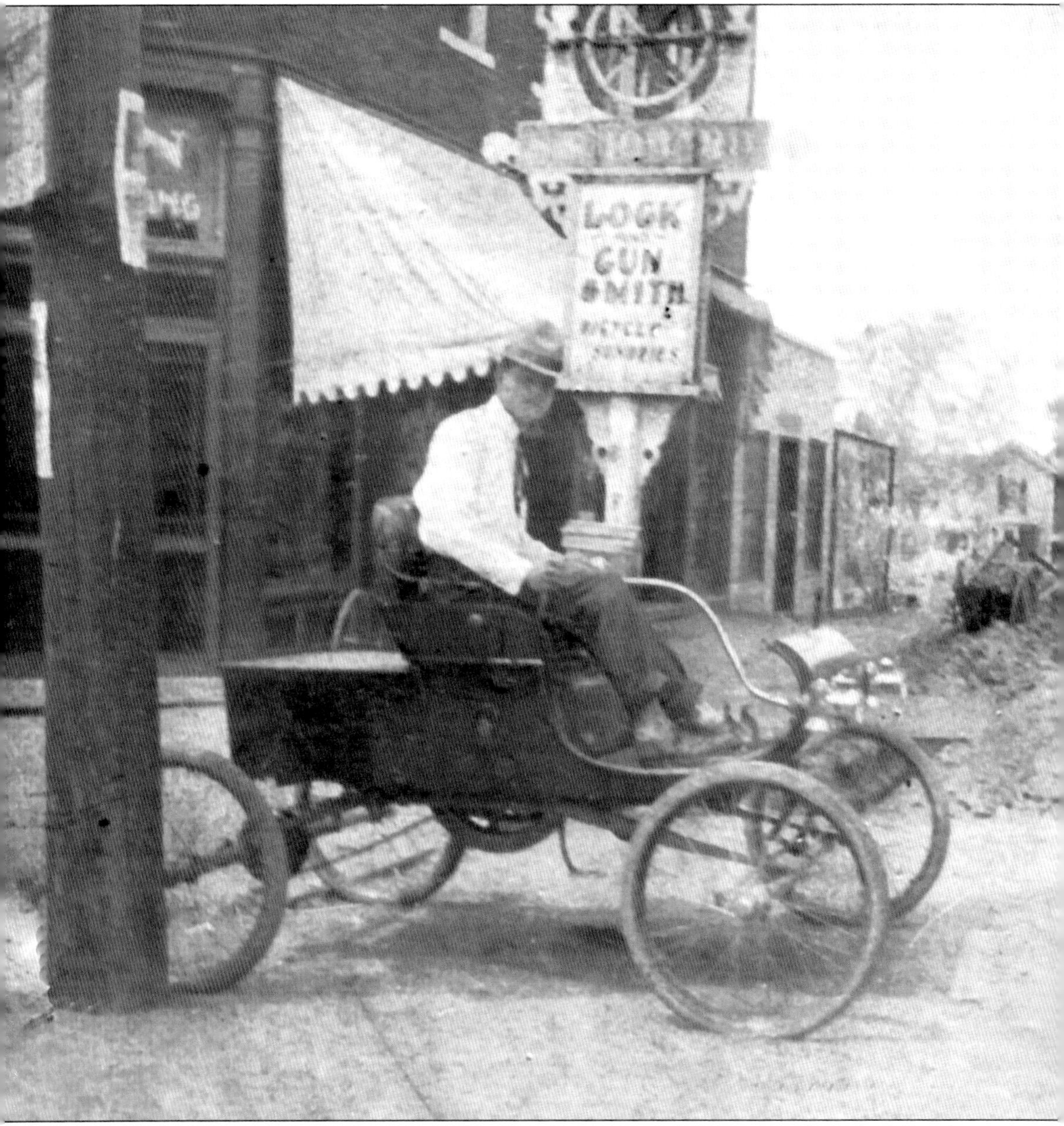

Sam Howard owned the first automobile in Mexico. He rented the car to others for $5 per hour. Usually a driver would head into the countryside, stall, and have to be towed back into town. L. M. White is driving the car in the photograph, which is thought to date from around 1905.

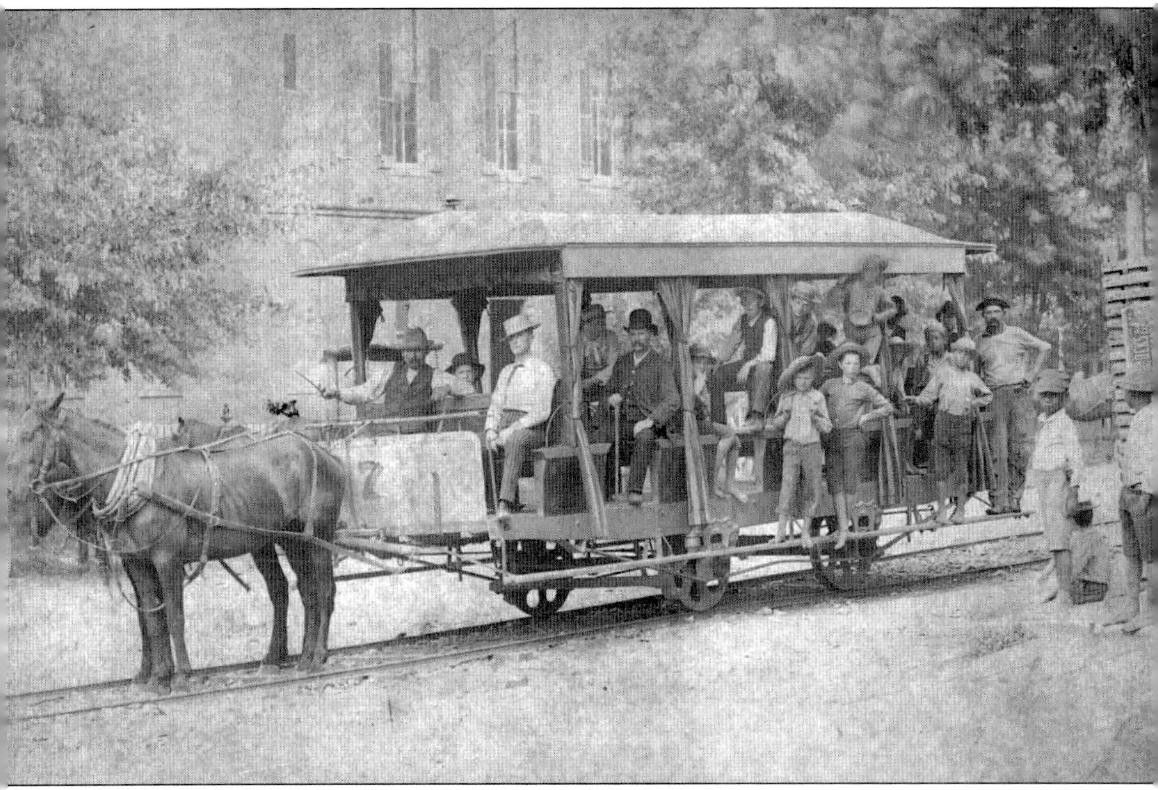

The city attempted a horse-drawn trolley in 1889, with tracks along South Clark Street and west along Hardin College Boulevard to the fairgrounds. Three cars traveled each line. Passengers, however, often had to jump off to lighten the load or help set the car back on track. One trip on the trolley was usually sufficient. In the front seat of this trolley in 1889 are driver Joseph Price and George Reynolds; the other passengers are not identified.

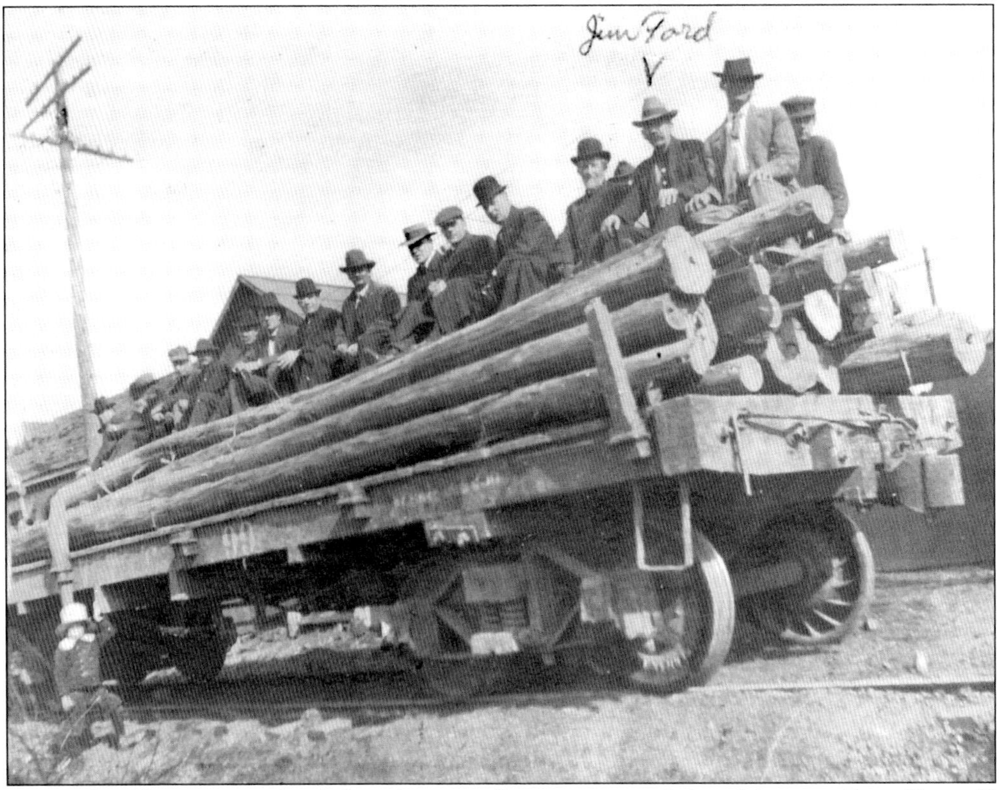

In 1909, local businessmen decided an electric trolley running north from Mexico to Santa Fe would fare better and the Mexico, Santa Fe and Perry Traction Company (MSF&PT) was born.

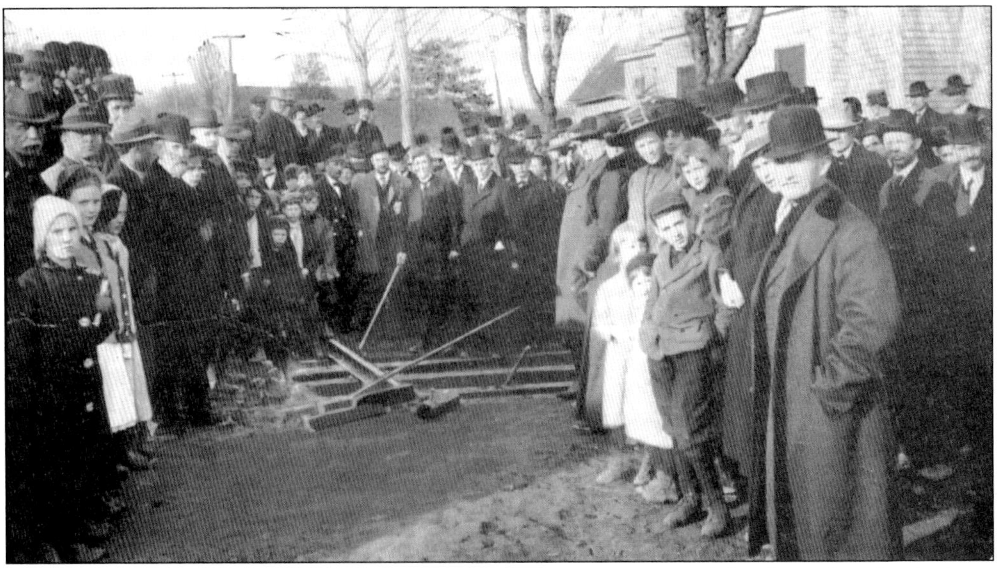

The trolley line was hopefully intended to carry both passengers and freight and make Audrain County and Mexico the center of an interurban transport system. On March 1, 1910, citizens gathered near Western and Love Streets for the ceremonial "Driving the golden spike" that signaled the beginning of laying the track for the MSF&PT.

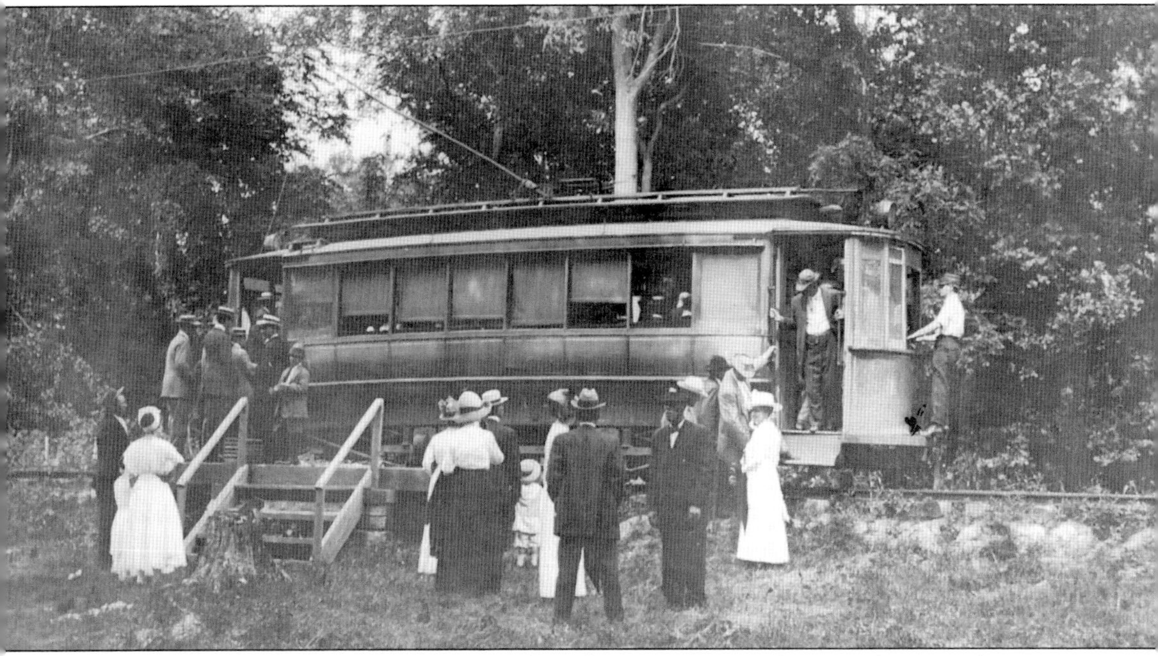

By 1911, passengers and freight could travel on the new system as far as Molino, 9 miles away. An additional 7 miles of track leading to Santa Fe was added by 1915. Tickets to ride on one of two passenger cars were 5¢ per stop. A ticket from Mexico to Santa Fe totaled 45¢. The growing popularity of autos and the improving road system led to the demise of the trolley in 1919.

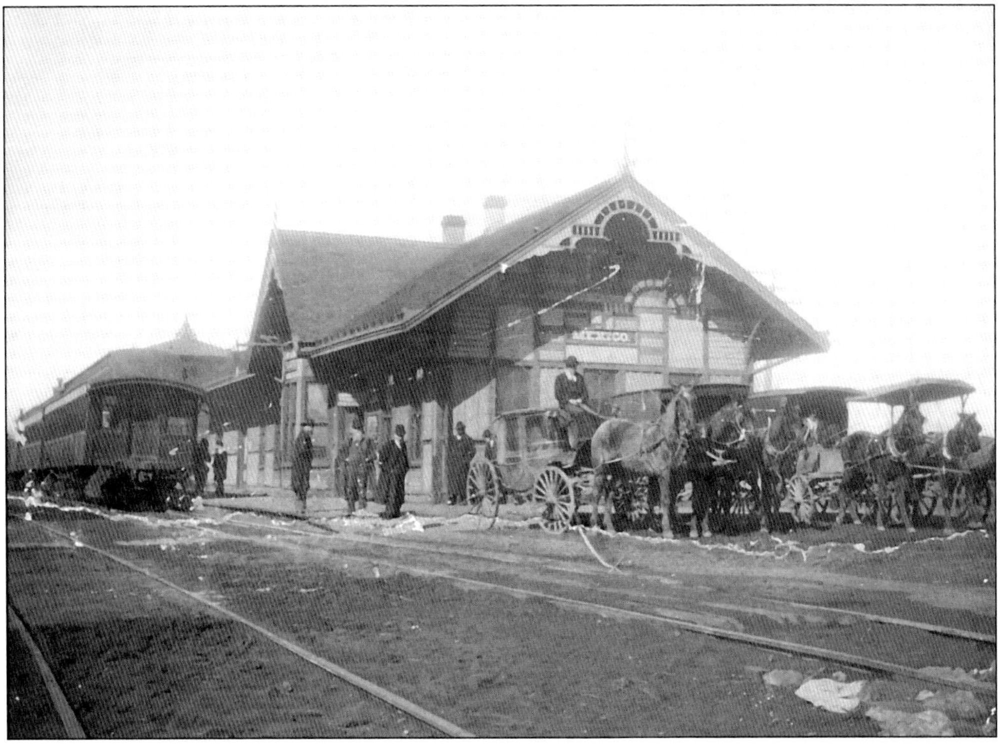

The coming of the North Missouri Railroad in 1858 signaled a new era in growth and prosperity in Mexico. The county supported the coming of the railroad to the tune of $50,000, which was an enormous debt at the time. At first, the train line was to pass north of the city, but Dr. Nathaniel Allison donated a right-of-way west of Jefferson Street and south of Liberty Street. In this picture, a Wabash train arrives at Union Station in 1898.

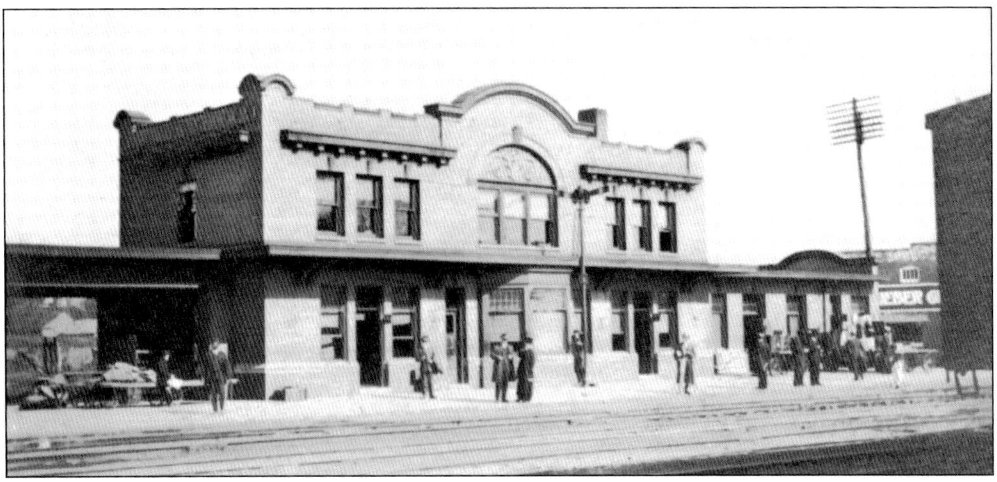

In 1868, the county subscribed another $300,000 to the Louisiana and Missouri River Railroad, which became the Chicago and Alton (C&A) Railroad. The Chicago and Alton depot is shown here in 1915.

The North Missouri became the St. Louis, Kansas City and Northern Railway in 1872. By 1879, the rail line was the Wabash, St. Louis and Pacific Railway. This 1890 image shows the Wabash line westward at Western Avenue, with the freight house on the left and the water tanks on the right.

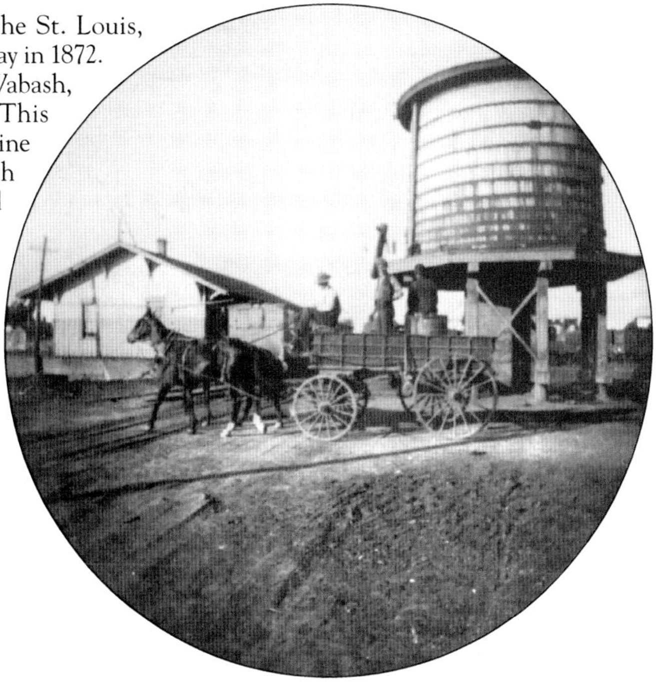

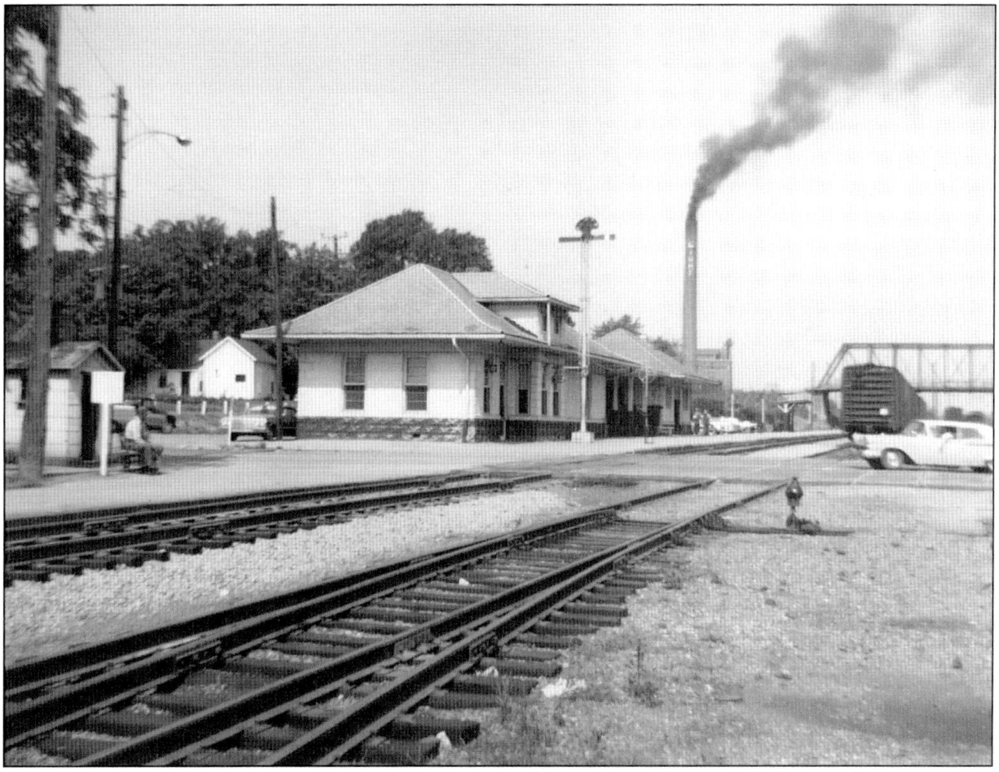

Rerouting the railroad from north of Mexico through the city was a blessing for businesses needing to send and receive goods. Residents trying to get across town, however, often cursed the Jefferson Street crossing, shown here around 1966.

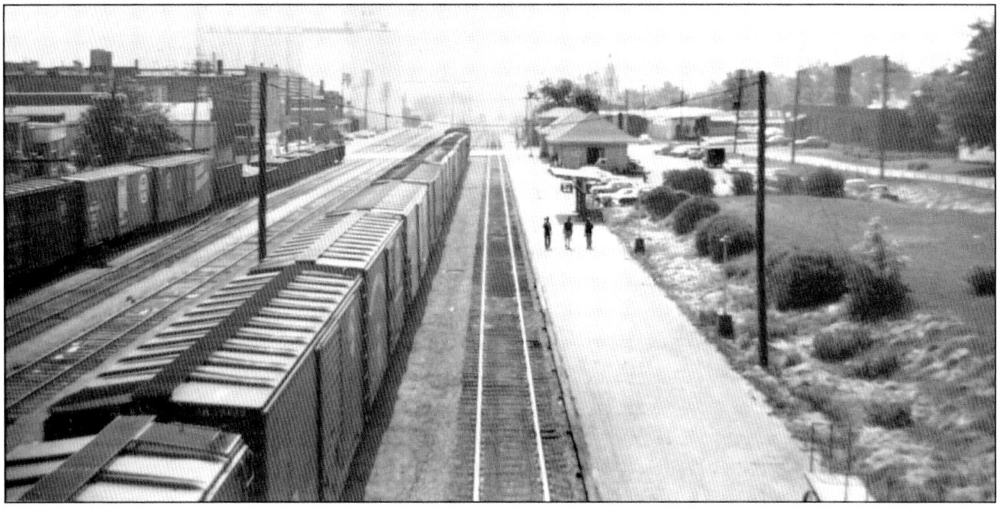

The Wabash, the Alton (part of the Baltimore and Ohio system), and the Burlington Railroads used two depots across from each other at the Jefferson Street crossing. This image shows an elevated view, looking east, of the railroad yards.

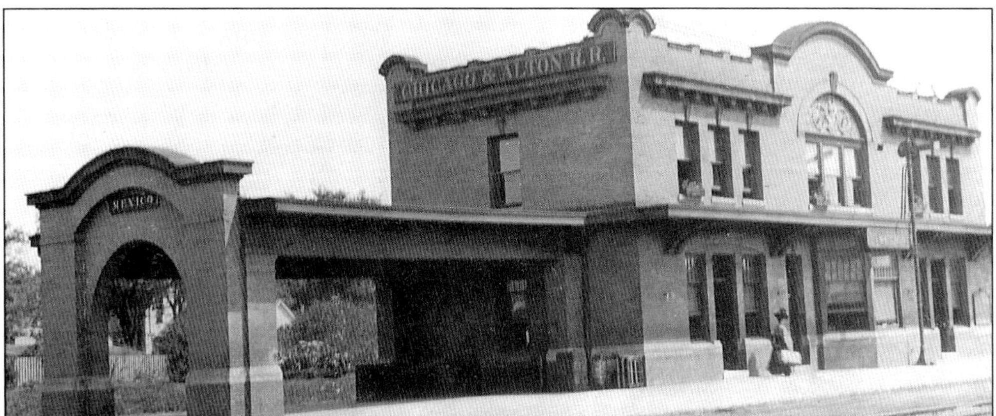

In the early 1900s, thirty-five passenger trains traveled in and out of Mexico daily, carrying more than 1,000 passengers. This c. 1915 photograph shows the C&A depot, which was both a freight and passenger station.

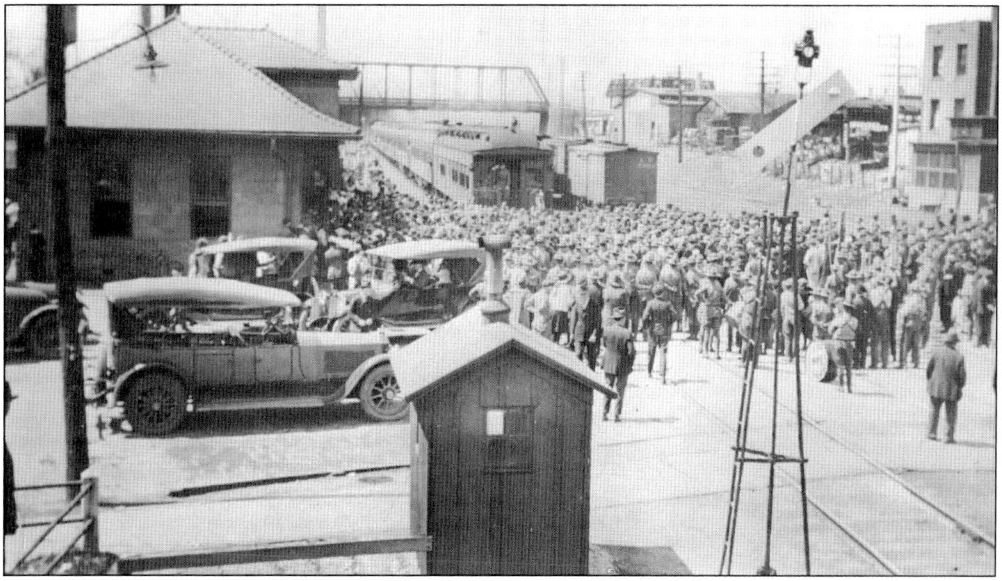

In the heyday of passenger traffic, many famous people, including royalty and U.S. presidents, chugged through the city. In 1919, Gen. John J. Pershing toured the country by rail, and Mexico was on his itinerary. Pershing salutes from the back platform as he passes the Wabash station.

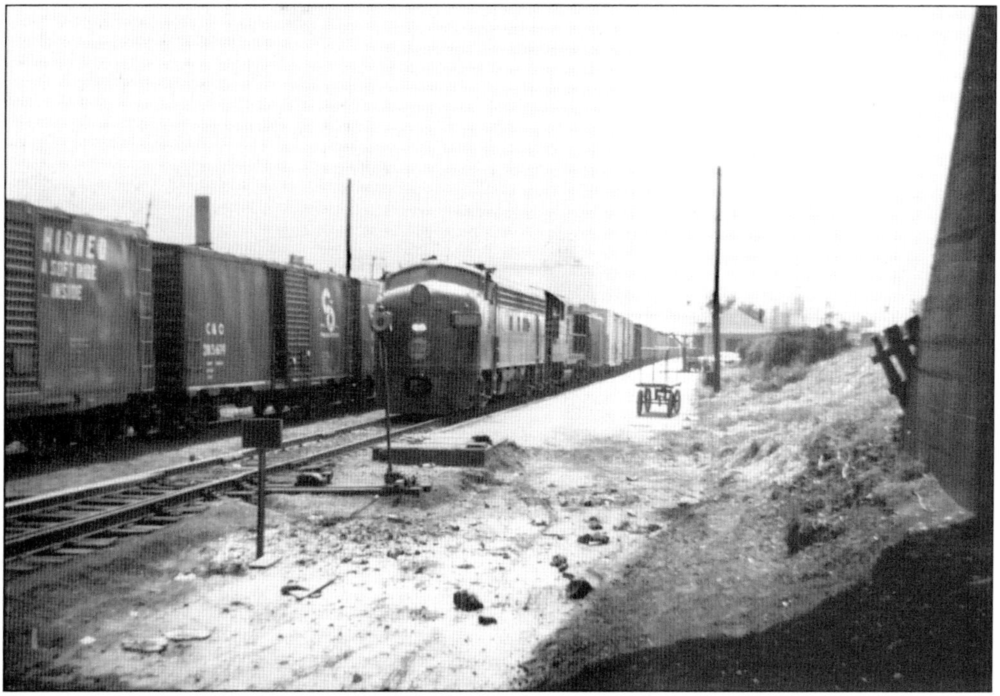

By 1969, no passenger trains ran through the city because of declining demand. Travelers could drive their own cars or fly much faster. Freight trains, however, were still operating, such as the westbound Wabash Redball train in this c. 1966 image.

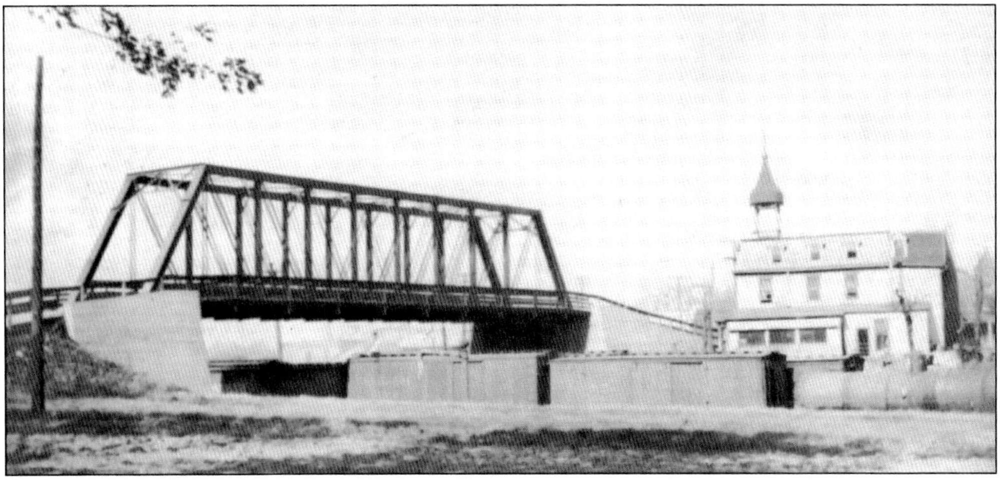

At one time, the Clark Street Bridge allowed cars to easily drive over the rail yards. With the demise of train traffic, the bridge, shown here around 1900 with the Liberty Hotel in the background, was demolished and replaced.

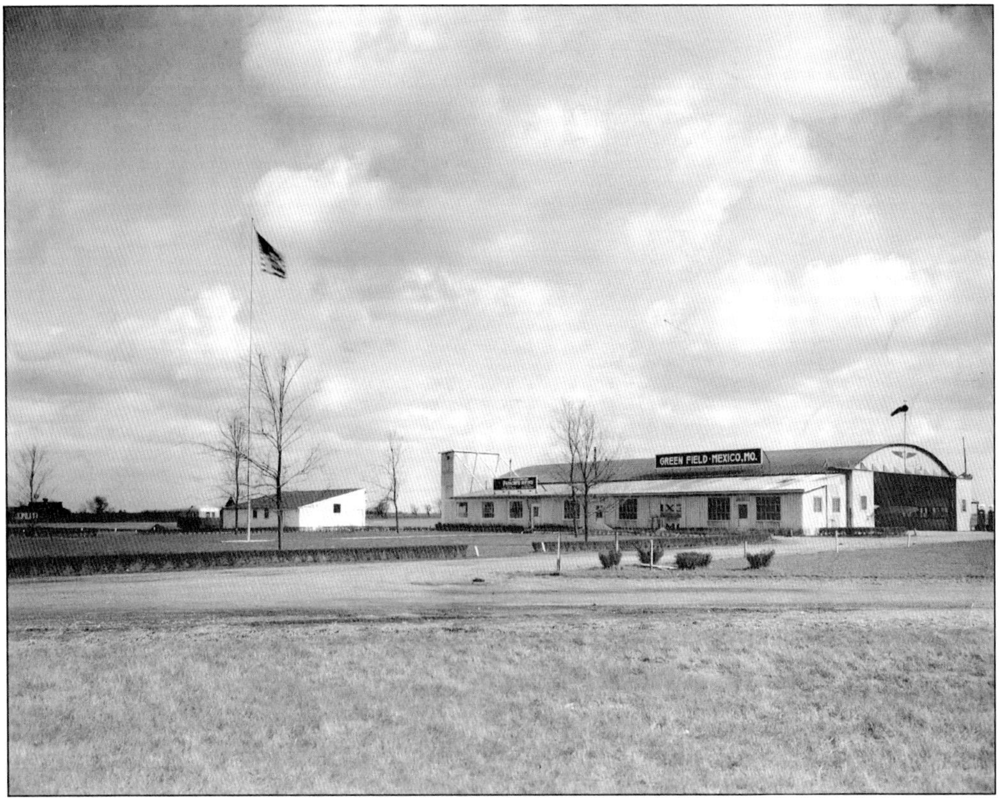

This photograph shows Green Field in 1939. In the early 1930s, the airport had been an unpaved runway. By 1949, traffic had increased and a 2,000-foot paved runway was added in 1951. Further additions have been made since, and today the Mexico Airport boasts two runways—one is 3,200 feet and the other 5,500 feet.

Six

INSTITUTIONS

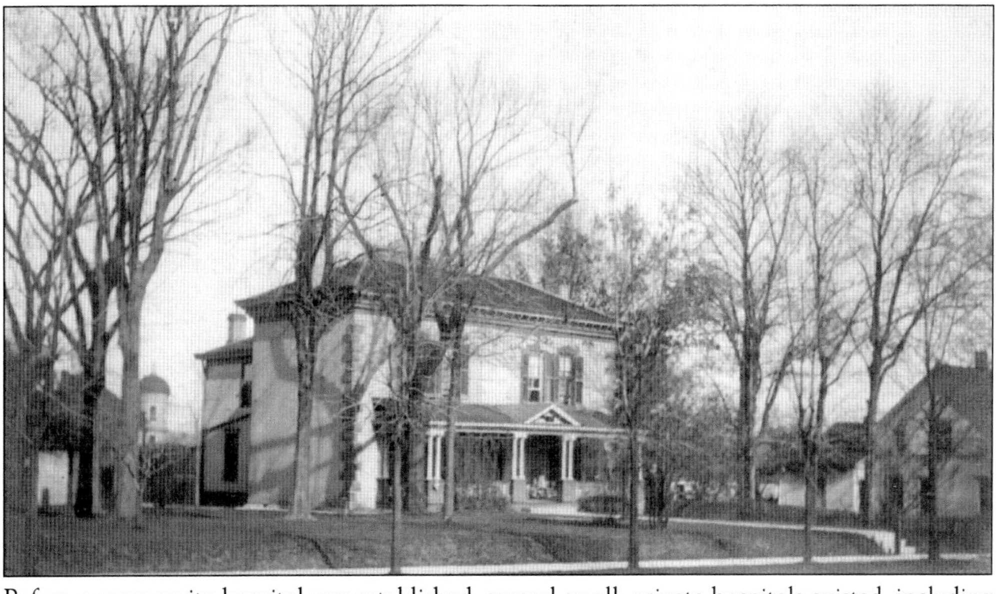

Before a community hospital was established, several small, private hospitals existed, including the Amanda Hospital shown here, located at 711 East Jackson Street. These hospitals were private endeavors of individual physicians and typically short-lived.

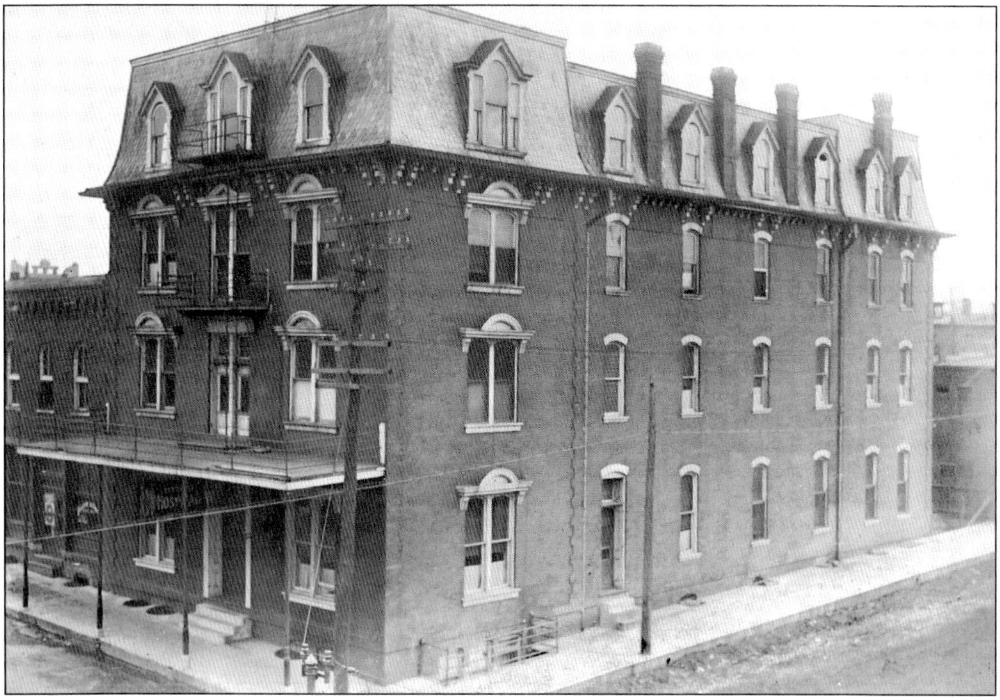

Around 1900, Mexico was home to the largest horse infirmary in the state but had no hospital to serve its citizens. Col. Robert M. White and A. P. Green provided funds, and with the support of the Mexico Commercial Club the Mexico Hospital Association was born. The association rented and equipped the Windsor Hotel, on the corner of Jackson and Clark Streets, in 1913.

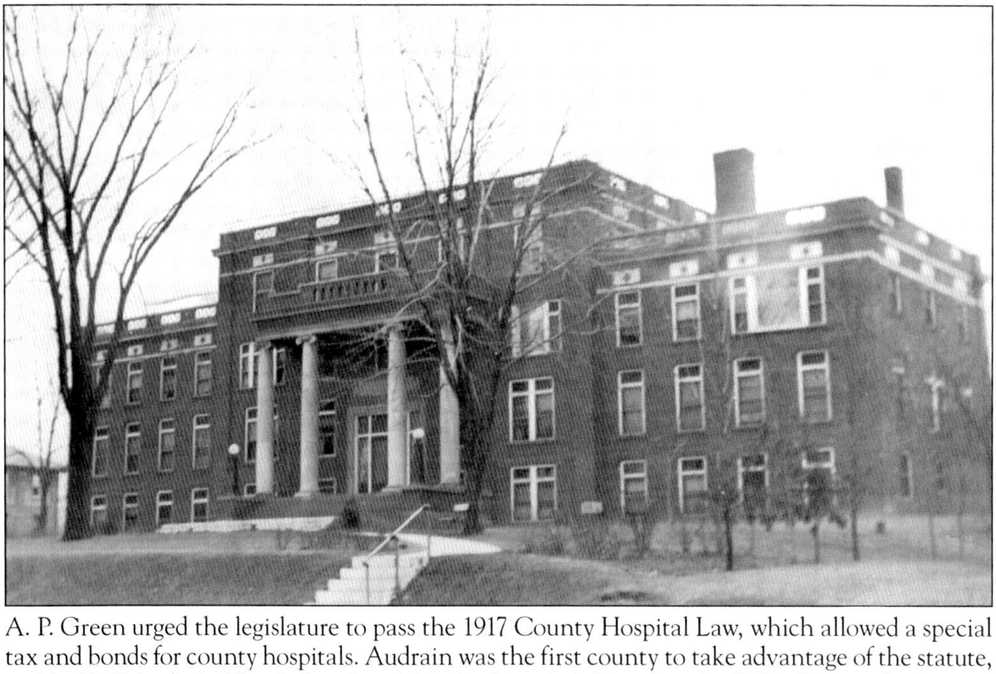

A. P. Green urged the legislature to pass the 1917 County Hospital Law, which allowed a special tax and bonds for county hospitals. Audrain was the first county to take advantage of the statute, and in 1920 Audrain Hospital replaced Mexico Hospital. Seen here in 1930, the new facility was located on East Monroe Street. A. P. Green is known as the "Father of Audrain Hospital."

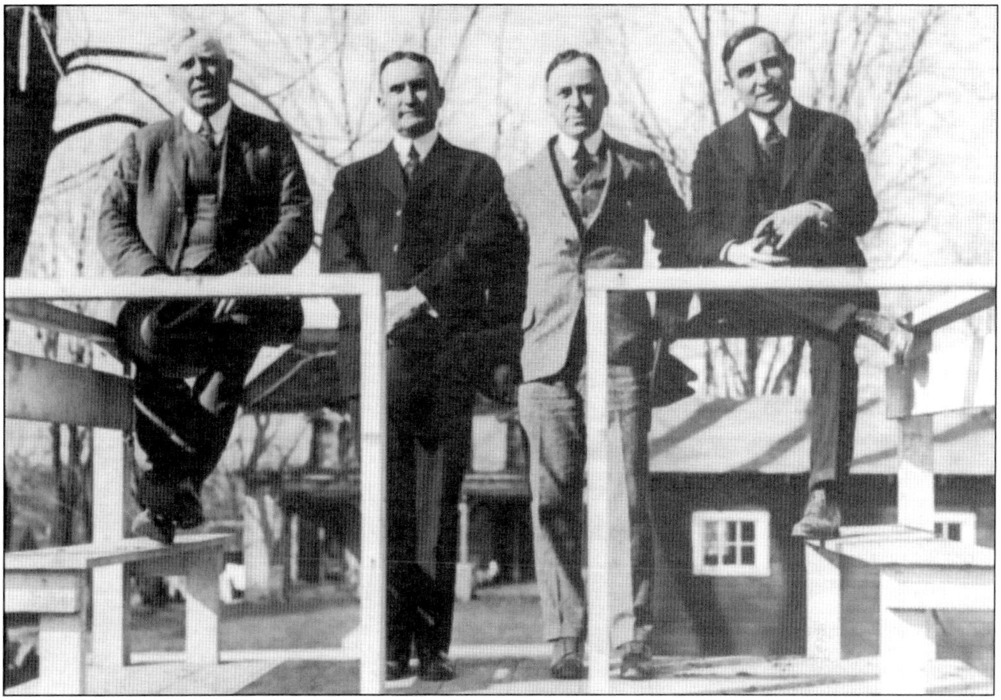

This March 18, 1919, photograph shows the first board of directors of Audrain Hospital. The board consisted of, from left to right, Joe Considine, J. W. Dry, Fred Pilcher, and Nate Phillips. The hospital required the passage of bond issues of $75,000 and $40,000, thus reinforcing the commitment of county residents to the project.

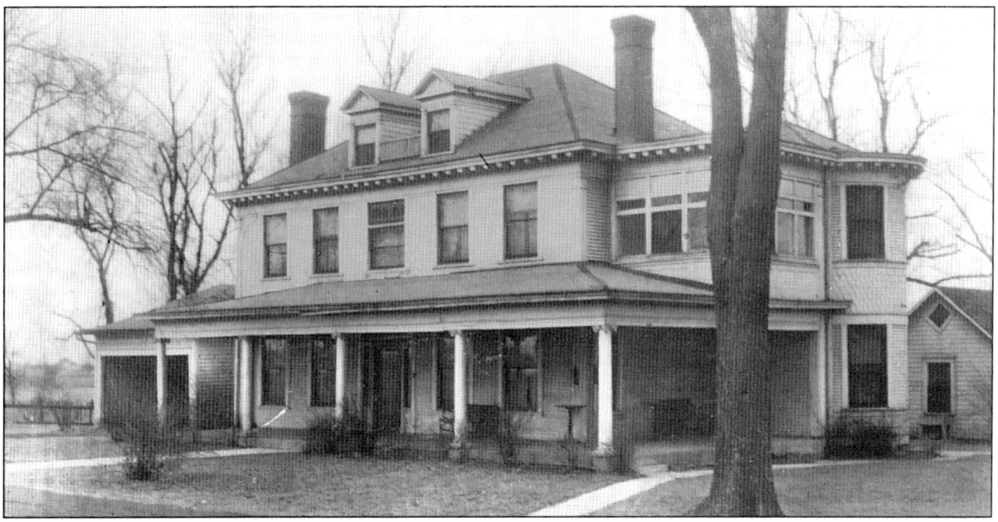

At the time Audrain Hospital was growing, controversy was brewing. Doctors of osteopathy were barred from practicing at the facility due to different philosophies and methods from medical doctors. After opposition from osteopaths and patients led to the defeat of bond issues to improve Audrain Hospital, the Missouri Court of Appeals determined that osteopaths did practice medicine as defined by law, and the doors of hospitals across the nation opened to them. This photograph is of the General Hospital that was owned by H. I. Nesheim, D.O., and operated from 1940 to 1955.

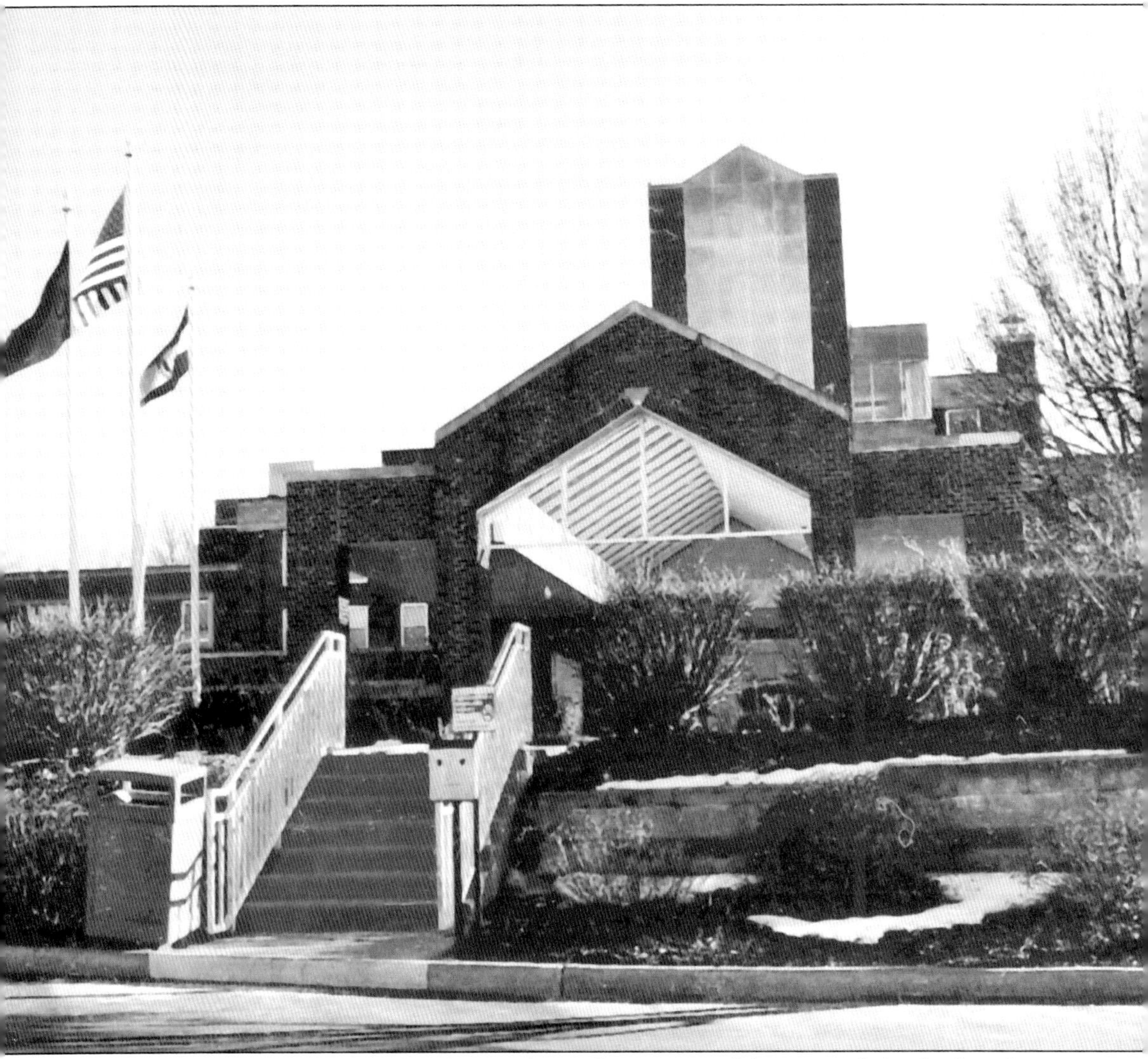

The Audrain Medical Center (until 1970, the Audrain Hospital) has expanded in both real estate and services and today offers a full range of care. It is a major employer in the region and recognized nationally for quality and value as well as for patient satisfaction. (Author's collection.)

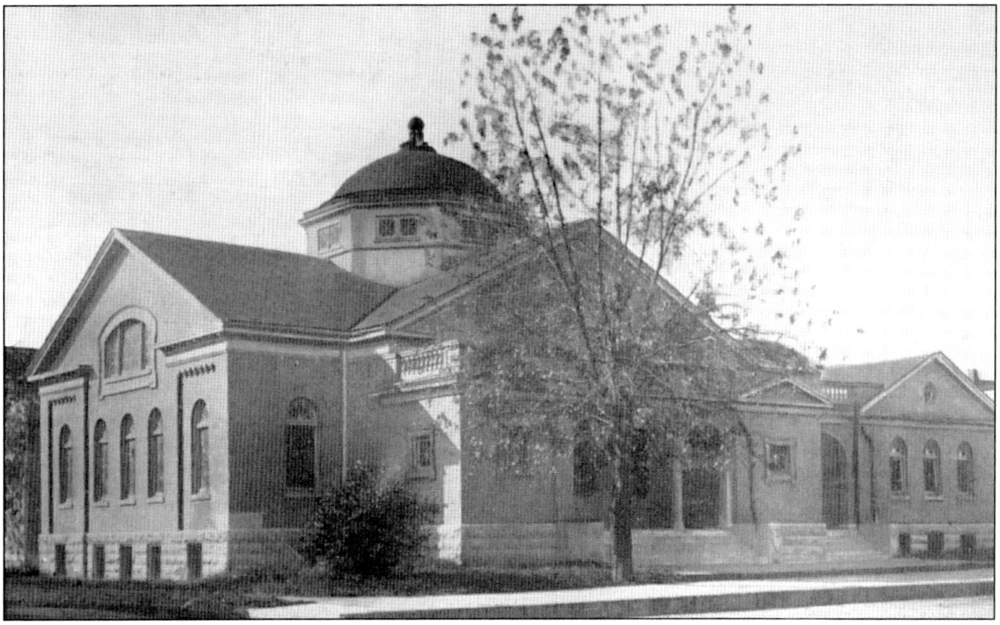

Early settlers in the area were mostly Baptists and Methodists. Baptists built the first permanent church, Hopewell, a little over a mile southwest of the courthouse in 1836. In 1838, the Methodists built the first church in town a block west of Jefferson Street on the south side of Promenade. The Methodist church (with additions) still occupies the site.

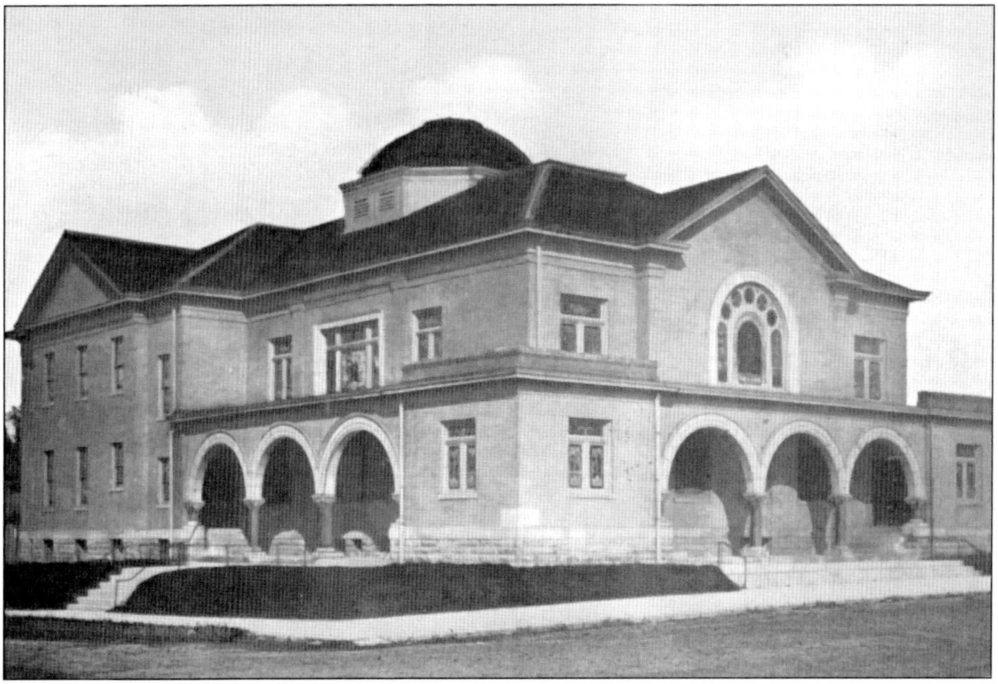

In 1853, the Disciples of Christ (Christian Church) built a church on Liberty Street at Water Street. There were two front doors leading to the worship area, one for women and one for men. By the early 1900s, congregations grew larger and the Christian Church moved to its present location on the northeast corner of West Jackson and Olive Streets in 1905.

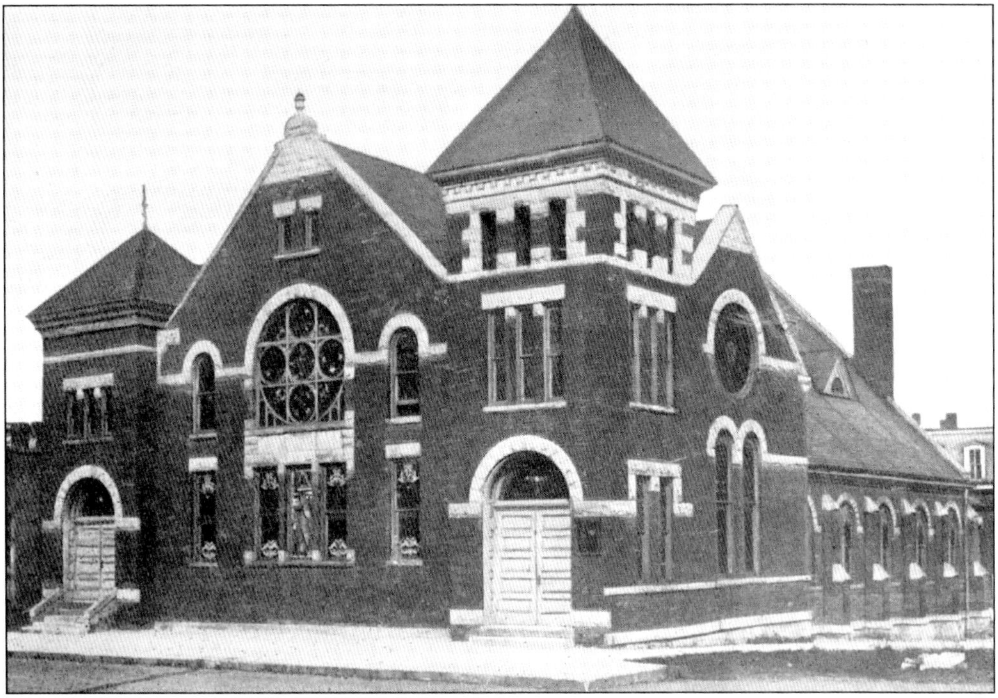

The Baptists built a new church in 1894 at the northwest corner of East Promenade and Coal Streets. This structure was later demolished and replaced by the telephone company building. The First Baptist Church is currently located further east on Promenade Street.

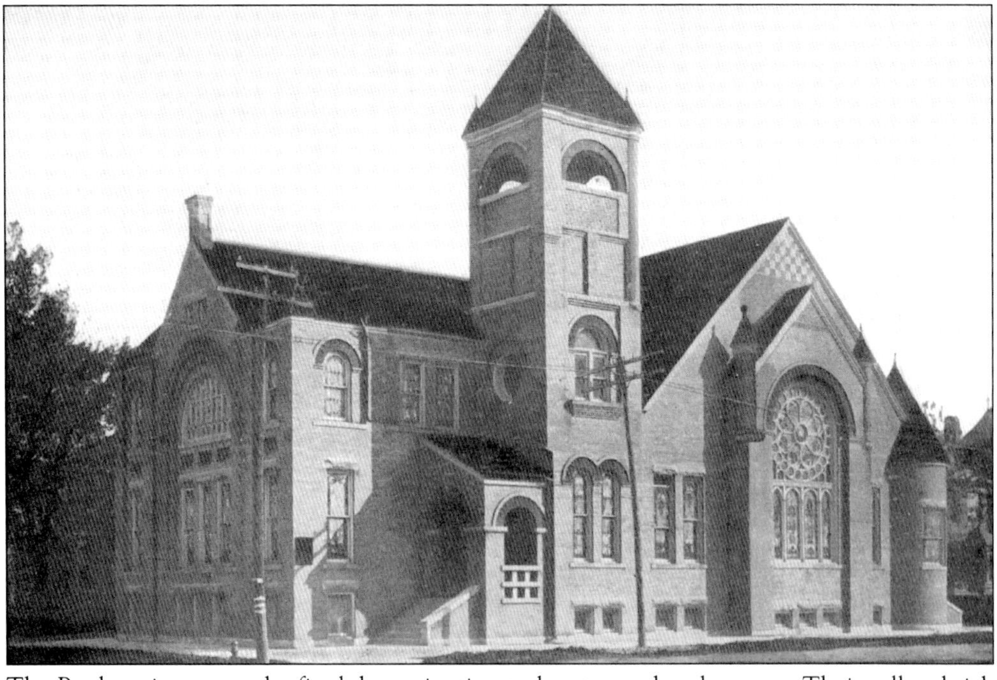

The Presbyterians were the final denomination to locate on church corner. Their yellow brick house of worship sat on the southeast corner of Promenade and Coal Streets. Currently the First Presbyterian Church is found on Lakeview Road.

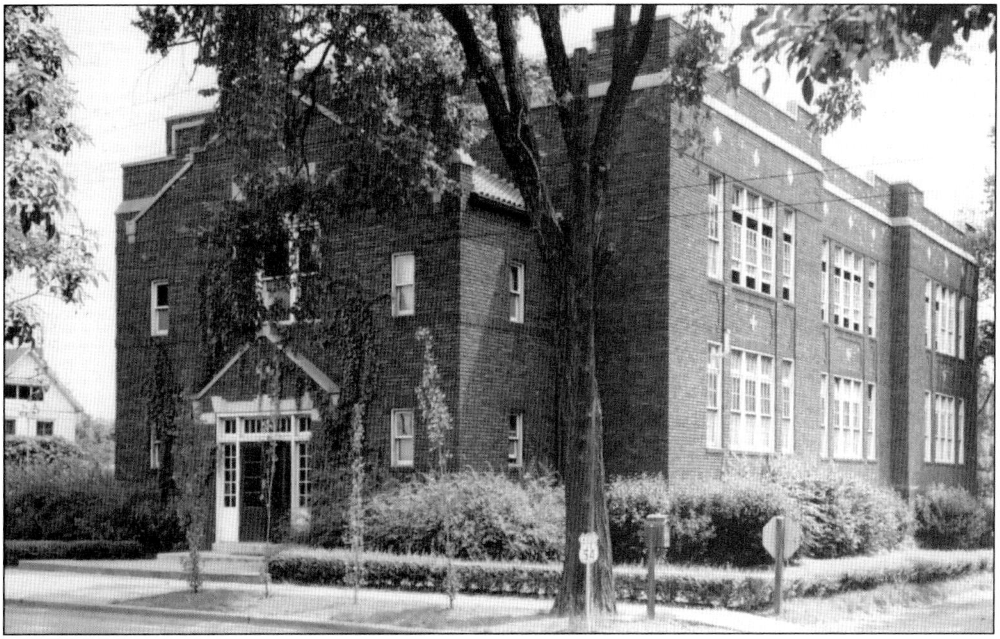

St. Stephen's was the first Catholic parish to locate in Mexico. In 1874, St. Brendan's, at the corner of Breckenridge and Clark Streets, was built. After serving as both school and church for some time, the building today is the home of St. Brendan's School. A newer structure sits slightly behind and beside the school and houses the congregation today.

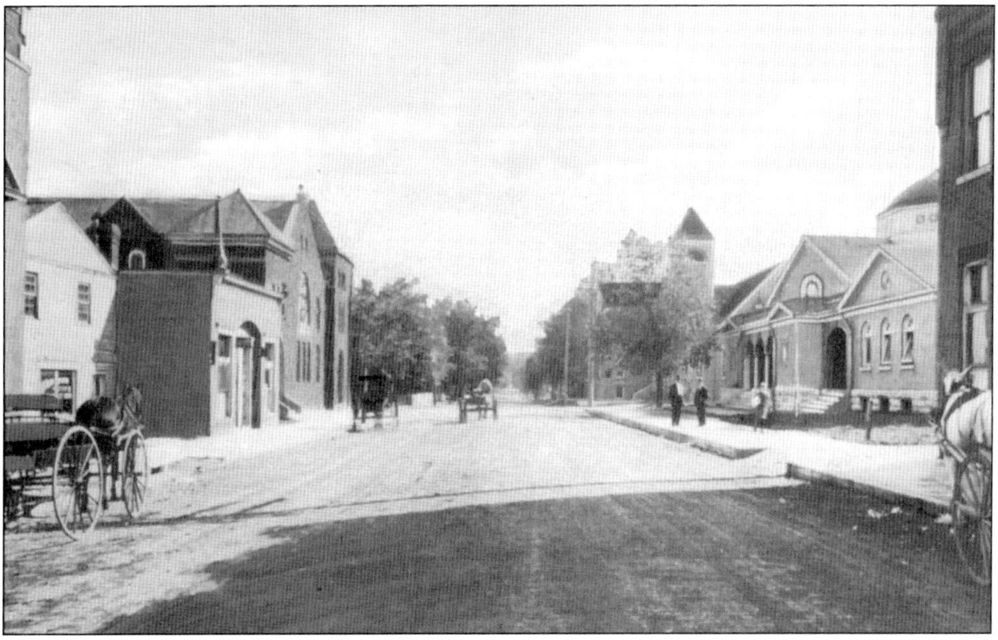

Many religions and congregations meet and worship in Mexico. The Episcopalians built a church in 1870; the Lutherans, by 1884. Three major churches served the early African American community—Methodist Episcopal, African Methodist, and Second Baptist. The intersection of East Promenade and Coal Streets overflowed with worshippers on Sunday mornings in the early 1900s and was known as "Church Corner."

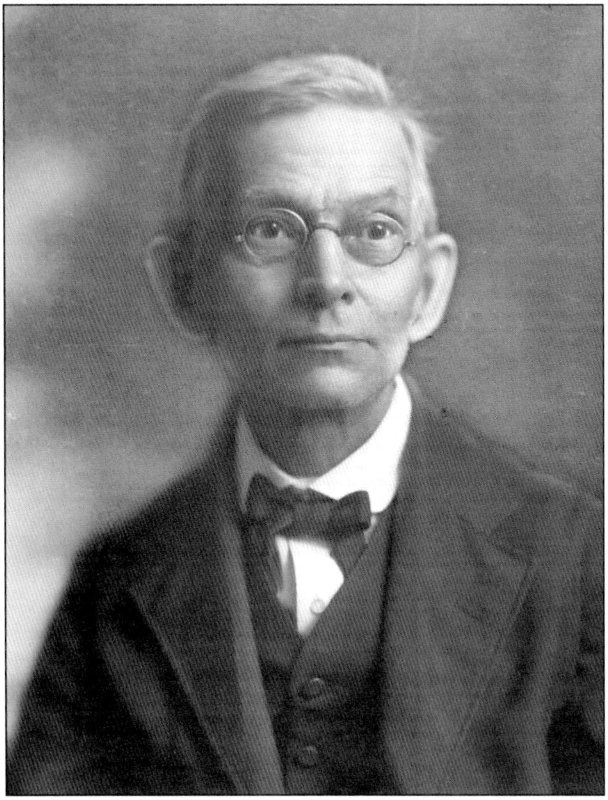

J. F. Llewellyn, druggist, weather recorder, and provider of electric light, also shared another important resource with Mexico's citizens—books. For many years, he provided a lending library on a shelf in the back of the drugstore. He, Mrs. (Sarah Caroline) Llewellyn, and Robert M. White were the catalysts in obtaining a Carnegie Foundation grant of $12,500 to fund a public library.

J. F. Llewellyn donated the land for the library as well as a generous number of books from his own collection. The library opened in 1914 with Esther Houston as the first librarian. Llewellyn served as president of the Mexico Public Library until he died in 1917.

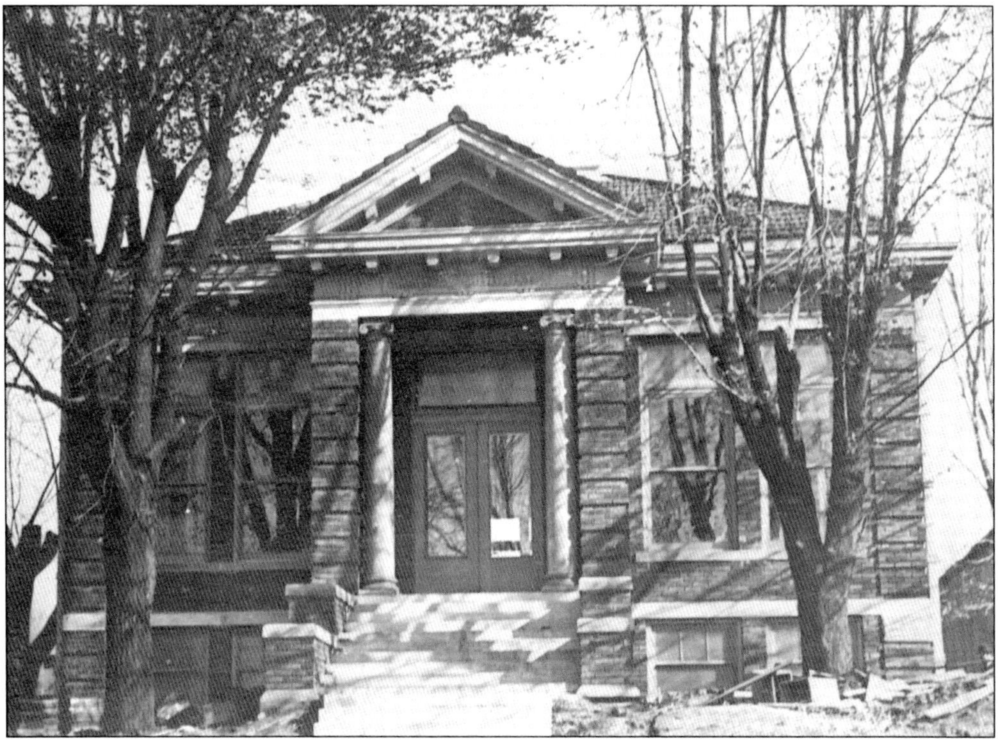

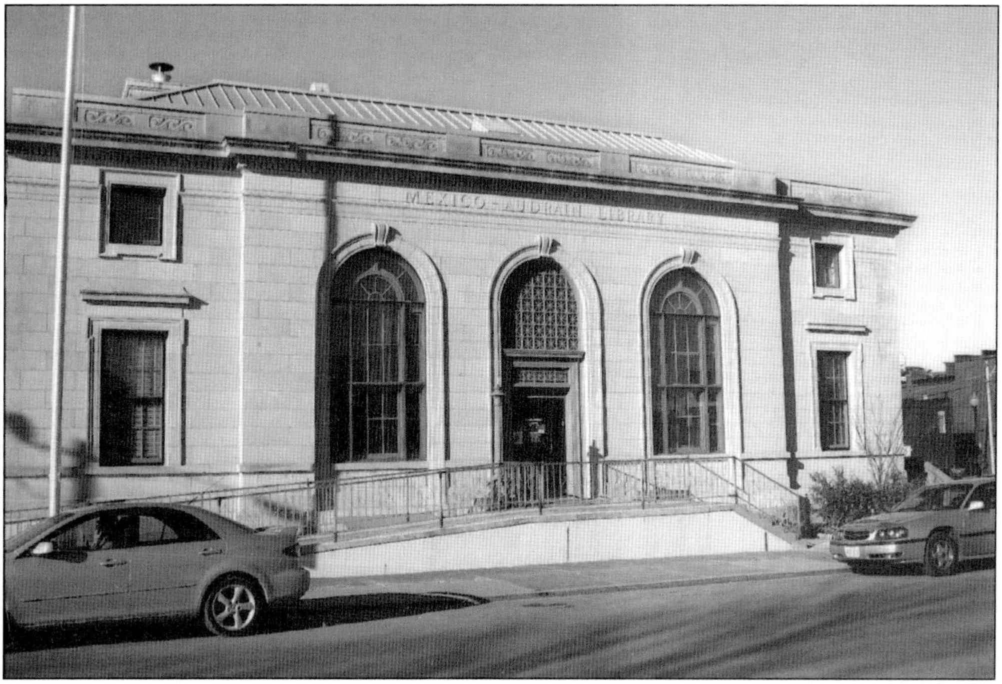

In 1967, the Mexico Public Library merged with the Audrain County Library District. To meet the demand for space, the Mexico Audrain County Library headquarters moved to the recently vacated post office building. (Author's collection.)

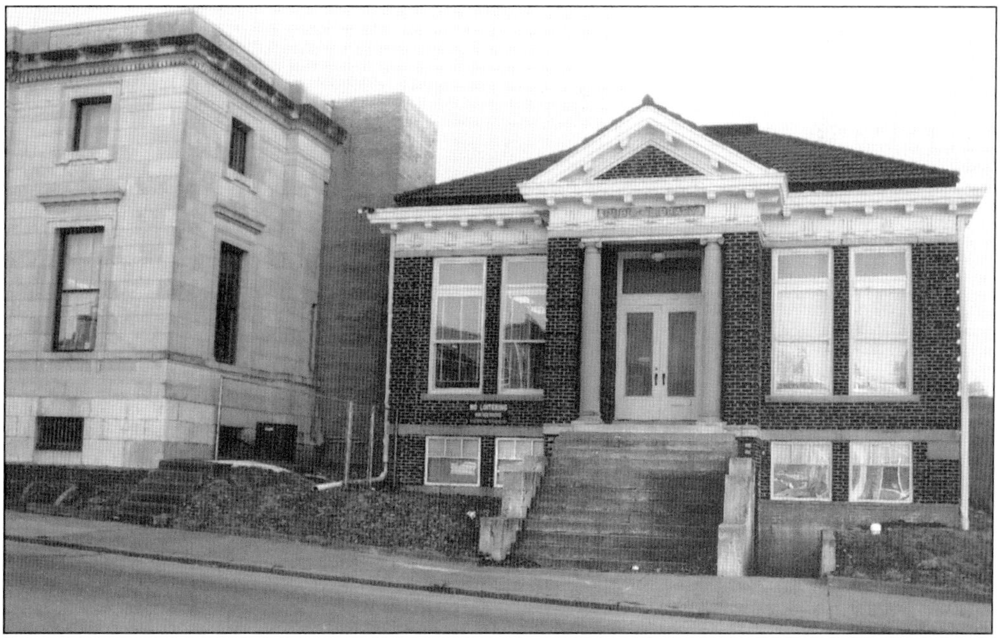

In 1990, the original library building was moved to a spot north of the main building. In addition to the book collection, the library also houses genealogy resources. (Author's collection.)

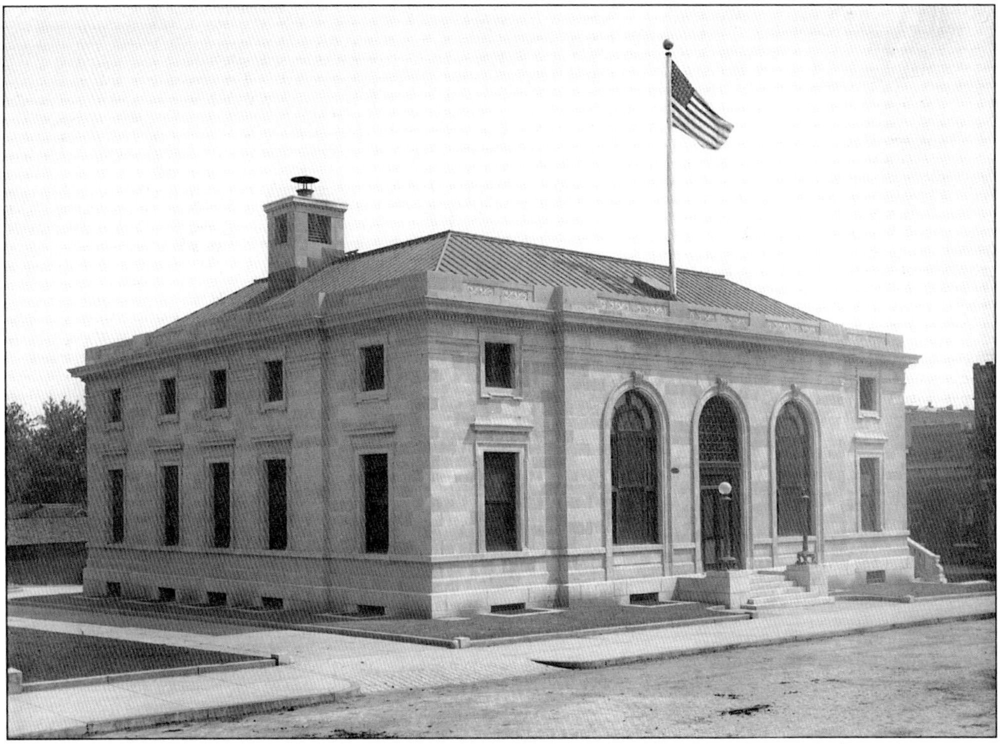

John Bingle Morris was the first postmaster in Mexico, and his post office was his Green Tree Tavern. The building pictured was the first permanent post office and Mexico's first federal building, which was constructed in 1913.

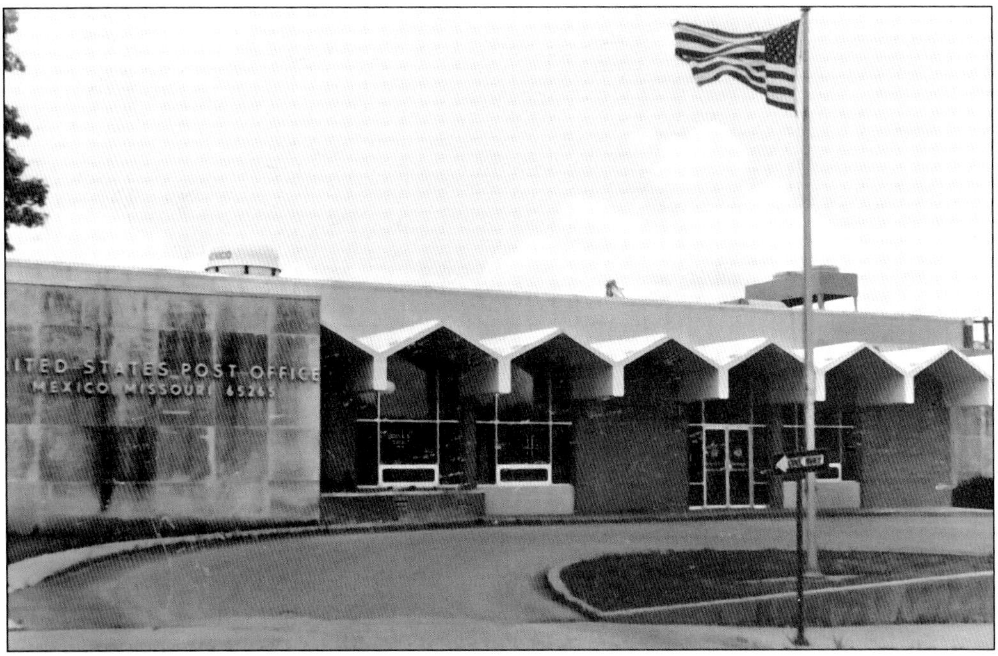

A new, more modern post office building further west on Jackson Street opened in 1967. This photograph dates from around 1983.

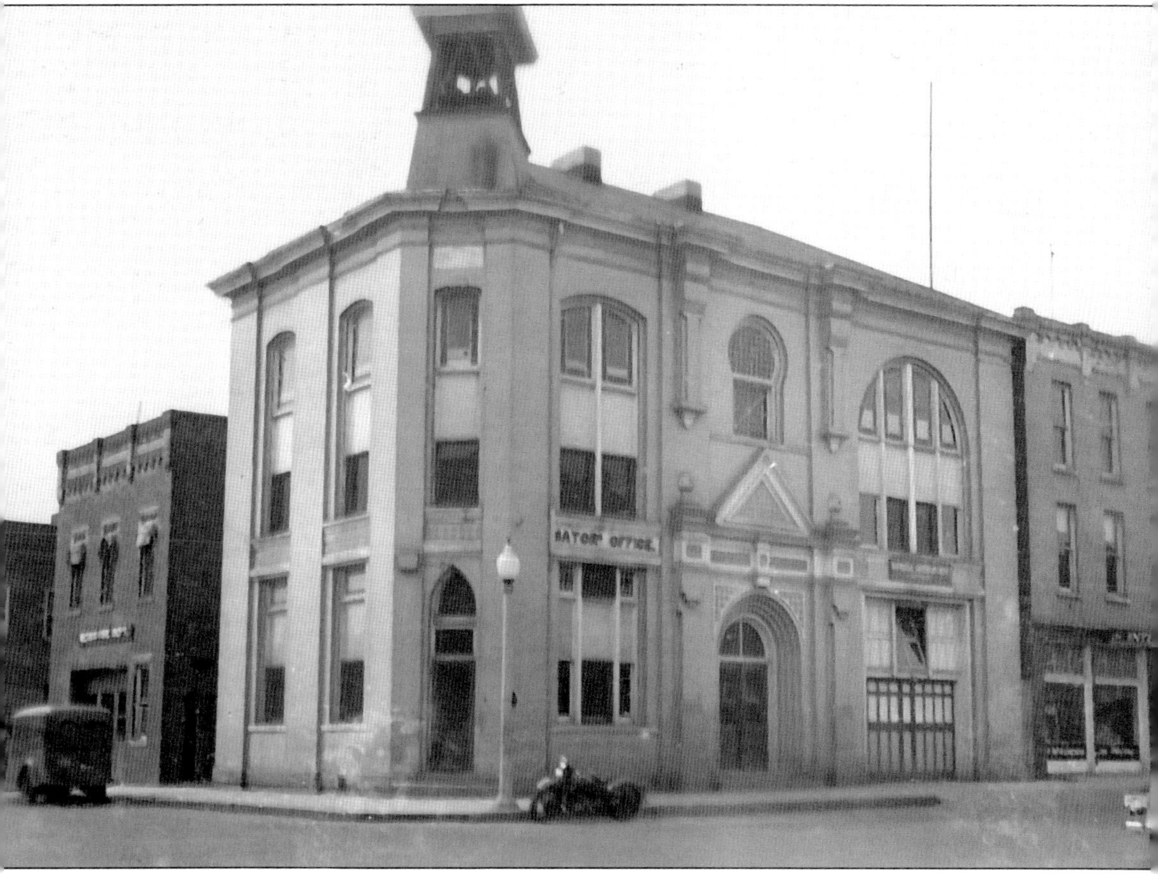

The original Mexico City Hall in this *c.* 1935 photograph was built in 1885 on the former site of the 1838 Methodist church. A fire station was added in 1906. The building was razed in 1975.

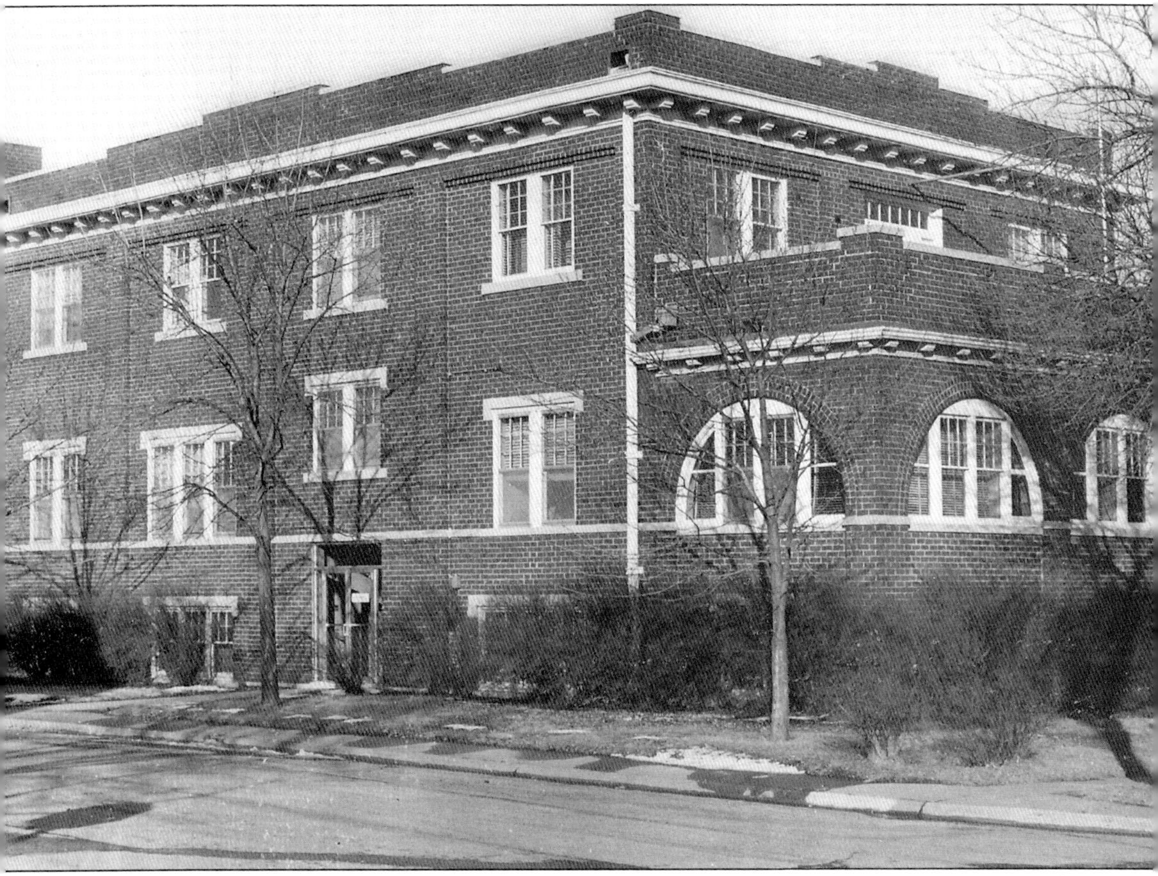

In June 1970, the city government moved to the renovated Kaiser office building (originally the Elk's Lodge). The Mexico Public Safety Department is located in the basement.

Seven

Schools

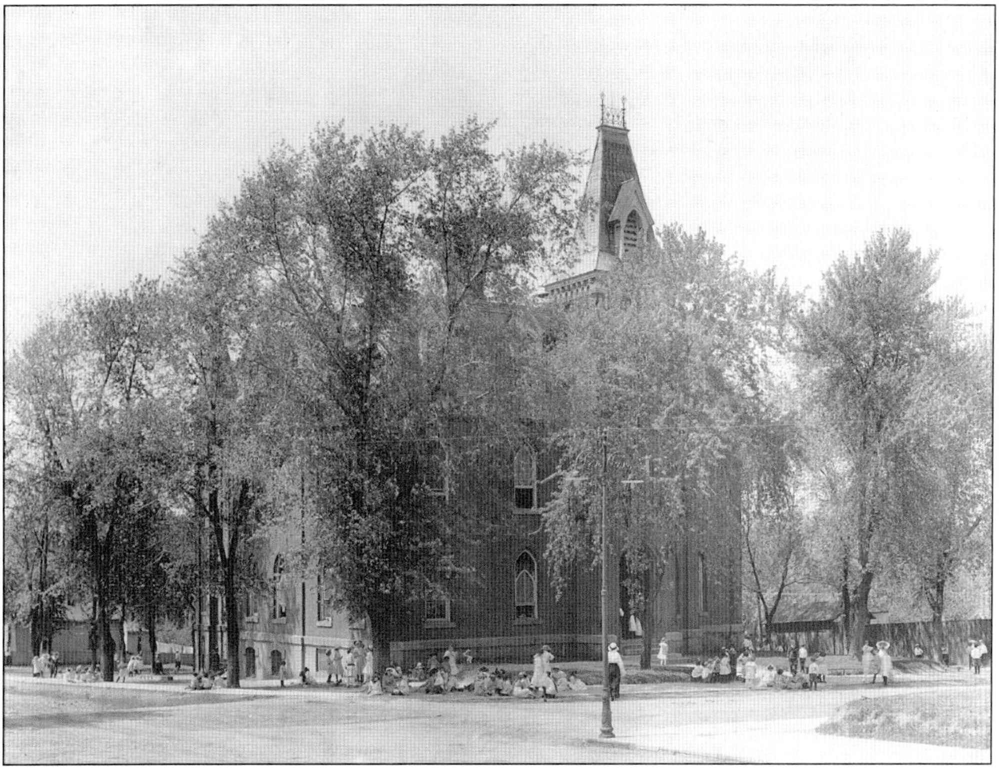

Although private schools existed, Mexico had no public school until after the Civil War. The first school was in the old Christian Seminary on South Jefferson Street. That location was considered too far from town, so lots were purchased two blocks off the square at Olive and West Jackson Streets. The three-story building opened in the fall of 1874 and welcomed about 200 children, grades one through eight. In 1882, the high school was added. The school closed in 1928.

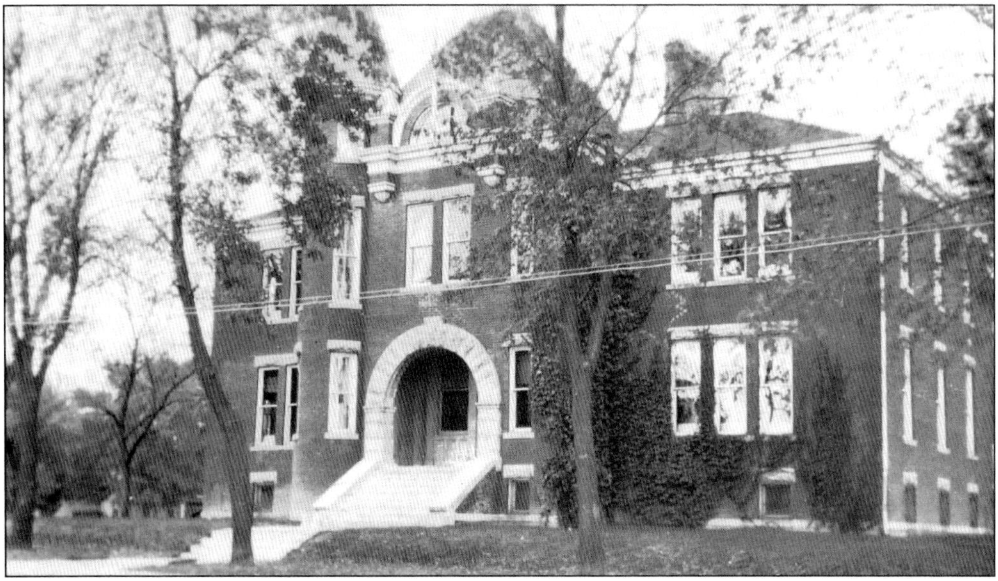

Located on Breckenridge Street, South Side Public School was the second to open in Mexico.

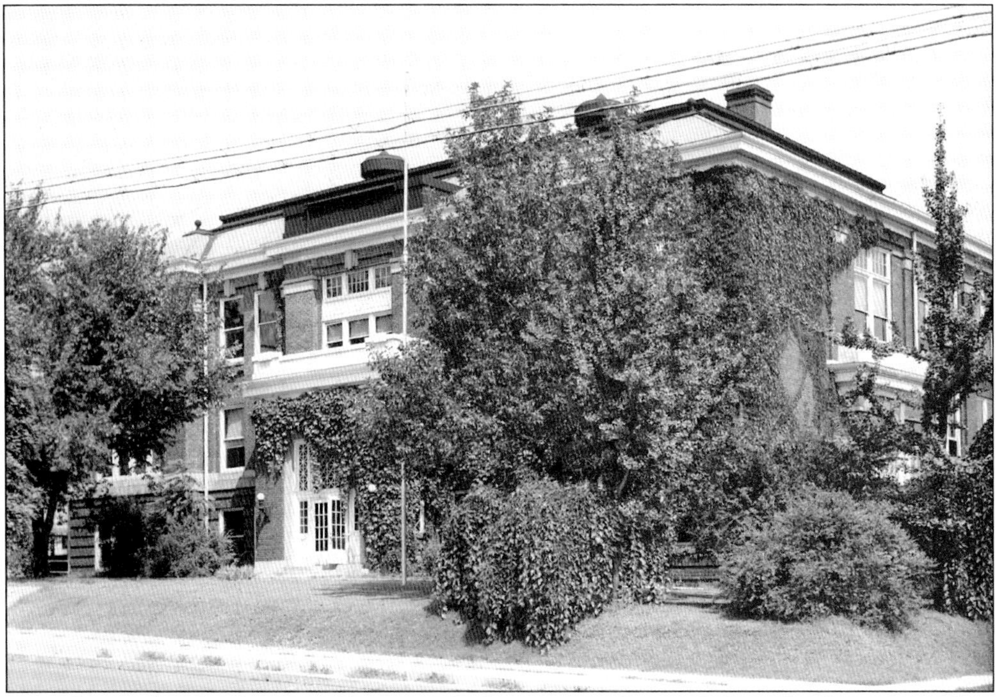

McMillan High School, pictured here, was built in 1908 and named after school superintendent D. A. McMillan. This building housed kindergarten classes in the 1950s and special education and sixth graders in the late 1950s and early 1960s when elementary schools were dealing with overcrowding. Before Mexico Public Schools were integrated in 1954, African American students attended Garfield School, which closed its doors in 1975.

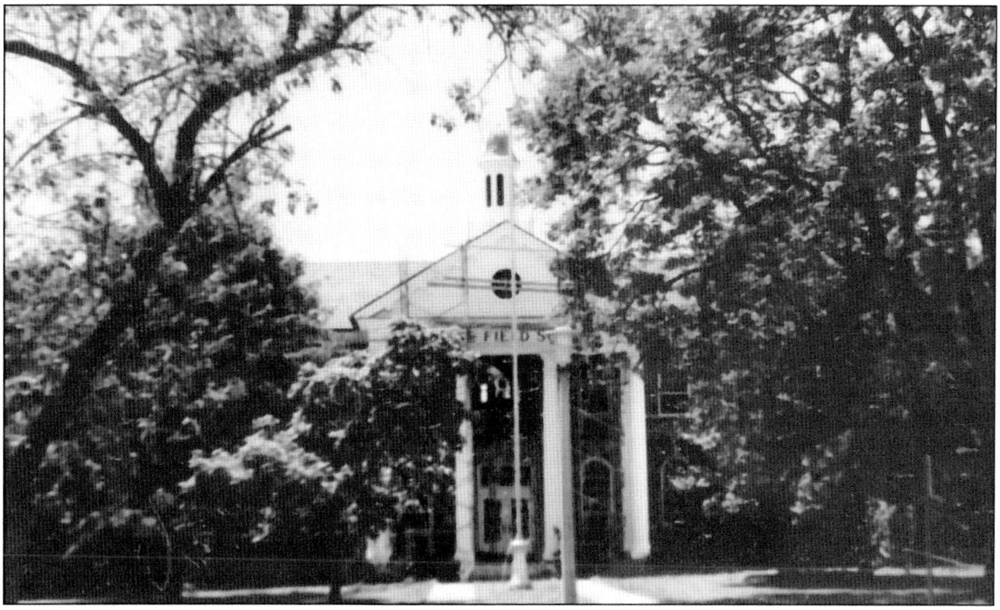

Opened in 1936, the Eugene Field School was named after the Missouri poet, and each grade memorized a Field poem each year. In 1955, ten rooms were added to accommodate newly required kindergartens and the postwar baby boom. A second addition was built in 1966. This is how the school looked in 1983.

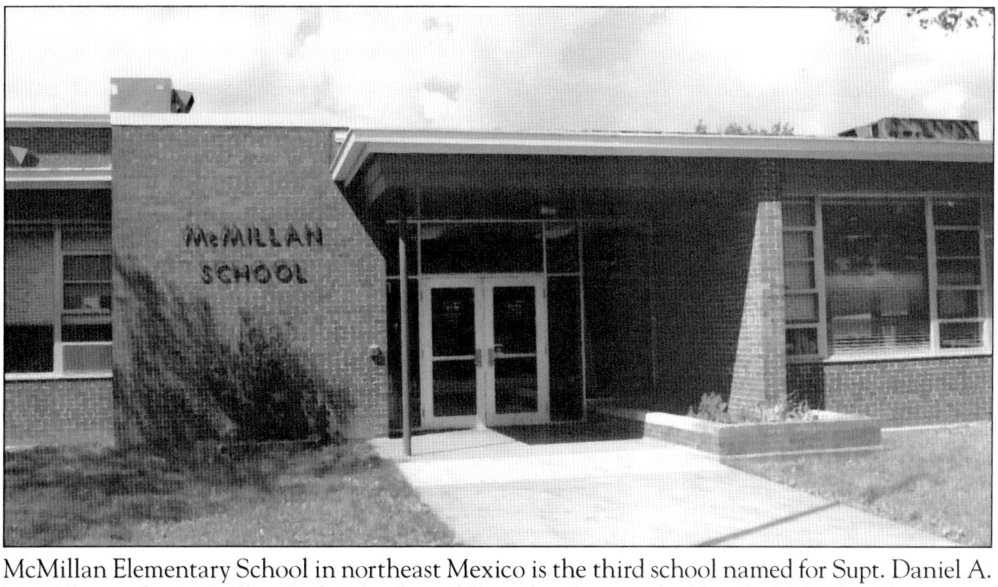

McMillan Elementary School in northeast Mexico is the third school named for Supt. Daniel A. McMillan—after McMillan High School was followed in the same building by McMillan Elementary. Space constraints led to the construction of the latest school carrying McMillan's name in 1955. This 1983 image includes two classrooms that were added in 1965. (Author's collection.)

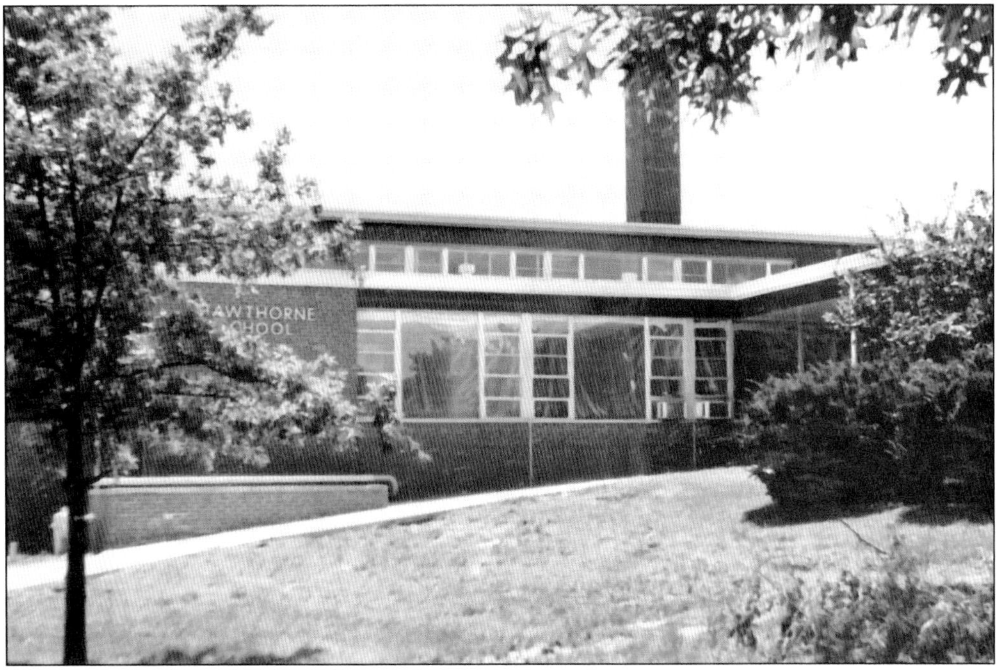

Hawthorne Elementary School, named after Supt. L. B. Hawthorne, opened in 1955 with 11 classrooms for students in northwest Mexico. In 1966, eleven classrooms were added to make room for additional students in the attendance area and pupils entering the district from rural school closings. The school is seen here around 1983.

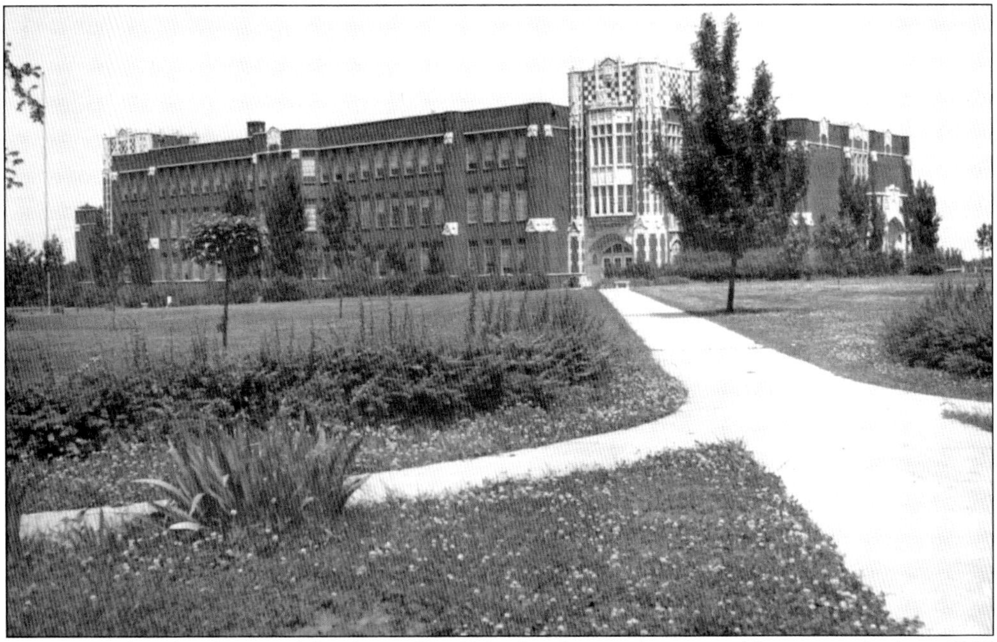

Mexico High School opened for the 1927–1928 school year. A major addition was built in 1962 and included classrooms, a cafeteria, a bigger gym, and a new shop department. The space meant ninth graders no longer had to attend the junior high school on the former Hardin College campus. This image shows the original school building.

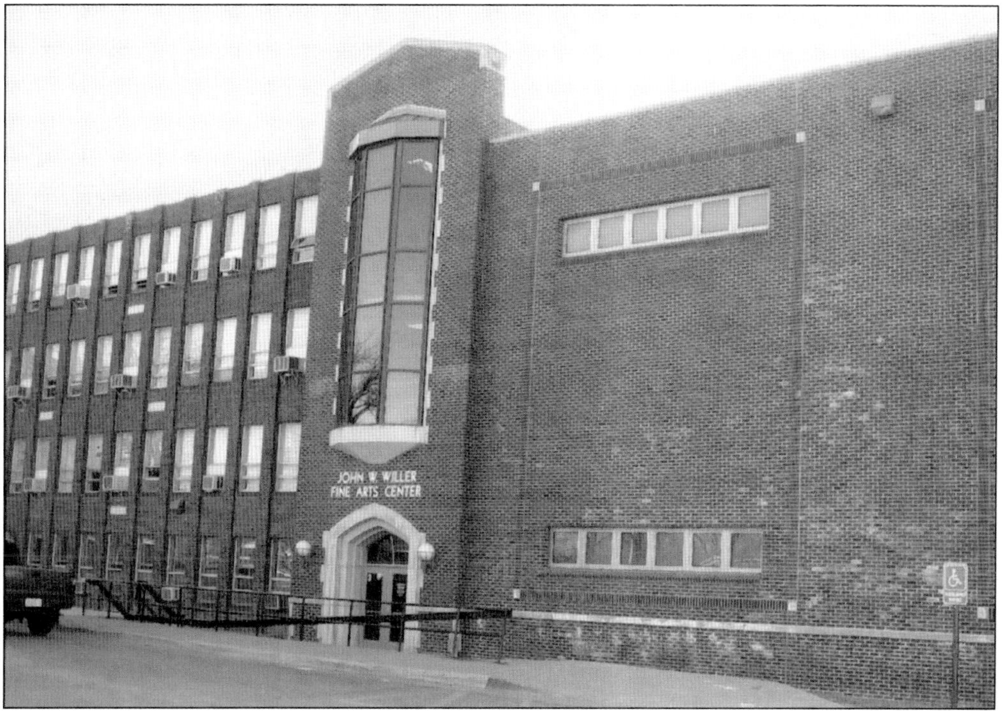

The John W. Willer Fine Arts Center is the second and most recent major addition to the high school. It is named after the longtime and beloved band director. (Author's collection.)

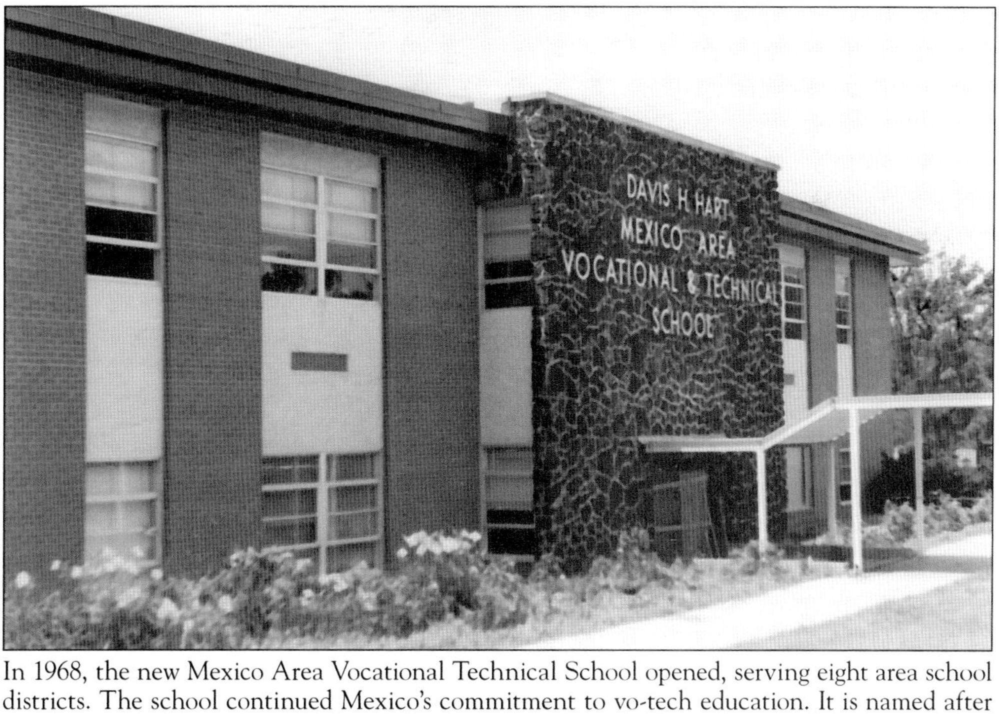

In 1968, the new Mexico Area Vocational Technical School opened, serving eight area school districts. The school continued Mexico's commitment to vo-tech education. It is named after Davis H. Hart, an early school administrator and the school's first director. This picture was taken in 1983.

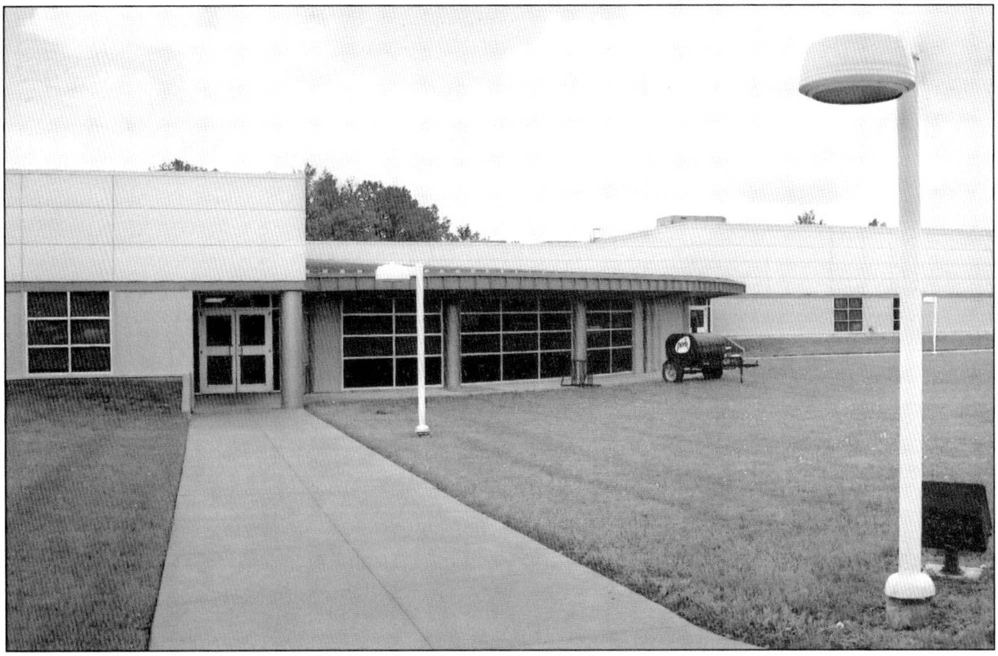

The Advanced Technology Center (ATC) is the newest entry into educational institutions in Mexico. Offering five degree programs, the ATC is a cooperative effort between the city, Linn State Technical College, Moberly Area Community College, and the University of Missouri Extension.

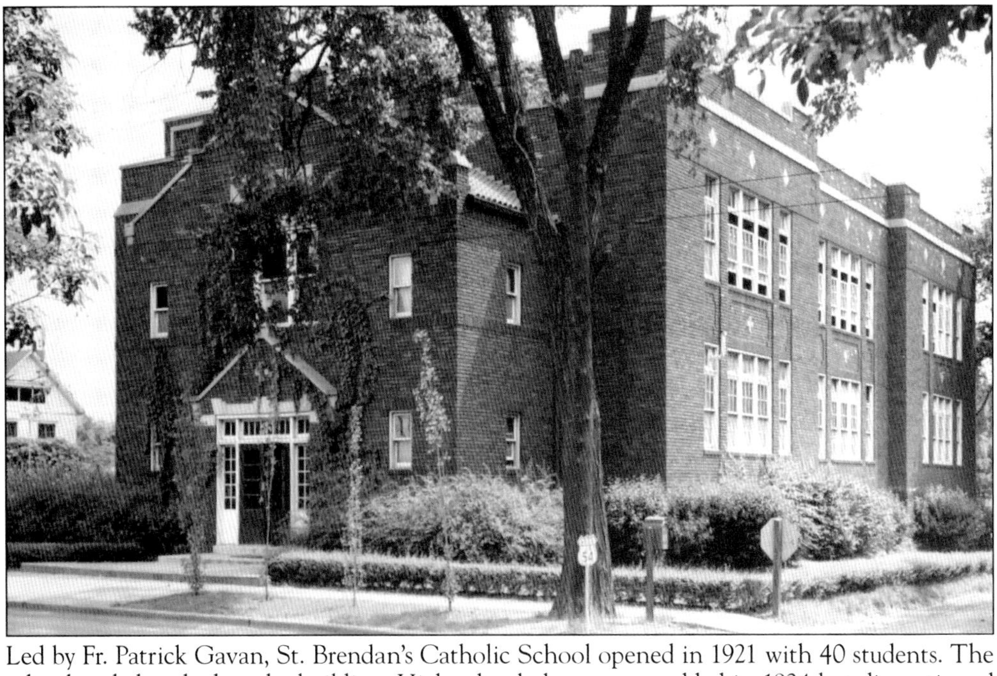

Led by Fr. Patrick Gavan, St. Brendan's Catholic School opened in 1921 with 40 students. The school and church shared a building. High school classes were added in 1924 but discontinued in 1959. Originally Sisters of the Most Precious Blood served as teachers, but today the school has a non-ecclesiastical staff.

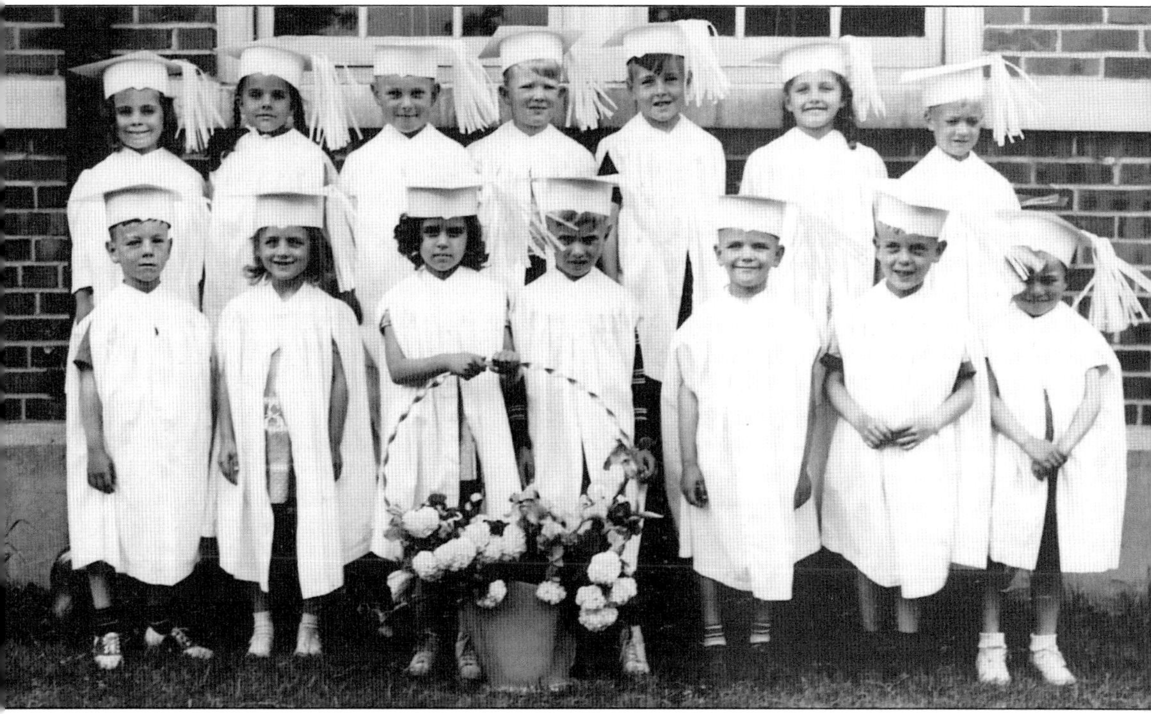

Mrs. Gilman's Kindergarten is a not-to-be-overlooked chapter in the education of young Mexicoans. Nora Gilman opened her school in 1936, meeting at McMillan School, and then Eugene Field Elementary School, before moving it to her home. The children gave programs throughout the year and graduated in cap and gown in the spring. Here is the class of 1940. After kindergarten was added in the public school, Mrs. Gilman ran a nursery school until 1972.

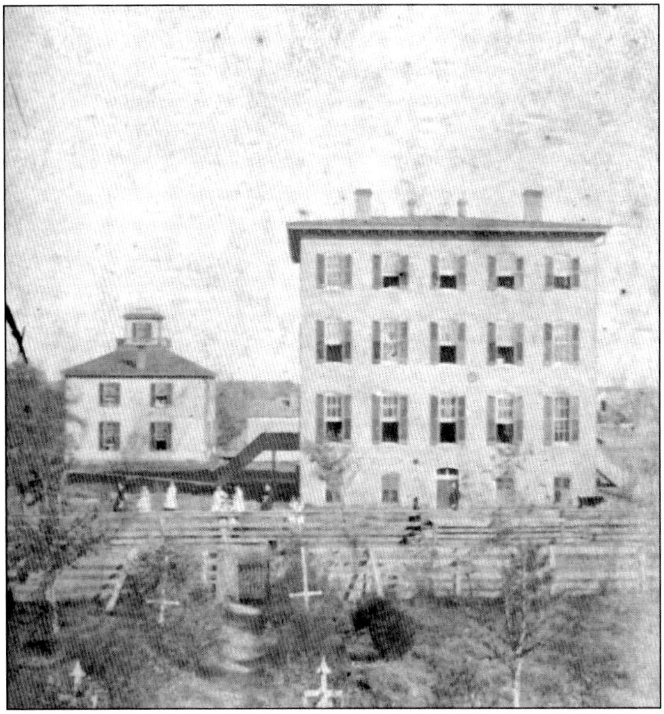

In 1873, Charles H. Hardin purchased 5 acres on South Jefferson for $3,500, including buildings from the Audrain County Female Seminary. His purpose was to establish an institution for the education of females in Mexico at what was to be known as Hardin College.

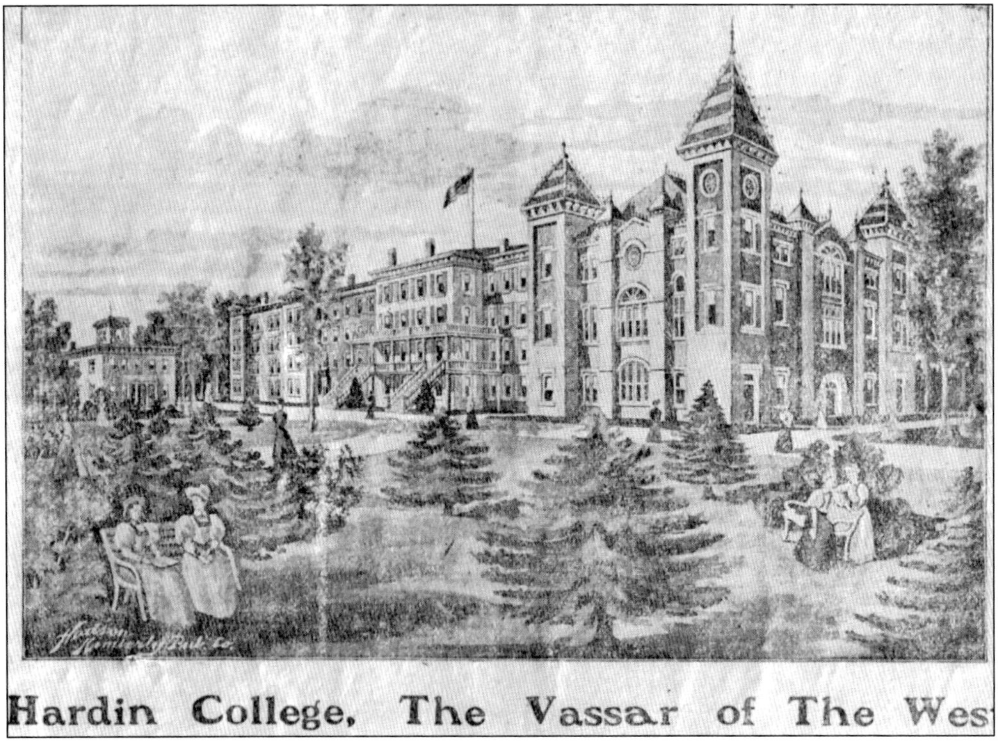

The first year, 90 girls enrolled—17 in the prep school (later discontinued) and 73 in the college; fees were $15 and $20, respectively, and room and board was $80. Because of its strong programs, Hardin attracted students from other states and advertised itself as "The Vassar of the West."

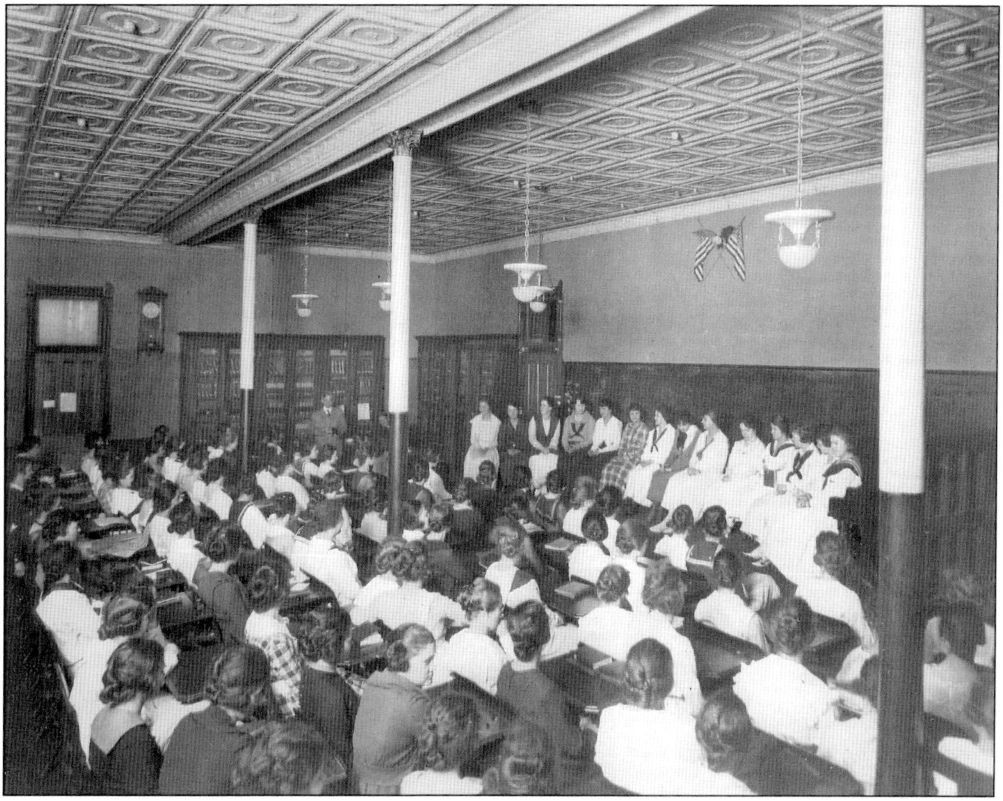

The college was associated with the Baptist church, and several Baptist ministers served as Hardin's president. The school believed in a course of both mental and moral training. These women are attending chapel as required.

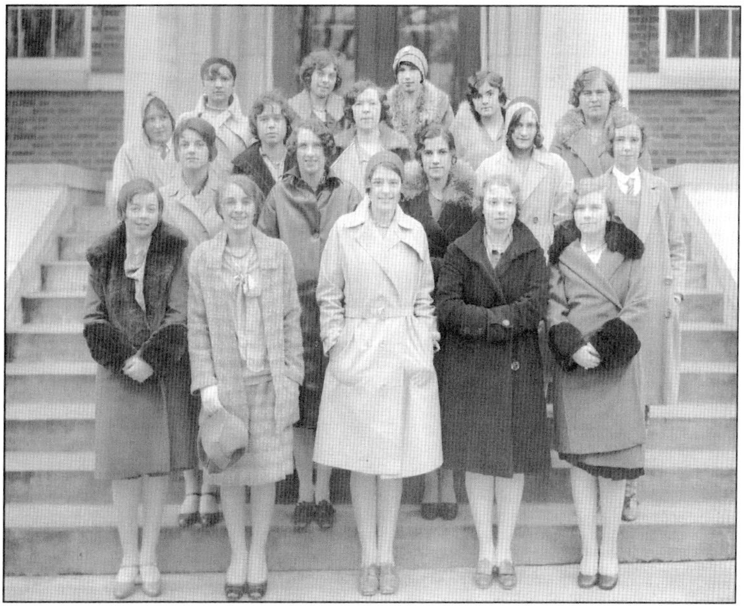

In the early days, uniforms were required, although this rule was later relaxed to allow the girls to wear "what best becomes them," as in this 1930s photograph of unidentified students.

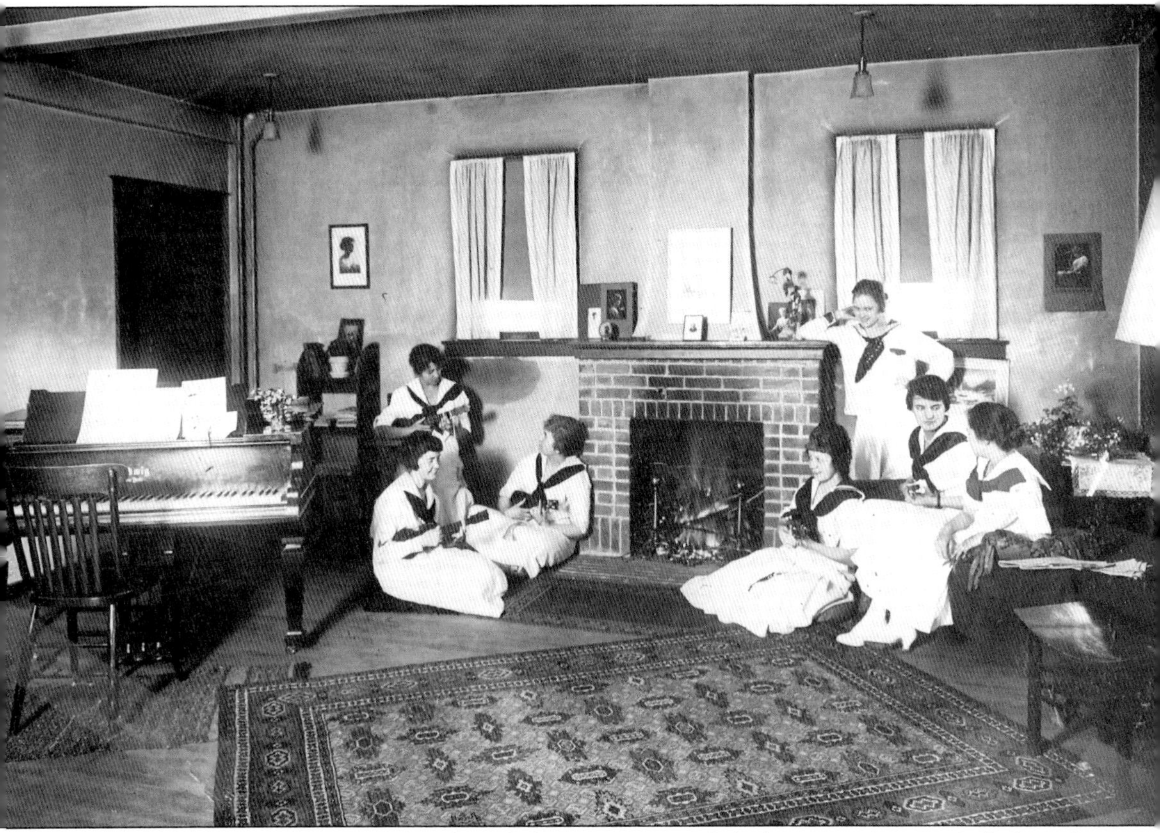

Students rose at 5:30 a.m. and study ended at 9:00 p.m. with bedtime at 9:30 p.m. Still the girls found time for fun and relaxation, as shown here in one of the college parlors in the 1920s. Music was seemingly even a part of off-school hours.

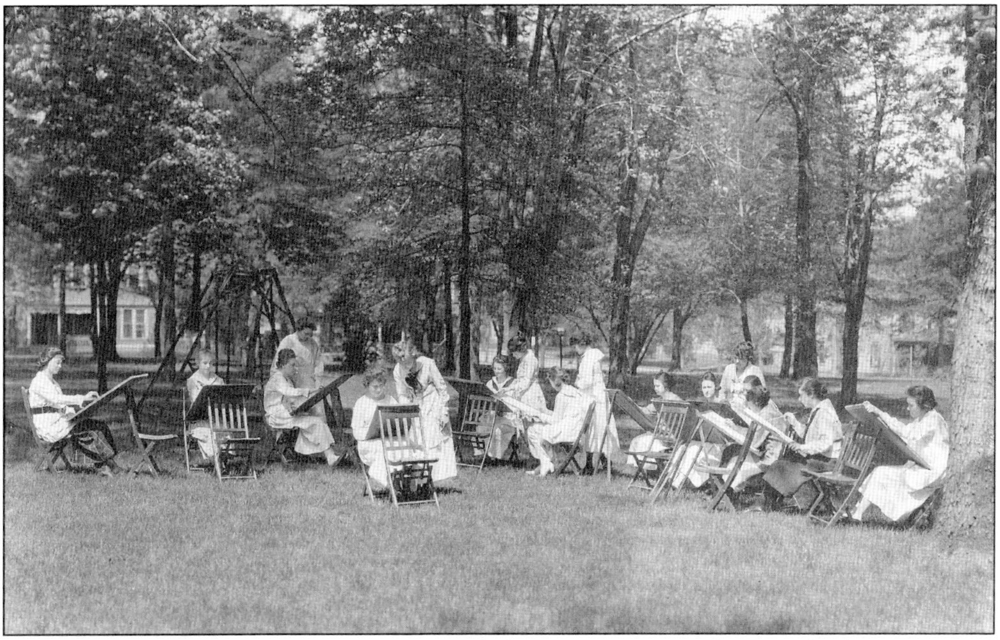

The first degrees at Hardin College were awarded in 1876. In 1901, it became the first recognized junior college in Missouri, which meant credits earned at Hardin transferred to universities all over the country. In 1913, Hardin students began receiving associate's degrees. Classes ranged from art to science. This photograph is of an art class in 1921.

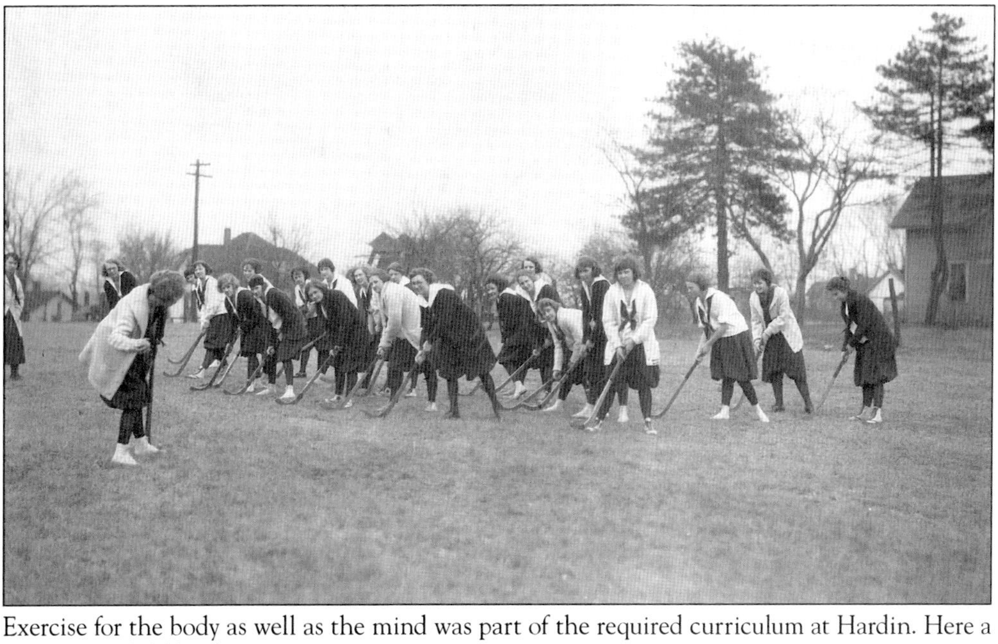

Exercise for the body as well as the mind was part of the required curriculum at Hardin. Here a group plays field hockey in 1922.

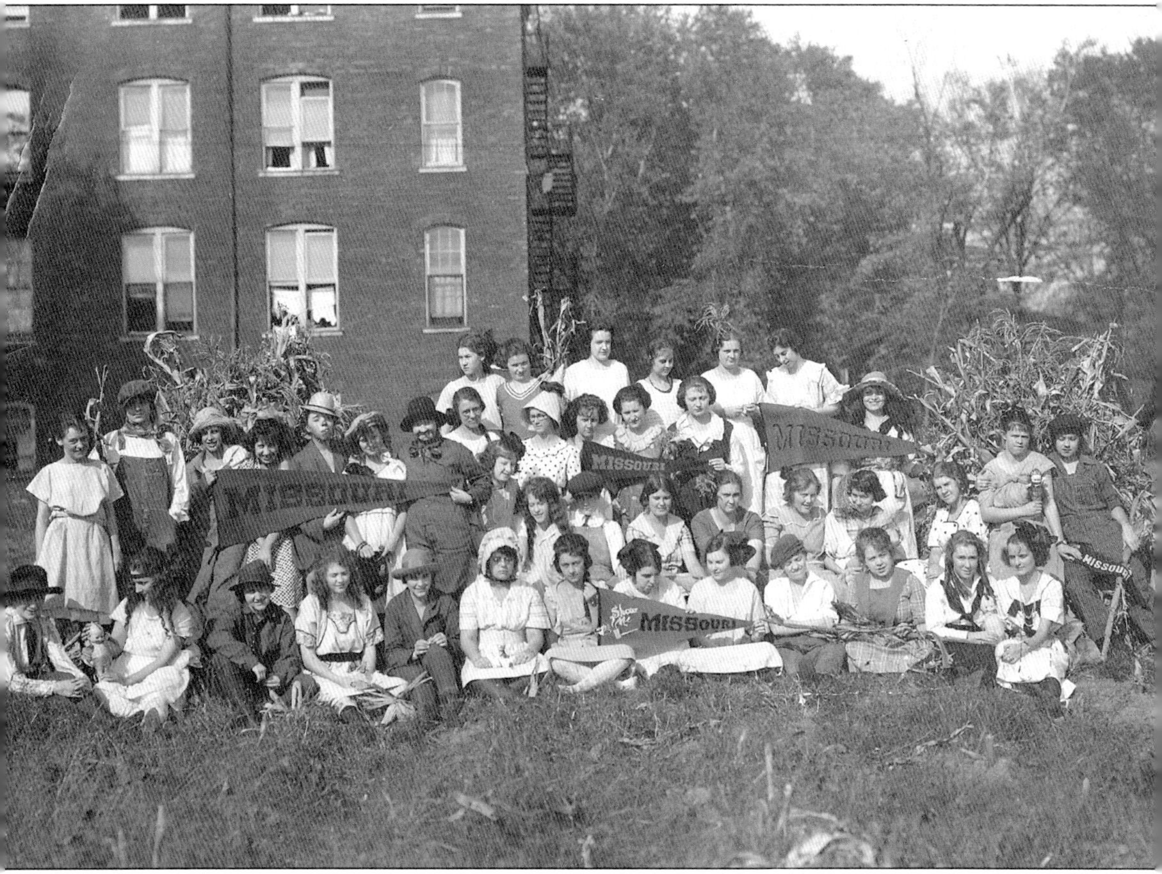

Plays, picnics, and clubs were also part of the Hardin College experience. Once the school attracted students from surrounding states, clubs celebrating home-state identities developed. This is the *c.* 1921 Missouri Club. Students from states such as Oklahoma and Nebraska also formed clubs.

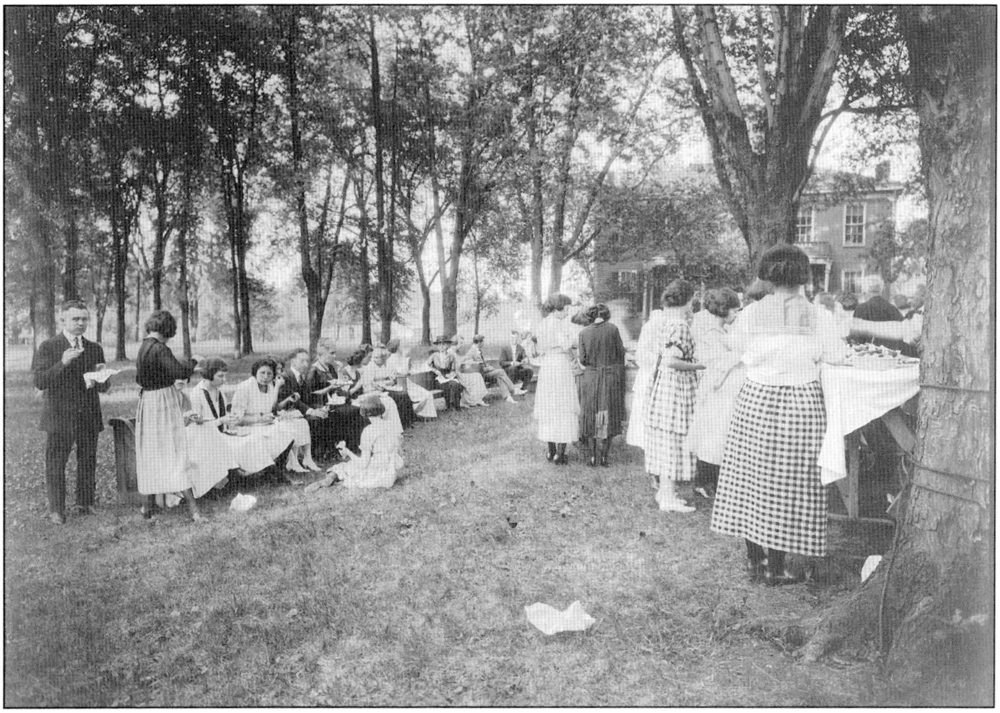

For 50 years, women attended Hardin College. Many sent their own daughters and granddaughters, and graduates sometimes returned to reminisce and reacquaint themselves with the campus and old friends. This *c.* 1921 photograph shows a Hardin College picnic.

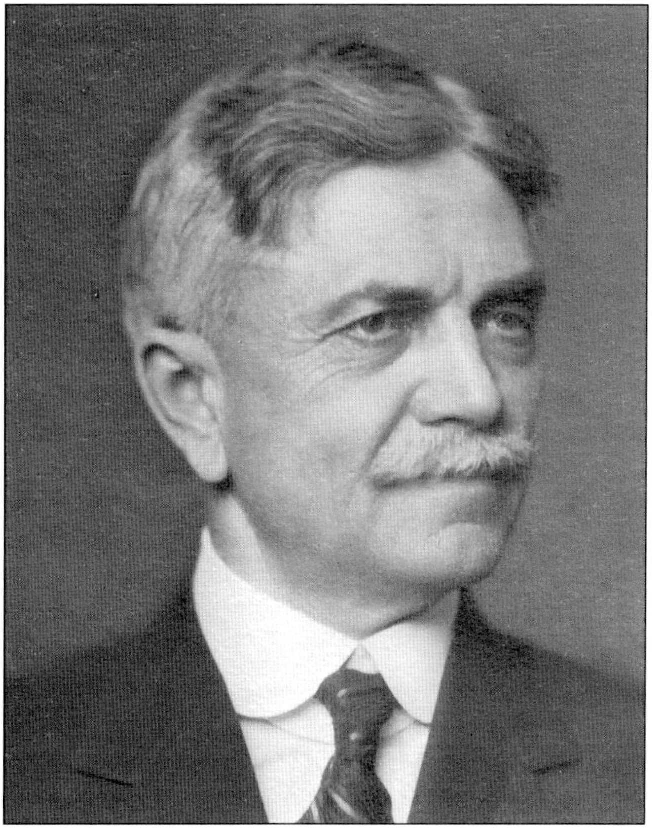

Dr. John W. Million served on the faculty and as president of the college for 26 years. He left in 1921, and the college had a series of short-term presidents until it closed in 1931.

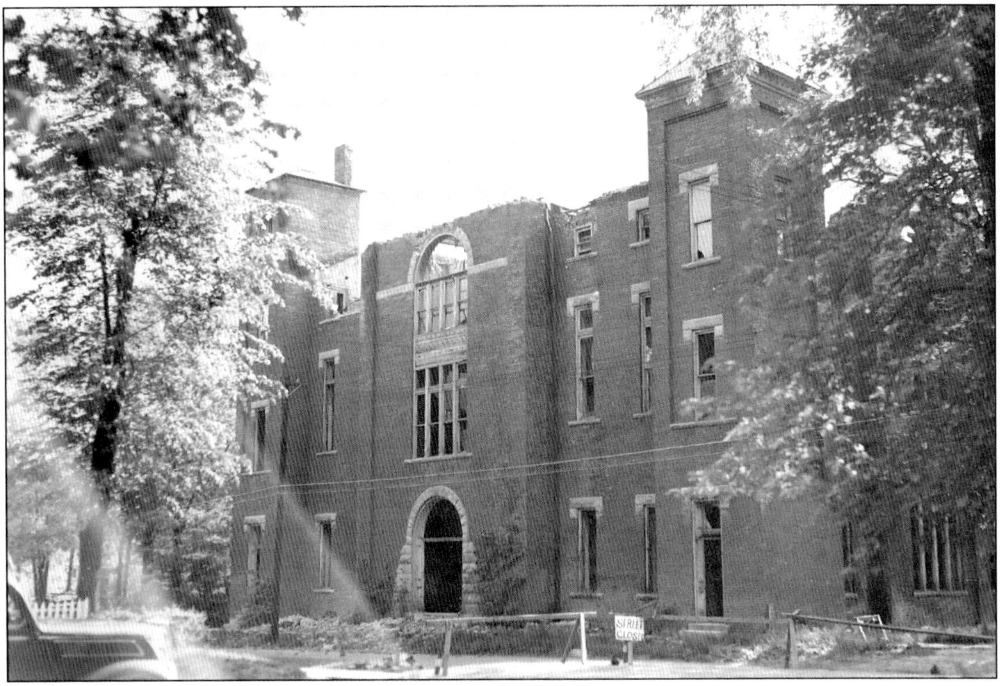

Charles H. Hardin contributed almost $40,000 in land, cash, and notes to fund the launch of Hardin College. Another $7,000 was raised at a courthouse meeting. Hardin served as president of the board from its founding until his death and created an endowment intended to keep the college running in perpetuity. Financial mismanagement and the Depression, however, led to the closing of the school in 1931. Hardin Hall was razed in 1939.

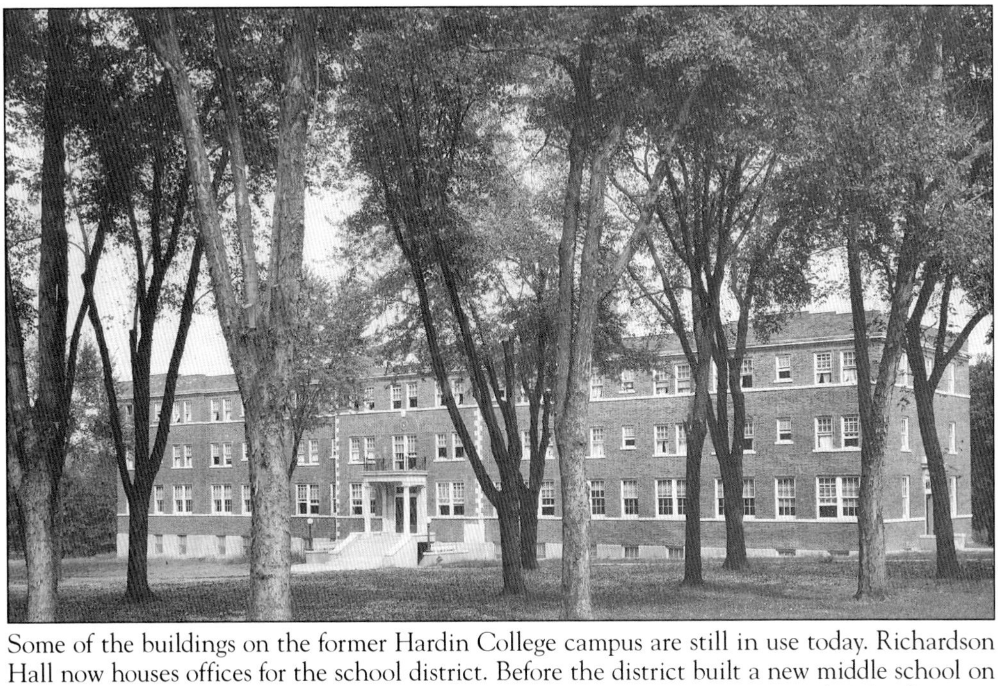

Some of the buildings on the former Hardin College campus are still in use today. Richardson Hall now houses offices for the school district. Before the district built a new middle school on the former fairgrounds, the former college campus served as Hardin Junior High School.

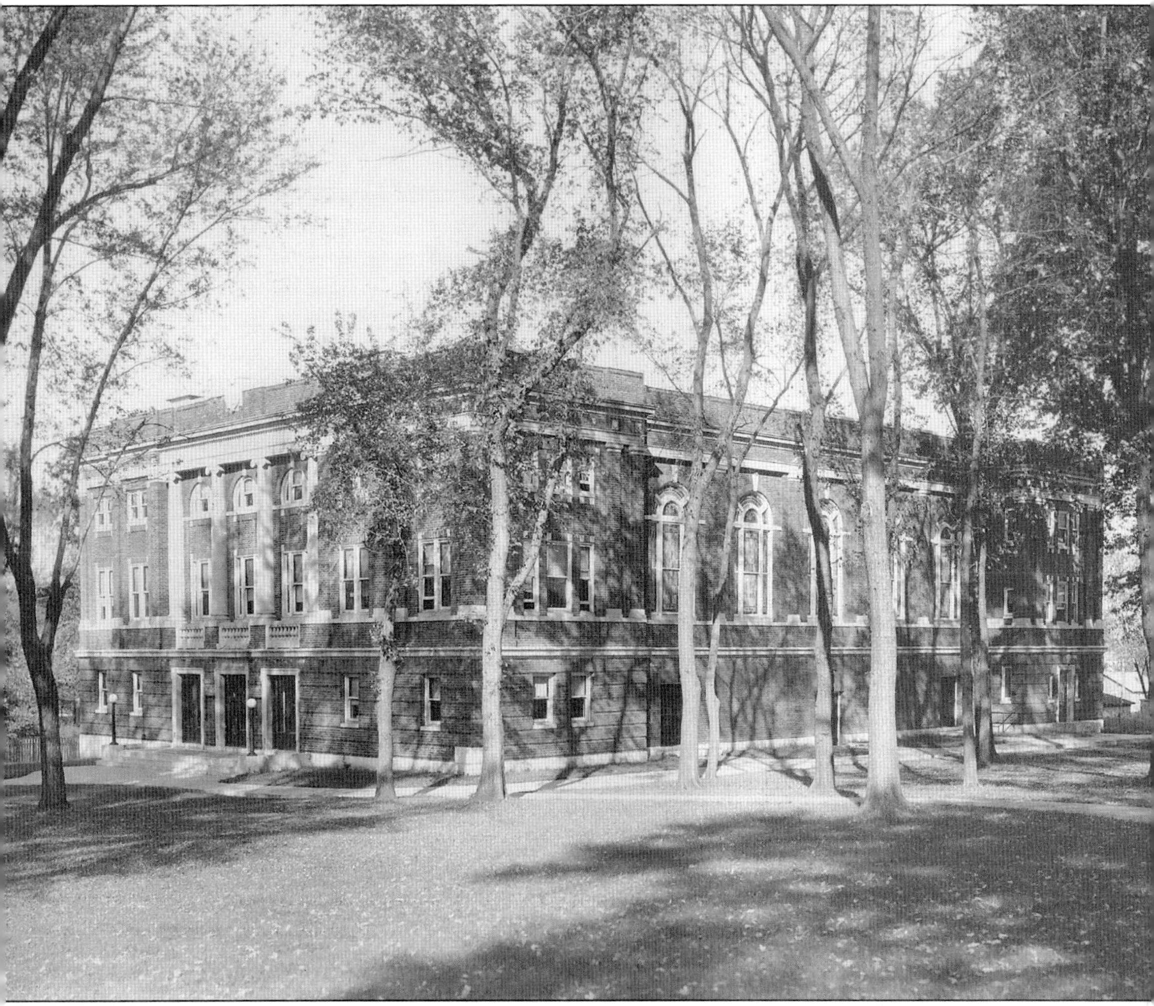

Presser Hall was the last building to be added to the Hardin College campus and served as a recital hall. The city and school district continued to make use of the building for performances. The auditorium was refurbished in the 1990s and hosts concerts, plays, and other educational, school, and cultural events.

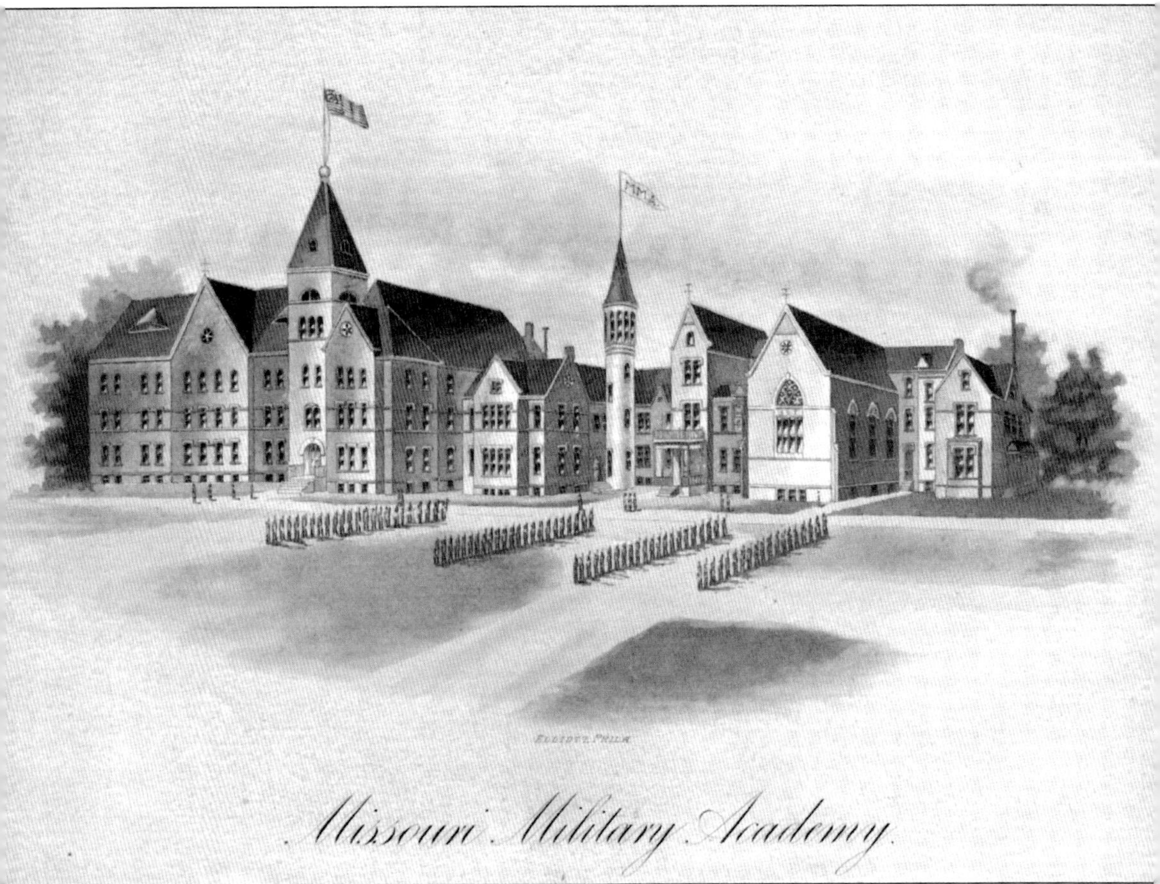

Missouri Military Academy (MMA) was founded in 1889 under the leadership of Col. A. F. Fleet and with the support of Gov. Charles H. Hardin. The academy was built on 20 acres on West Boulevard and opened on September 16, 1890, with an enrollment of 60 cadets. A September 24, 1896, fire that burned the campus nearly ended the dream of a private school for young men.

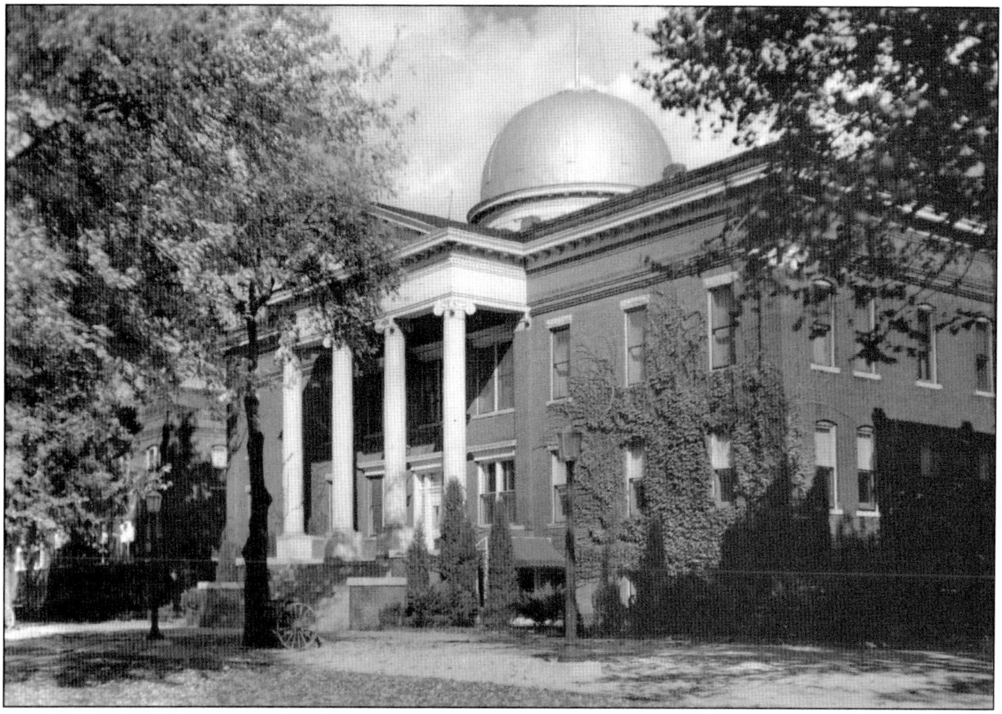

Mexicoans were convinced that a school like Missouri Military Academy could only benefit the city, and it reopened on September 20, 1900, at a new location on the eastern end of town. Col. W. D. Fonville headed the school, which grew in stature and reputation during his tenure. The resurrected Missouri Military Academy sported a more classic design, as seen in this 1930s image of the Administration Building.

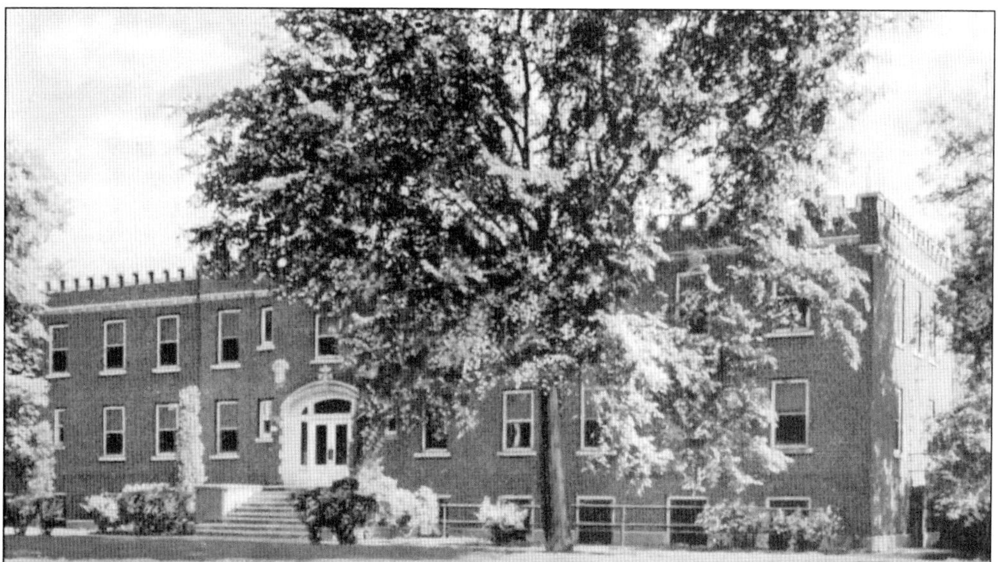

Under the leadership of Col. E. Y. Burton (1915–1933), the U.S. War Department named MMA an Honor Military school, one of 10 in the country. The school was known by this time for its integrity and high academic achievement. This 1930s photograph shows one of the barracks.

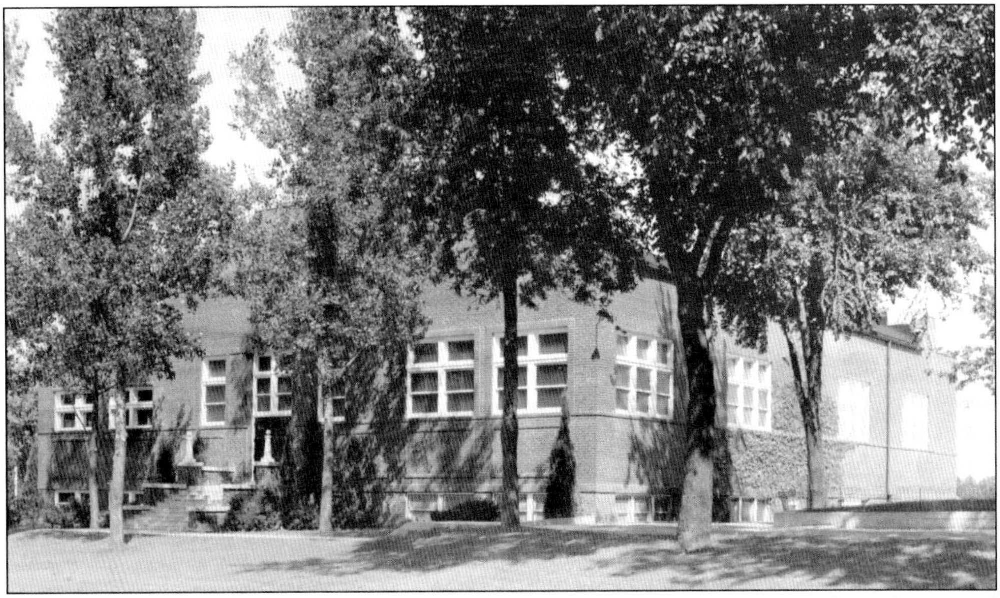

Taught to "Look like a soldier. Act like a gentleman," MMA cadets have come from the United States and from abroad. The curriculum aims to develop young men academically, morally, and physically. The academy's gym is pictured here in the 1930s.

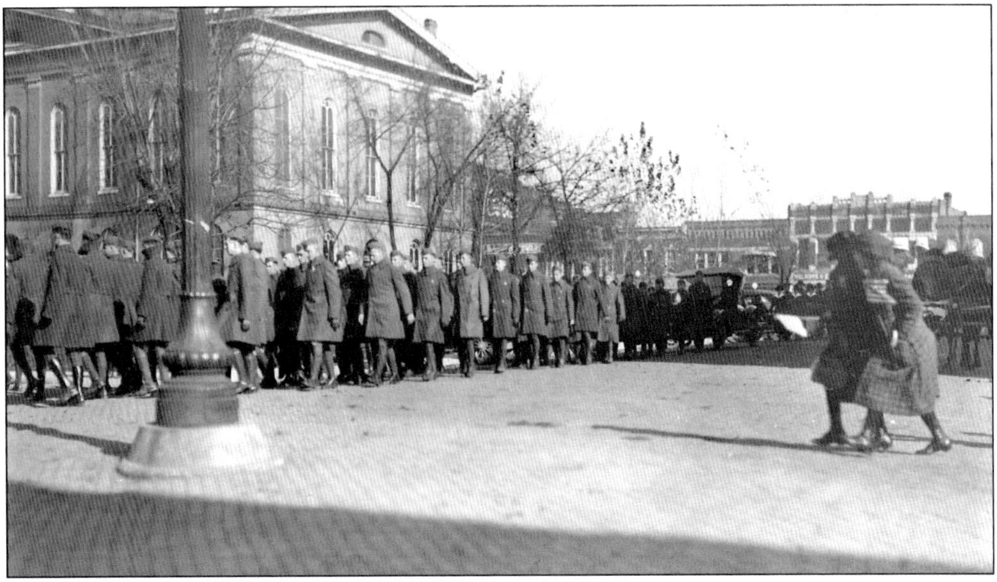

Often seen marching in formation downtown, cadets are part of the life and local color in Mexico. This image of an MMA parade dates from around 1920.

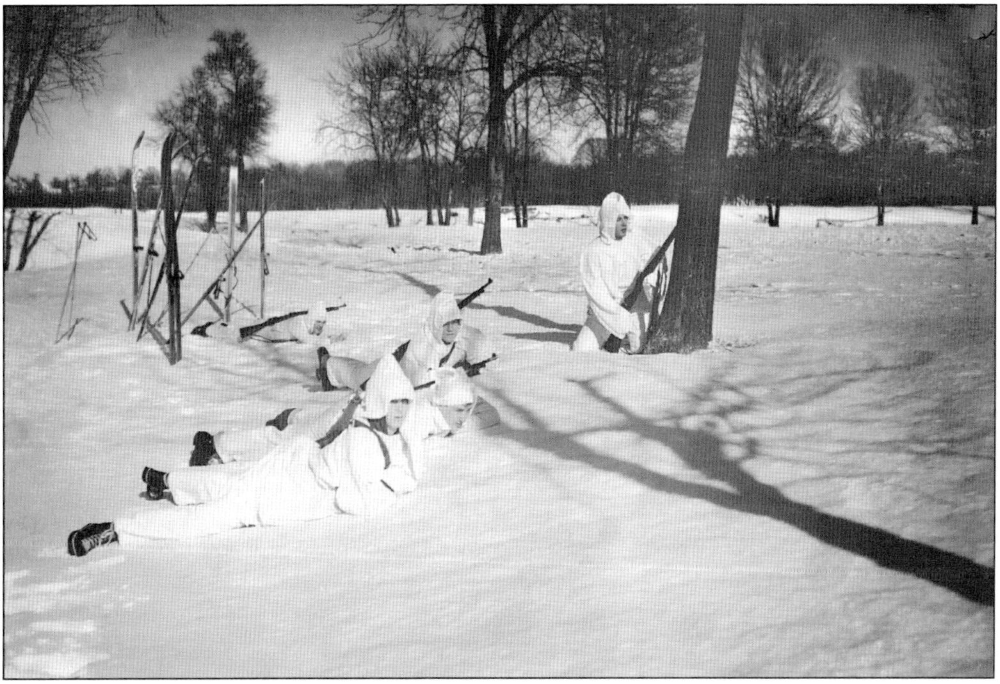

Studies include military exercises. In recent years, MMA has been cited as the top Junior ROTC unit in the Midwest. Cadets are shown here during winter exercises in 1940.

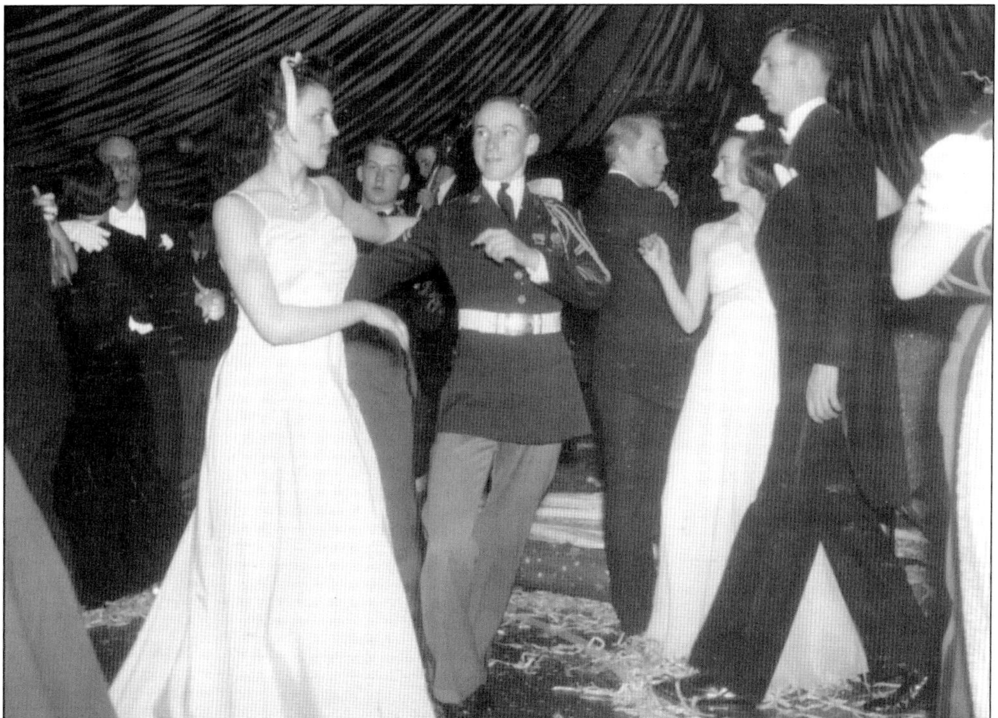

Even with the emphasis on academics, cadets also take part in social activities on campus. This couple dances away the evening at a Valentine Ball in 1940.

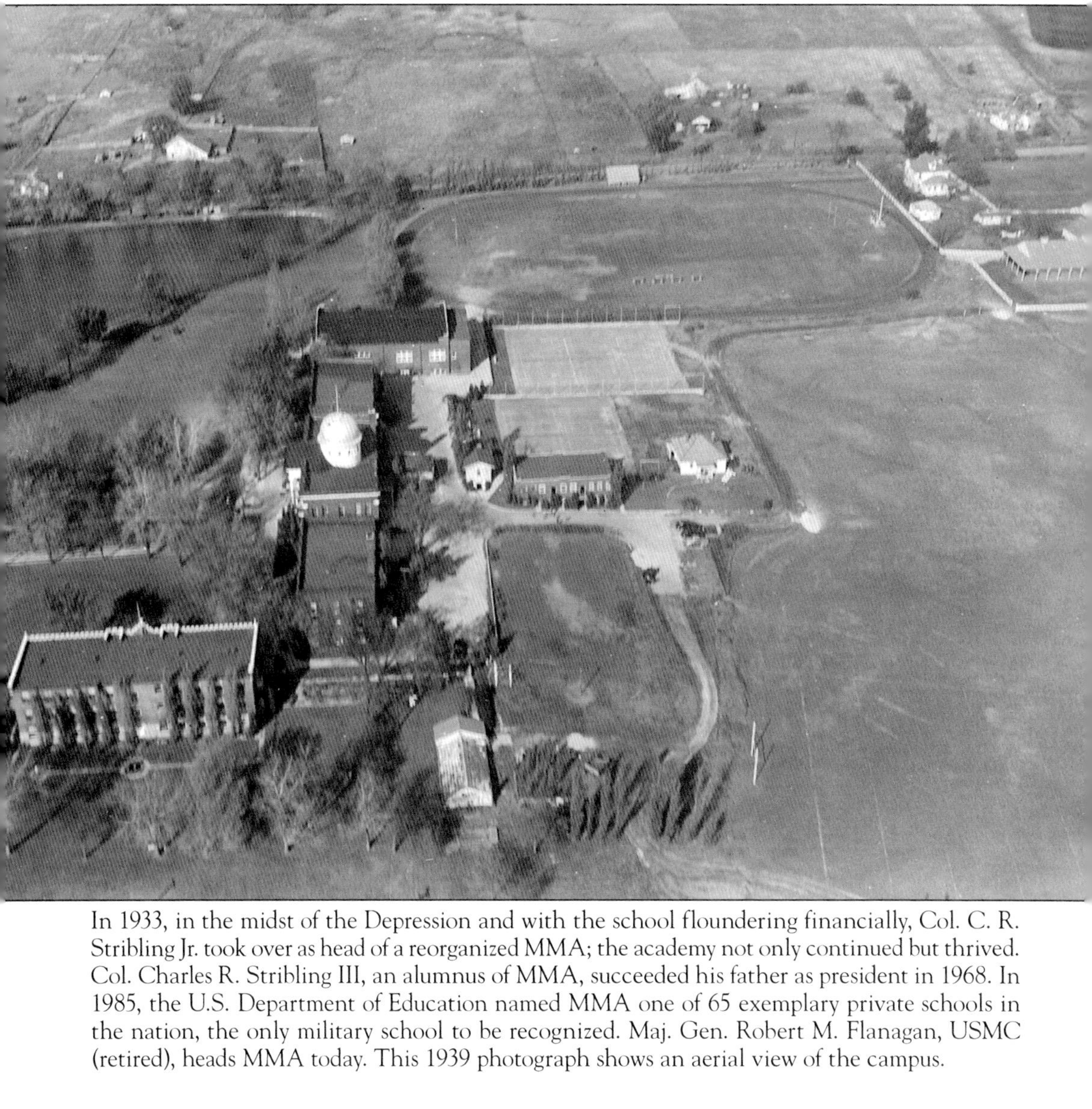

In 1933, in the midst of the Depression and with the school floundering financially, Col. C. R. Stribling Jr. took over as head of a reorganized MMA; the academy not only continued but thrived. Col. Charles R. Stribling III, an alumnus of MMA, succeeded his father as president in 1968. In 1985, the U.S. Department of Education named MMA one of 65 exemplary private schools in the nation, the only military school to be recognized. Maj. Gen. Robert M. Flanagan, USMC (retired), heads MMA today. This 1939 photograph shows an aerial view of the campus.

Eight

The Fair

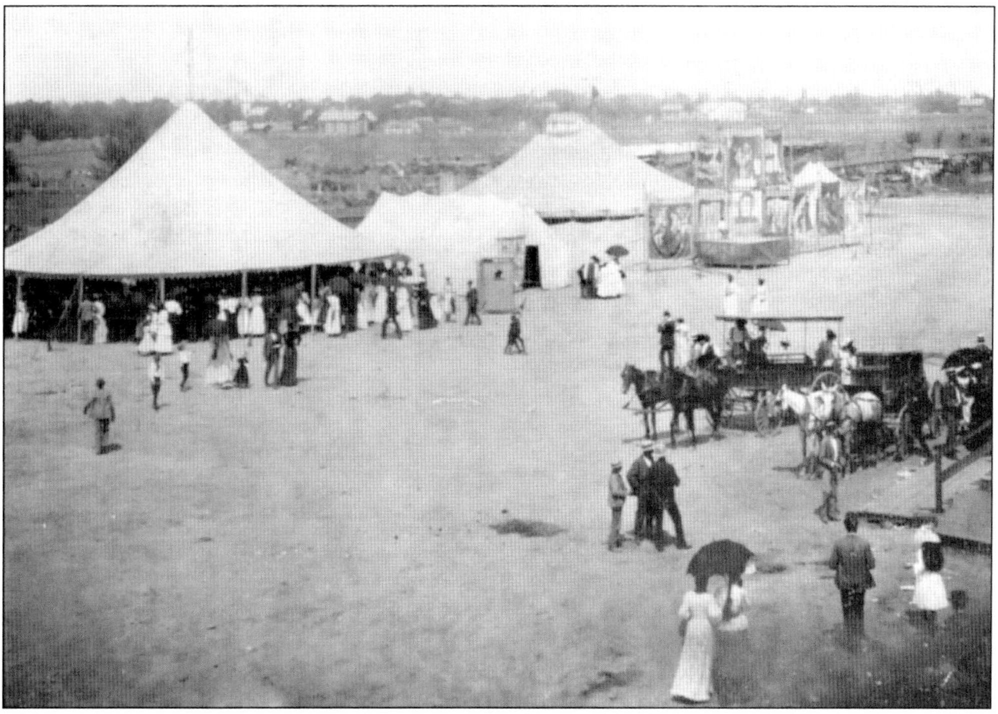

The Audrain County Fair Association traces back to 1860 when a group of citizens created a track at the end of East Promenade Street and held horse races. The fair was suspended during the Civil War but resumed in 1866. Due to growth, it was moved in 1880 to West Boulevard, where a permanent racetrack was created that remained as the heart of the fairgrounds until its demise. In 1892, the year this image was made, over $14,000 in premiums were paid out.

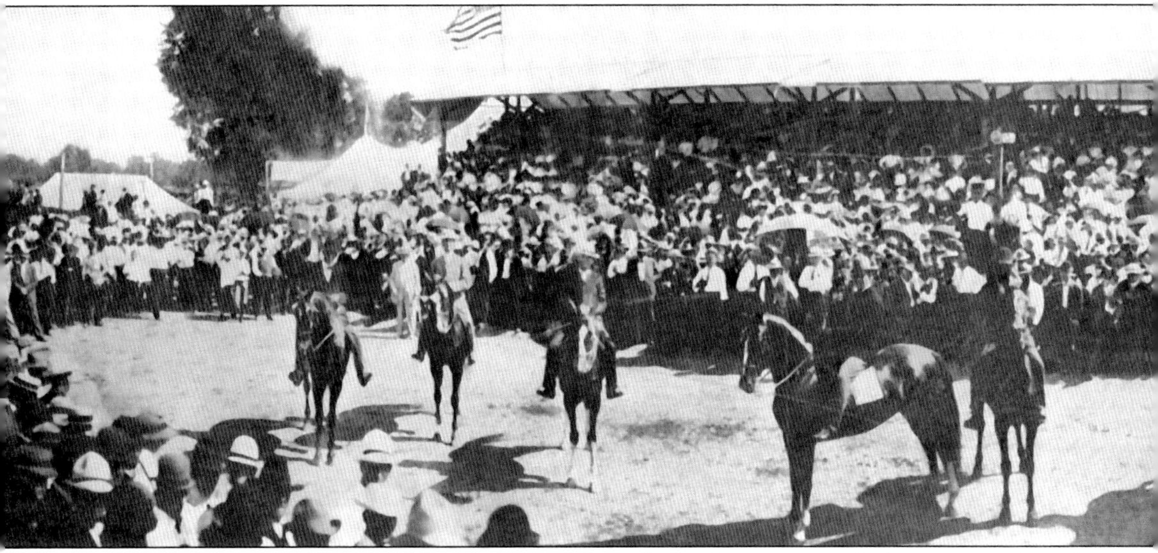

In 1893, the county fair yielded to the Chicago World's Fair but continued afterward until 1916, when World War I took precedence. Between 1894 and 1915, horses gradually became more important. The competition, sales, and prize money at the county fair contributed to Mexico's growing recognition as the "Saddle Horse Capital of the World." At the horse show in 1908 pictured here, a $1,000 prize was awarded the winner.

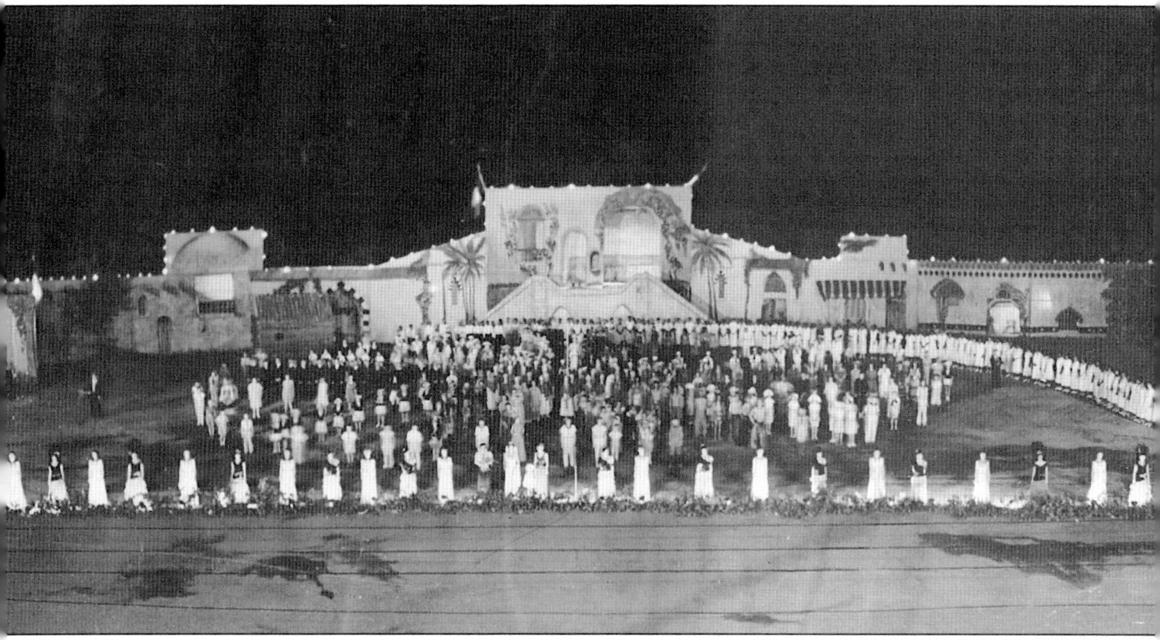

The Centennial Pageant, Mexical, was the centerpiece of the Centennial Fiesta Fair in 1936 and was presented Wednesday, Thursday, and Friday nights with a total estimated attendance of 20,000. The population of Mexico at the time was 8,721 and the county was 22,000. The extravaganza featured over 1,000 citizens and included singing, dancing, costumes, a queen (Darlene Nichols), and horses of course.

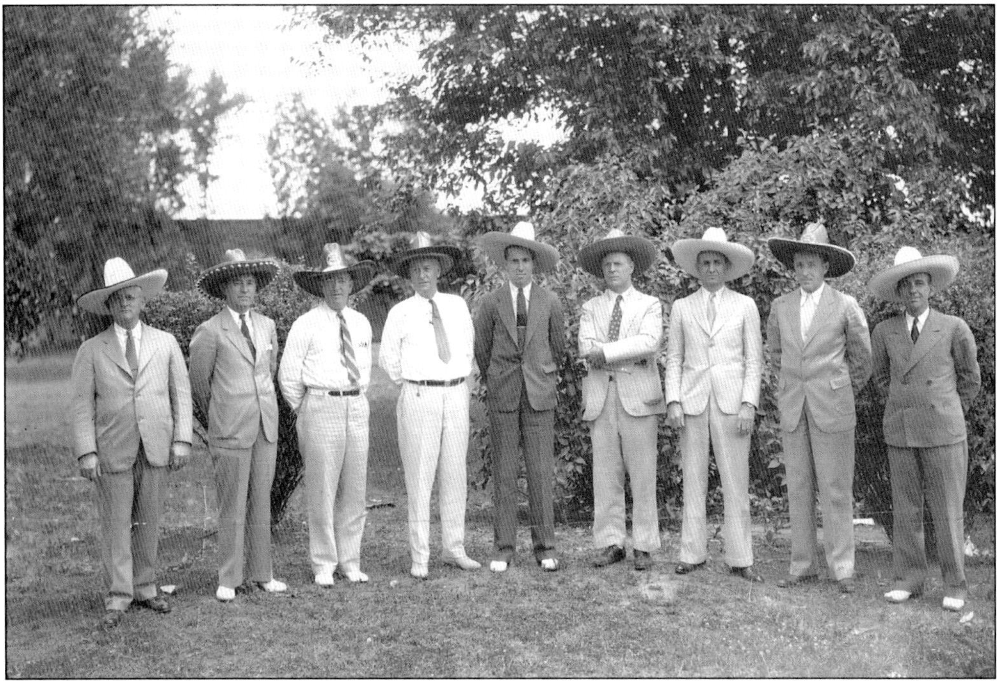

For the week of August 16 to 22, 1936, Mexico celebrated its centennial in the style of its namesake. A committee made up of, from left to right, O. P. James, James Eckenberger, Ed Pearl, Mayor Gus Graham, Charles Arnold, Paul Ekern, Rodes Jesse, Walter Staley, and Turner Williams created the Mexico Centennial Fiesta Fair. Officials from the country of Mexico attended as well as American government officials, from the governor of Missouri to congressmen and senators.

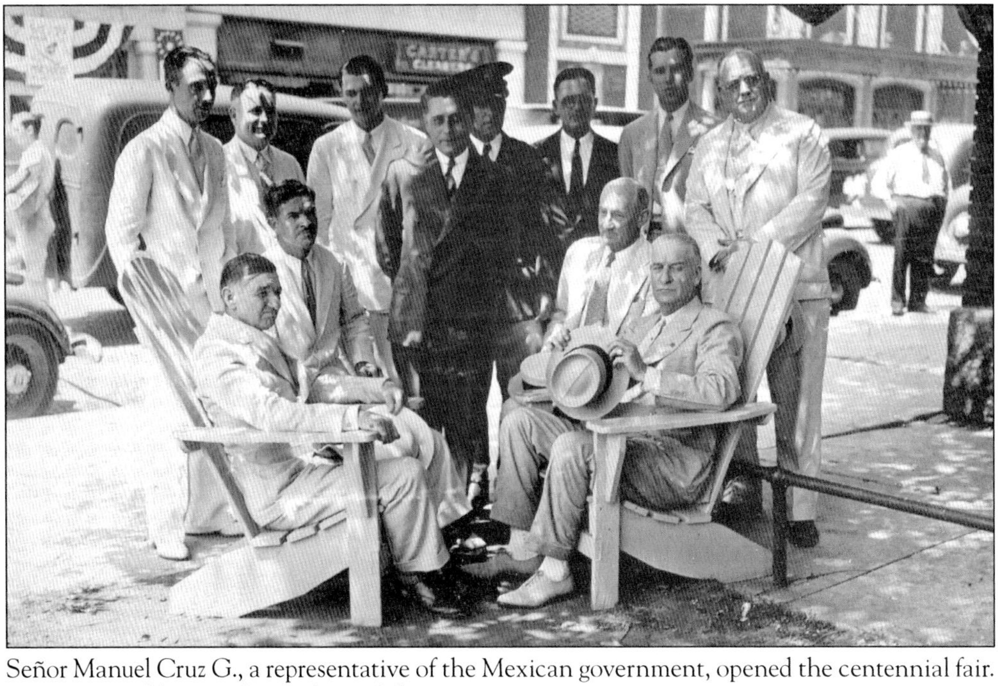

Señor Manuel Cruz G., a representative of the Mexican government, opened the centennial fair. He is pictured here with members of the organizing committee.

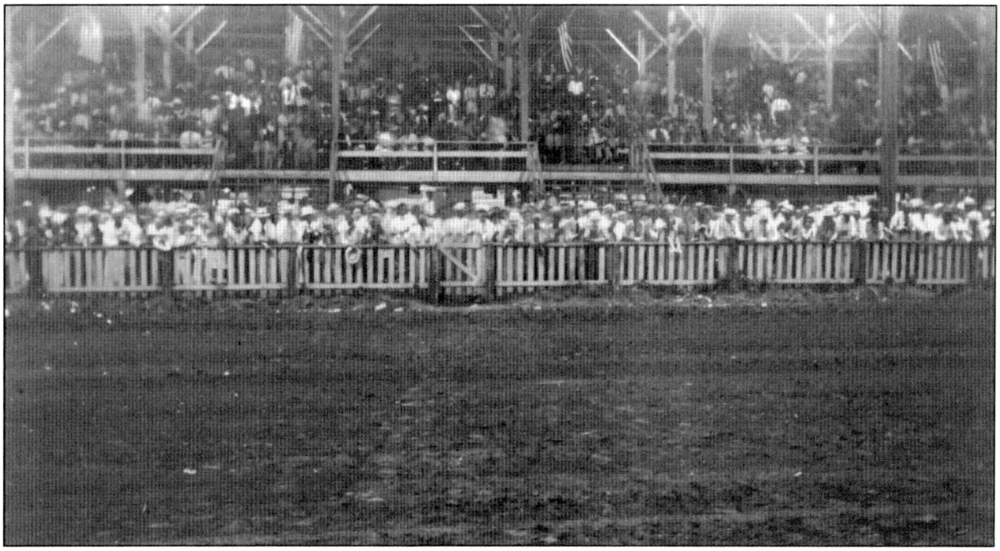

Horses continued to command crowds as seen in this photograph of onlookers at the August 7, 1937, show.

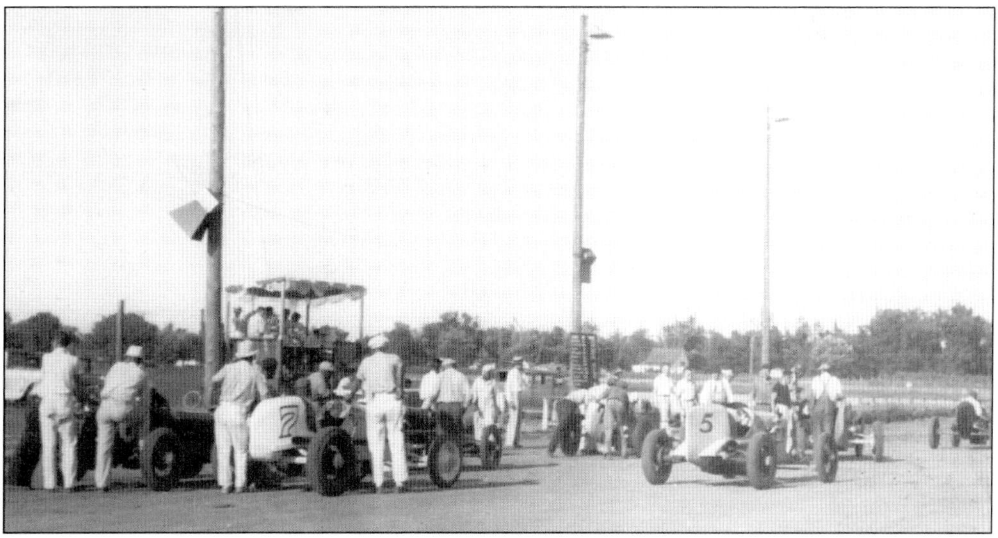

At the new fair, the track was used for more than horse races; car racing debuted in 1937.

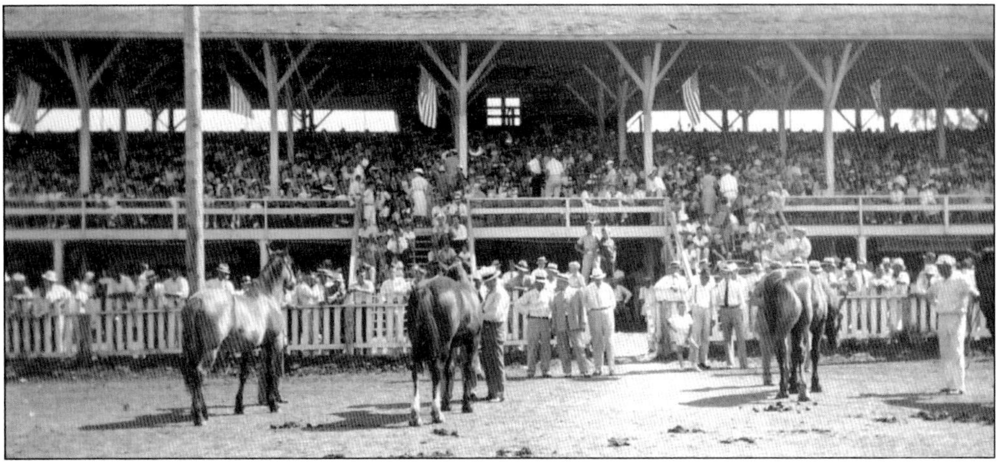

Even given new life by the centennial, the income from tickets, concessions, entry fees, and program sales barely covered fair expenses. In 1937 (date of this photograph), the income was $7,995 and expenses were $6,060.

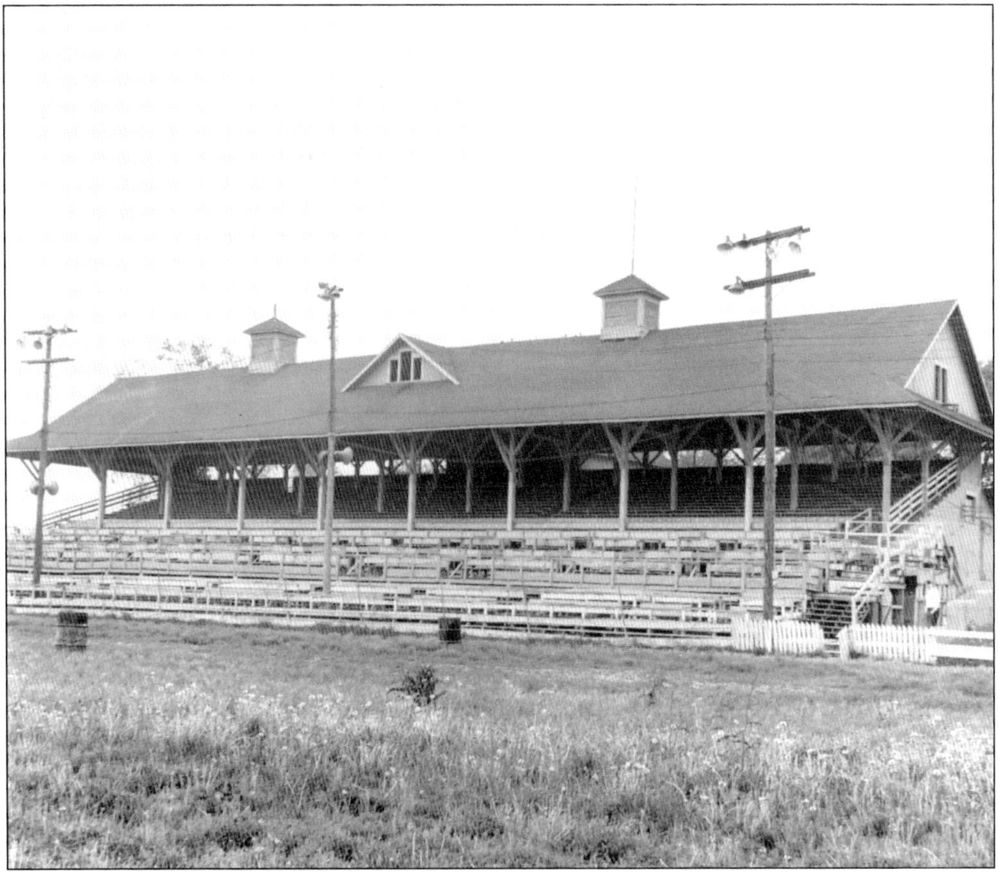

The debt grew until 1967, when the fair was again suspended. The school board and the city purchased the fairgrounds, turning it into a middle school campus and recreational area. For a while the only evidence of the former use of the property was the abandoned grandstand, pictured here. The structure burned in the 1970s.

Nine

Mexico at War

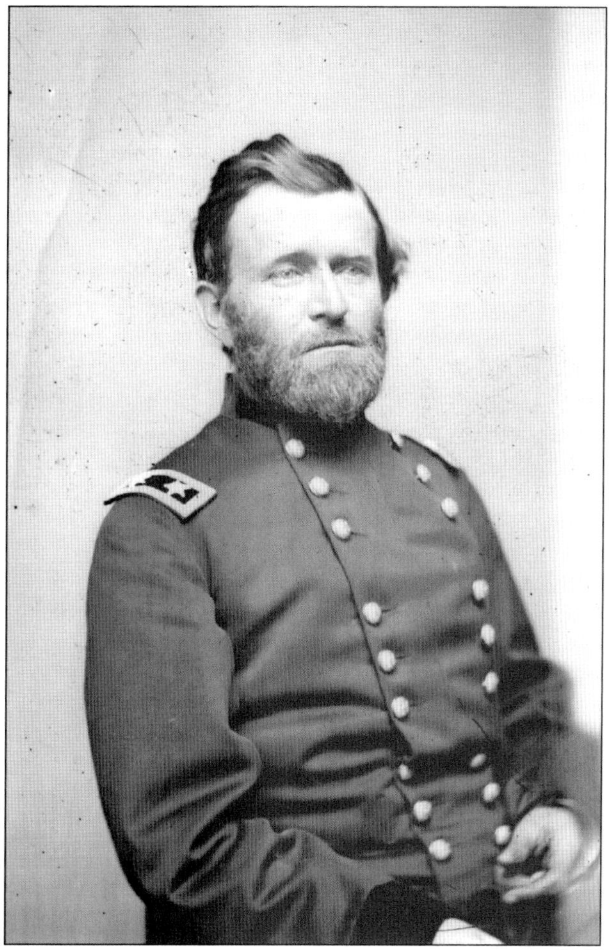

Gen. Ulysses S. Grant was in charge of the Federal troops in Mexico during the spring and summer of 1861. Until he arrived, the soldiers were in much disarray; during his command, conditions improved. Mexico remained under martial law for the duration of the occupation. (Courtesy of Library of Congress.)

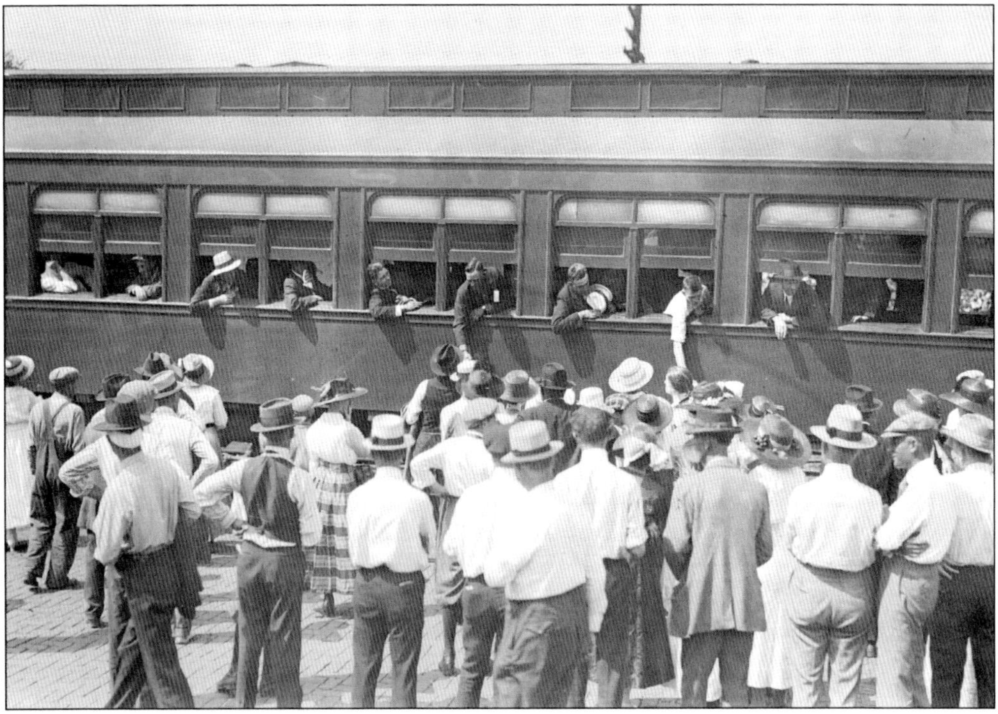

Mexicoans were generous during World War I, oversubscribing every quota set; citizens donated $3,231,905.55 to the war effort. An estimated 943 men and 10 women from Audrain County served from 1917 to 1919; 27 young men gave their lives. Over half of those who served were volunteers. In this undated photograph, men depart for service from the train station.

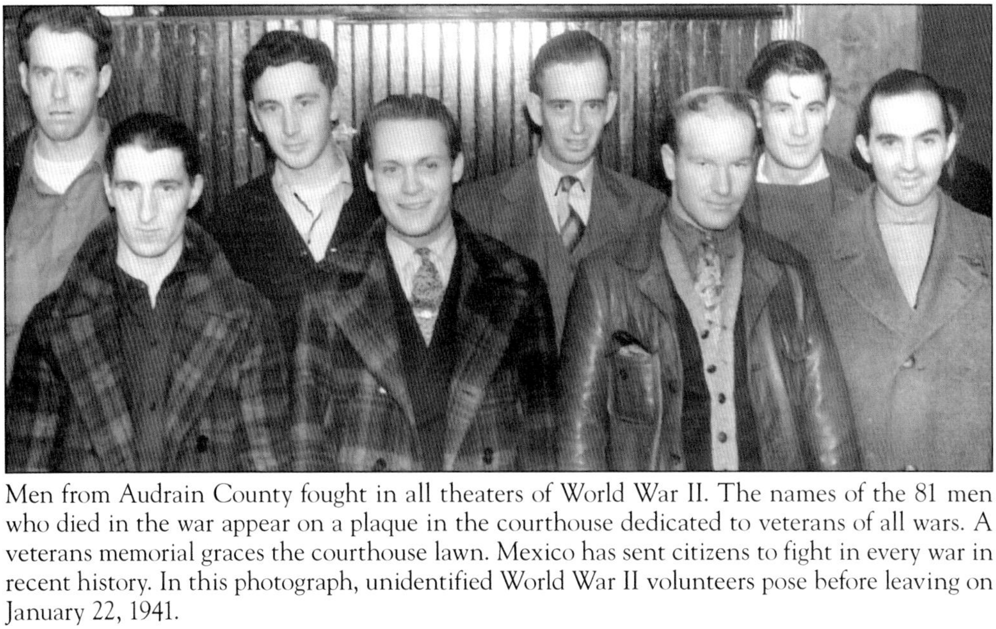

Men from Audrain County fought in all theaters of World War II. The names of the 81 men who died in the war appear on a plaque in the courthouse dedicated to veterans of all wars. A veterans memorial graces the courthouse lawn. Mexico has sent citizens to fight in every war in recent history. In this photograph, unidentified World War II volunteers pose before leaving on January 22, 1941.

GOVERNORS FROM MEXICO

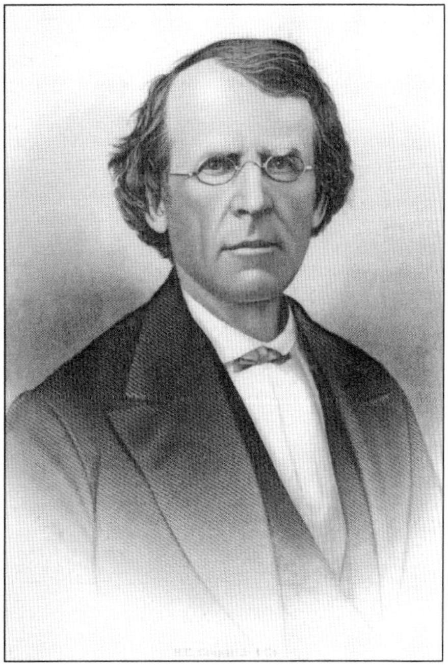

Mexico is the hometown of two Missouri governors. Charles Henry Hardin (right) served from 1875 to 1877. During his term, he was credited with putting the state on a more solid financial ground. Hardin is also known as the governor who proclaimed a day of prayer and fasting on June 3, 1875, in order to end a plague of grasshoppers that was ruining Missouri crops. This met with controversy regarding the separation of church and state, and Hardin did not seek reelection. Christopher S. "Kit" Bond (below), grandson of A. P. Green, was elected governor in 1972, the first Republican governor of Missouri in 30 years. At 33, Bond was the youngest governor in the United States when he was inaugurated on January 8, 1973. He was elected to a second nonconsecutive term in 1980. Governor Bond became Senator Bond in November 1986. He has announced his retirement at the end of his current term.

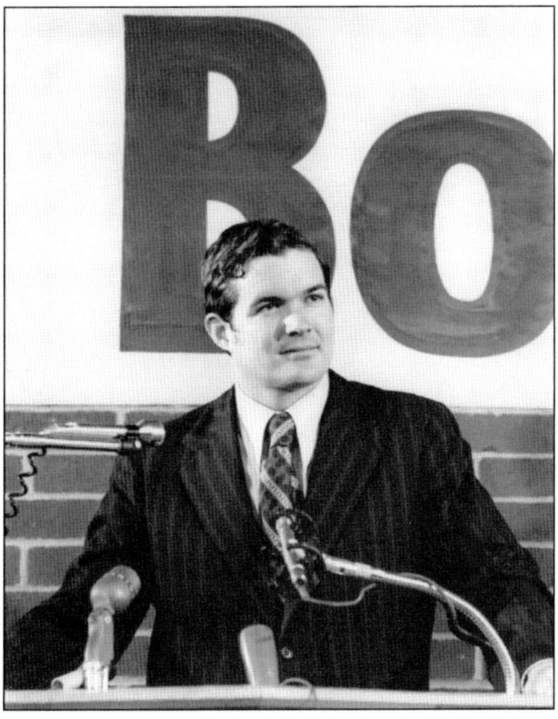